"Today, psychiatry offers medication for genetic bipolar disorders, but there is no way to repair the broken limbs in one's family tree caused by the disease, save that of retelling the tale with the salve of forgiveness. I admire Linda's courage and perseverance in writing about the primal pain of mother abandonment."

—Tristine Rainer, author of
Your Life as Story: Discovering the New Autobiography
and director, Center for Autobiographic Studies

"I have long been one of those who avoided dealing with death, who dodged sentiment, who felt that stories about the loss of a loved one were a bit indulgent, a way of saying, "my pain is greater than your pain." That was before I lost my father and my wife lost her mother, both within ten days. And that was before I read Linda Joy Myers's *Don't Call Me Mother*. This is powerful stuff, insightful, detailed, layered, emotional without being manipulative, insightful without being indulgent. It's a wonderful read, a marvelous examination of life and its inevitable conclusion. I loved it."

—James Dalessandro, author of *1906*

"This haunting story chronicles a lonely child's attempt to understand her complex and difficult family and make sense of a confused and chaotic world. Myers does what a good memoirist always does. She reveals a great deal about herself and, at the same time, helps us to understand more about our own lives."

—Susan Wittig Albert, best-selling author of
Writing From Life: Telling Your Soul's Story

"Could you still love your mother, even if she left you? In this gut-wrenching, poetic memoir, Linda Joy Myers explores three generations of maternal abandonment in her family—and movingly explores her own quest to break the chain."

—Melanie Rigney, former Writers Digest editor

"Linda Joy Myers's *Don't Call Me Mother* is a moving testimony to the resilience of the human spirit and the power of writing to trigger insight and healing. With unerring honesty and painstaking detail, Linda explores and re-experiences her family's many generations of loss and grief, and in the process frees herself from her history and uncovers her deep ability to love. Her memoir will inspire readers with the courage to record their own inner journeys".

—Elizabeth Fishel, author of *Sisters and Reunion: The Girls We Used To Be, the Women We Became.*

"Linda Joy Myers eloquently renders the details of her past in this transformative memoir, allowing all of us to find redemption through her honest courage. For anyone yearning for self-discovery, *Don't Call Me Mother* serves as a compelling guide on a journey to wholeness.

"I love the book."

—Michele Weldon, assistant professor, Northwestern University and author of *I Closed My Eyes*, and *Writing to Save Your Life*.

"Beautifully written, *Don't Call Me Mother* is an aching history that holds out a torch to the child inside us who longs to connect with her mother. A story of healing and, ultimately, love."

—Jessica Inclan, author of *One Small Thing*

"*Don't Call Me Mother* is an acutely moving story of one woman's yearning for tenderness and truth. Linda Joy Myers's exquisite language stirred my own desire to find my mother, who was once lost to me."

—Teresa LeYung Ryan, author of *Love Made of Heart*

"Many have experienced the heartache of emotional abuse, but few have written about it with such insight and beauty."
—Jacqueline Marcell, author of *Elder Rage* and host of "Coping with Caregiving," an Internet radio program

"This compelling memoir proves that stories have the power to transform and to heal. Myers takes us along on her hero's journey to exorcise the pain of abandonment by her mother and to find a fuller self. While this mother-daughter story is uniquely Myers's, it is also strangely universal. Haven't we all lived our own versions of this primal loss, and haven't we all struggled to sustain our own odysseys to survive and thrive? In the end, this story of the search for self is a valuable guide as we enter our own labyrinth of experience."
—Denis Ledoux, founder of the Soleil Lifestory Network, writer, and teacher

"Powerfully written, this memoir of a life filled with pain leaves the reader with a profound respect for the resilience of the human spirit. Bravo, Linda Joy Myers, for having the courage to unveil your past and for your compassionate commitment to helping others survive living with mental illness."
—Beth Proudfoot, director, East of Eden Writers Conference

"*Don't Call Me Mother* is beautifully launched by the image of the train station in the middle of the Great Plains. The reunions and partings that take place there will be both heartbreaking and healing for many readers, as they were for me."
—Barbara Gates, author of *Already Home: A Topography of Spirit and Place*

Don't Call Me Mother

Breaking the Chain of
Mother–Daughter Abandonment

Linda Joy Myers

✳
*helio*graphica

*helio*graphica

For information:
Heliographica
2261 Market St., #504
San Francisco, CA 94114
www.heliographica.com

Library of Congress Control Number: 2005923714
ISBN 1-933037-56-3

Printed in the United States of America

The loss of the daughter to the mother,
the mother to the daughter,
is the essential female tragedy.

— ADRIENNE RICH

Contents

Don't Call Me Mother

Preface

Don't Call Me Mother is both a healing memoir and a spiritual autobiography, a story about pain and transformation, of darkness and light that weaves itself through generations. This book is more than a specific tale of mothers and daughters struggling with the abandonment and undiagnosed mental illness that burned through my family history. It goes beyond abuse and loss, hatred and the holding of grudges. It is a testament to my belief that, under all the hurt and anger, love is buried deep inside each person.

As a child, I could see this love. I also saw that most adults had forgotten how to find and express it. It gave me joy whenever the beauty of this inner treasure shone through in the grown-ups around me, and I felt deep disappointment when some remained stubbornly blind to it.

Now, as a psychotherapist and teacher of memoir writing, I have learned that most humans are on the same path that I traveled—trying to reconnect with the love that was lost, trying to understand how and why things sometimes go terribly wrong.

The gestation period for art and healing can't be measured in ordinary time. The final draft of this memoir—woven through with dream and fantasy, memory, and personal history—has been "becoming" for fifteen years, ten years, five years, and two years, each version having a rhythm, direction, and resolution of its own.

For months at a time, I would try to ignore my family legacy of undiagnosed mental illness, and generations of mothers leaving daughters, despairing of any hope of resolution—but the story kept tugging at me, refusing to leave me in peace.

At first, I wrote it as fiction, until a fellow workshop member—said, "This is unbelievable. No family acts this way or does these things."

I replied, "But it's all true."

"In fiction," interjected the teacher, "the literal truth doesn't matter."

It was then that I knew the story had to be written as a memoir, a distillation of the truth and the history I had lived and witnessed.

Like so many children, I made a promise to not to be like my parents when I grew up. But the effect of childhood conditioning is often more powerful than will. The archetype of the wounded healer applies: like many people who are raised in dysfunctional homes, I became a therapist. Psychiatrist Alice Miller, a respected authority on childhood trauma, says that therapists are compassionate witnesses who help re-weave our brokenness.

After working on the story of my life and my family through art, photography, and poetry for many years, I needed to tell the truths that resided beneath the oil on a canvas and between the lines of a poem. I needed to reveal the story that I had implied, hidden, buried, or alluded to, but never put in a scene for open viewing.

Writing the whole story helped to hasten the healing process that I'd been searching for years in therapy. Wrestling with words and images, putting myself into the story as a character, in the first person, present tense, forced me to integrate the self that I was with the witness I have become. This memoir has given me a profound sense of completion with the past and a wonderful freedom. As I healed through the writing of this book, it too has evolved into a love song to my mother and grandmother, to my great-grandmother and my aunts, my father and grandfather and friends—to all those who saw the spark of love in a little girl and fanned it into flame so I could survive. The women who had once been curses—my eccentric, wild, emotion-wracked mother and grandmother—became my teachers. I believe that the emotional pain I experienced as a child has given me a depth of compassion that benefits my clients and enhances all my relationships.

Two schools of thought exist about memoir. Some people hunger to find out how other real people struggled, lived, and came to terms with difficult circumstances. Others find the idea of a healing memoir too trite or simplistic.

As a therapist, workshop leader, and author of *Becoming Whole: Writing Your Healing Story*, I stand in the former camp. I know that this work—writing down our lives as a journey of healing—is important to us as individuals and to the world. I humbly offer my own story as one of many that cries out to be told.

Even though the details described in this book are about me, aspects of the story are universal. I hope this book gives you hope and comfort, and helps you to know that you are not alone.

Tracks to My Heart

THE TRAIN BISECTS *the blue and the green, parting wheat fields by the tracks. Mommy and I rub shoulders, sitting in the last car, watching the landscape move backward, as if erasing my childhood, all those times when she would board the train and leave me aching for her. Now, in my dream, we rub shoulders, her perfume lingering. The old longing wrenches my stomach.*

Click-clack, click-clack, the train's wheels on the track, the language of my past, my future.

Her face is soft. Her wine-dark eyes glance at me with promise, an endearing look that gives me all I ever wanted. The click-clack ticks away the time, the mother time, moons rising and falling as the years fall like petals in a white garden, our body-and-blood song haunting my dreams. Mommy, where are you.

Even as she is with me, she is gone.

❧

The train station is the center of the universe, with tracks going and coming in all directions. People stand shivering in the ever-present plains wind, their hair kicked up violently when a train blows by, especially a freight bound for Chicago where, as I understand it, all sensible trains end up. To me, the Windy City, as I hear my mother and grandmother call it, is the end of the known world. It is where I began and where my mother is off to as the three of us—my mother, Josephine, my grandmother, Frances, and I—stand in a miserable clutch. I am sure they are as miserable as I am, my mothers, standing there with their arms across their chests, hips slung out, like bored movie stars competing for the same part. Maybe that's what they are doing—vying for the part of good mother, or bad mother, depending on how you define things. To me both of them are beautiful and thrilling.

But underneath their beauty and power, a secret is buried. A secret that runs in the blood. This moment repeats for the third time what has happened before—a mother leaving a daughter, repeating what Gram did to my mother so long ago, and her mother before her. It will be years before I find out the whole story about the three generations of women who will define my life. At this moment, the ticking bomb is set to go off when my mother gets on the train. No one here claims any knowledge of this dire pattern. I can feel it, though, deep in a silent place inside me, a place of desperation, the beginning of a crack that will split my life open.

The sun pinks the sky in the west, a place where the eye loves to rest in this open land. Already the lore of its history tickles my curiosity, even though at this moment I am four years old. I hear of Indian chiefs and the frontier, if not from books, then from the pictures all around town proclaiming our cowboy heritage—neon signs, billboards showing an Indian chief in full headdress, peace pipe slung from an arm as casually as a gun. Right now the picture of an Indian, wearing only a blanket and standing in front of the Santa Fe Chief, hangs on the waiting room wall, wreathed in smoke rising like a mysterious code to the ceiling.

I read the code here, tapping feet in open-toed suede shoes. I stare at my mother's toes, as if to memorize an intimate part of her, bringing my gaze up her shapely legs, my stomach in a pang, the scenes that brought us to this moment fresh in my mind.

⟨✶⟩

Mommy and I came here a few months ago from Chicago, where we had lived after my father left. I don't know much about him, except that he went off to the war, and came back too, but not to us. She cries when she looks at his pictures. Every so often she shows me a small black-and-white photo of a man wearing an army captain's hat and grinning as he leans casually against a brick building. The crease in his pants is knife sharp. With her slim fingers, she caresses a photograph of herself against the same wall, wearing a big fur coat.

"That was the night before you were born, a cold night in March. What a wonderful thing that was for your mother." Mommy often talks about herself like that, as if she wasn't in the room.

I remember our time in Chicago, when Mommy would talk on the phone forever in the evening, twisting her hair in tiny ringlets all over her head, or knitting scarves and sweaters. I remember the amber light that shone over her like a halo, and I remember that I'd do anything to get her to scratch my back with her sharp fingernails.

But a few months ago, we left Chicago—my first time on the train. The ride was thrilling: the sound of the whistle, huge clouds of gushing steam, great deep rumblings of the engines that sounded like scary monsters speeding us by green fields and blue skies all around, with little towns along the side of the track and people waving, waving as if they knew us. The whistle tooted a special hello to them. What fun.

That night the porter unfolded the special bed that was our seat, pulling down a shade made of thick green cloth. I loved the little tent he made for us. My mother had a dreamy look on her face, staring at the sights as the wheels click-clacked beneath us. She wore her cotton nightgown, and I my pajamas. We cuddled between fresh cotton sheets. The train rocked us back and forth, back and forth in a sweet rhythm that one day I would remember as the best moment we ever had, Mommy and me. On the train, together. The next day, we arrived in Wichita where I met Gram, Mommy's mother.

She looked like my mother, with the same pretty face. Her voice was soft as she sifted my fine hair away from my forehead in a gentle gesture and smiled at me with soft brown eyes so dark I couldn't see the pupils you can see in most people's eyes. She was nice to me and called me Sugar Pie. But Mommy and Gram—whew—they sure did surprise me by fighting all the time. I'd watch, or hide in the hall, while they yelled, screamed, and cried. Almost every day. It was terrible to hear; it made my skin itch. I scratched the itch, making red marks on my arms. Their cigarette smoke filled the air.

When Mommy rushed off to work each morning it was quiet and nice in Gram's little house. Windows let in the sun through the Venetian blinds, making pretty patterns on the hardwood floors. Gram read stories to me, and we made bubbles with soap in the sink. She taught me to eat prunes every morning. I began learning how words make stories come alive—Cinderella, Snow White, the Three Bears. Every day I waited for Mommy to come home. I loved her throaty voice, the way she touched my hair for a moment. I was always slinking around trying to get more hugs out of her, but she was not much for that.

***

One evening, everything seemed different. Mommy yelled. Threw down her purse. Lit cigarette after cigarette, the frown between her eyes deepening with each puff. Gram edged around her, as if she were looking for a way to either blow up or not fight at all. Finally the explosion came, my mothers opening and closing angry mouths. I kept my eye on them while I put dishes on the table.

"I hate this place," Mother said, stomping her heels on the floor.

Gram made a nasty face. Their voices had sharp edges, and got so loud I had to put my fingers in my ears. They were so loud, so angry, sound-

3

ing like screeching birds. Then something happened. Mommy got really quiet, which scared me even more, and said, "That's it; I'm going back to Chicago." I can't say how I knew it, but I could tell that she wasn't going to take me, and that if she left me now, it would be forever.

I watched her walk back and forth across the floor. The seams in her hose were crooked. Mommy never had crooked seams. I sat on the floor, my stomach in a knot, while I traced the patterns in the Oriental rug. I wanted to get lost in those swirls, like in a dark forest in the fairy tales. I could get lost and never be found again.

❦

So here we are, waiting for the train. My chest is tight; there is darkness and ice all the way though me. I am shivering. How can she leave? She knows I don't want her to go. My mother stands apart from me and from Gram, far enough to show that she is the one leaving, the one who will go alone on the train. I dread the train that's about to take her away. All around me everyone acts normal. People bustle around getting ready, the train men push luggage carts, kids jump up and down. Words that I cannot say gather in my mouth, fill my whole body. Every muscle wants to run to her, grab at her and scream, "Please don't go," but I know that she and Gram don't want me to do this. I don't want to make them mad; I don't want them to look at me with those dark eyes of disapproval. I couldn't stand it. So I pretend.

The wind blows through me, whirling my dress. Then the sound of the whistle cries out, as if in pain. A deep sorrow lurches through me. I hold my breath to keep myself from crying. The light appears at the far end of the tracks and gets bigger. I can't stop any of this. The huge train tears into the station, rumbling the earth beneath my feet, kicking up my hair with the blast of wind. A scream comes out of my mouth, but no one hears me. The locomotive is too huge, too powerful and frightening, and it is coming to take my mother away.

Mommy and I are wrapped in invisible gauze, wrapped tight so it can't break, but as she touches me softly with her fingertips, and leans over to give Gram a kiss, I can feel the fabric unwrapping, unwinding us until just a thin piece is left. She hugs me lightly, as if she's afraid I'll cling to her. Her musky smell clings to me. She click-clacks toward the train on her high heels, almost as if she's glad to get away. Her seams are straight, and she is so beautiful with the sun on her face as she climbs into the train car.

Mommy, Mommy, I chant silently, putting my fingers to my nose to inhale her memory, her scent on my skin.

How I want to be on the train, to cuddle up with Mommy the way we did before. But when Gram looks at me with such sadness in her eyes, I know that I need to stay with her. It's funny that she was so mad before, but now I can tell she is sad, though she doesn't say it in words. I take her hand and stand with her as we watch the train disappear down the track in a puff of smoke.

The train whistle cries its lonely song, lingering in the wind that crosses the plains. It will call for me all my life, in my dreams and while I am awake. The train song, the train's power and promise, are etched deep in my soul from this day forward.

There Be Dragons

At the edge of the world, there be dragons.

—FOURTEENTH-CENTURY CARTOGRAPHER

I HAVE NO idea how long my mother has been gone because each day stretches out forever, with prunes in the morning, songs on the radio, and The Shadow and The Lone Ranger, too. Gram is nice and sweet, as if she feels sorry for me. Today she bustles around, vacuuming and dusting, and tells me to make my bed because we're having company. Gram always dresses up for company, so she puts on a silk dress, powders her face, and slicks on her red lipstick. (11/12pts)

I hear a knock and rush to the door. Two very tall people look down at me—a thin-faced woman who smiles with big teeth, and a skinny man whose lips are zipped in a tight grin. A small girl and three skinny boys with sharp noses and glinty eyes bounce around behind them. (11/13pts)

"Vera, Charlie, come on in." Gram is gracious as she leads them into our living room. She serves iced tea and perches at the edge of her chair, acting her company self, her good manners like frosting on a cake. She is passionate about good manners. This morning, she kneeled down and told me, "Remember to say 'please' and 'thank you.' Call them 'mister' and 'ma'am.'" She tells me that all the time. I told her I would. Gram gives me a wonderful smile when I do what she wants.

The boys swoop into the living room, a noisy bunch of lip-snapping, finger-popping kids. The adults tell us kids to go outside. I want to stay in and play with my dolls in my bedroom, but Gram obviously has adult business to attend to and sweeps us all outside. The boys scuffle; the largest one seems really tall and maybe is in high school. The middle one fights back at him with punches in the arm. The one close to my age has a gap between his teeth and smiles at me, as if to apologize for his brothers. The little girl whines and bangs on the door for her mother after the middle one pulls her pigtail.

"Boys—come here this instant." The mother stamps her foot. "Be nice to your sister." I want to come in, but Vera tells me to stay out. Why is this lady I don't even know telling me what to do?

I look at Gram, but she seems to be on Vera's side. Adults stick together, I know, but Gram is acting peculiar. I put a smile on my face and shuffle back out the door. I don't much take to boys. Most are noisy and rough, and this crew is full of mischief. They are wrestling on the grass and pummeling each other.

"What's your names?"

"She wants to know our names. Shall we tell her?"

"Tell her? Why should we talk to her?" They point at me and laugh, then announce that the oldest one is Bruce. Then comes Terry. Earnest is the youngest boy.

"Betsy, my name is Betsy," says the little girl with her thumb in her mouth.

Charlie comes out to tell the boys to play marbles and to include the girls. I don't know how to play marbles, but they are nice and show me how. They let me take my turn and even let Betsy try. Earnest is especially nice. Shadows are long on the grass when the adults come to the door and tell the kids to get in the car. I am tired from all the activity and the bossy, rowdy kids. When the Ford pulls away, I figure that this is the last we'll ever see of them.

<hr>

Two weeks later Gram goes into housecleaning action again, moving the couch and vacuuming under it. She washes the living room windows and gets dressed in another shimmery silk dress.

"Linda Joy, put on your pink dress and socks. We're having company."

I ask who, and she tells me Vera and Charlie. I'll have to put up with those boys again. I ask her why they're coming again so soon, and she just shakes her head. She's hiding something, but I can't figure out what. When the car drives up, everyone spills out like ants.

The boys bark and jump around on the grass. Vera plants a kiss on my cheek. I turn my head to wipe it off so she won't see. Her toothy smile scares me. To my horror, the kids thunder into my room and begin to tear it apart, looking through my books, dolls, and toys, tossing them to the floor. Finally Gram and Vera come to the door, urging us outside. I ask Gram if I can stay and clean up my room, but she says no.

"Children should be seen and not heard, and today we don't even want to see you," Vera says.

The boys play hide and seek. They cheat. Betsy cries. I hate them. I don't like being shut out of my own house and forced to be with these wild kids. Gram comes to the door, her dark eyes looking disturbed.

"Sugar Pie, are you all right?" I tell her I am, but cringe at her use of that affectionate name in front of strangers.

Sure enough, it gives them a reason to tease me in their sing-song cadence: "Sugar Pie, Sugar Pie. Eat it and you'll die. Sissy, sissy."

I sit on the porch, waiting for them to just leave. Clouds blow across the sun; raindrops splash on our Nash Rambler. The boys use the drops to make drawings with their fingers, creating muddy puddles on our shiny car. Vera comes out and puts her hands on my shoulders. My skin starts burning. She leaves her hands on me and says, "We'll see you soon." Charlie pats my head. I shrink away from both of them, and slip in the front door as soon as I can. Gram tells them goodbye, then turns to see the trails of dirty finger marks on her car. She wipes them with the palm of her hand and then leans against the car, burying her head in her arms. Her shoulders shake. I've never seen her so upset.

My stomach starts to hurt. "Gram, what's wrong?"

"It's just adult stuff. Don't worry." Her eyes tell me she is lying. She kneels down to fold her arms around me. I can feel her breath against my neck, the flutter of her fingers on my back. "Oh, my Sugar Pie, my sweet little Sugar Pie," she croons with so much sorrow that I feel broken. Something is terribly wrong. When I ask again what it is, she shakes her head. For the rest of the day she moves around woodenly, fixing lunch, washing dishes. I straighten up the mess in my room, putting my dolls nicely on the bed. I line up my story books in a row, a heavy feeling on my shoulders where Vera's hands had rested.

After I go to bed, Gram makes a long phone call to my mother, pleading with her, "No, it's wrong. I don't trust them." Her voice travels the scale from high to low, from sharp anger to quiet sorrow. I shake in my bed. I know this conversation has to be about me. Gram is acting too funny, and she doesn't look at me in the same way. I lie there, trying to figure out what is happening, but I can't. The veil of sleep finally falls on me in spite of my tense body and tumbling thoughts.

<hr/>

The next morning the sun splashes patterns on the wooden floor by my bed. When I shuffle out to breakfast, the look on Gram's face gives everything away. She kneels before me, tears running down her face, her arms grabbing me tight. I hold my breath. I know there's bad news about me.

"Honey, I have to tell you . . ." Her fingers trickle along my arms that are hanging heavy from their sockets. "Your mother and father . . . they think you should live with Vera and Charlie and the kids."

Those sharp-faced children? Vera and her bossiness? My insides shrink away from my skin. I don't know what to say. I stare at her, trying to understand why she wants me to go away. How bad have I been?

"I'm so sorry, but they think this is best for you."

"I don't want to live with them. Why can't I stay with you?"

"They think you should have kids to play with. I'm just your old Gram, you know." She shrugs her shoulders and smiles sadly.

I notice there are two parts to me. One part sees how she is trying to joke about this, to help me take the news lightly. The other part of me stands alone in a field under a gray sky, the wind blowing against me, sucking out the marrow of my bones. My lips try to form words, but for a few minutes I can't find them.

I already know that what adults decide is what will be, but I protest anyway. "I don't like them. I don't want to go. Can't I stay with you, Gram? Please don't send me away." Gram breaks down and sobs.

I bargain with her. "Call Mommy and Daddy. Tell them I don't want to go. I'll be good, I'll eat my prunes, I'll have good manners. I promise!"

These words make Gram cry even harder. I can hear her in the bathroom, sobbing and blowing her nose. I watch elm trees swaying in the wind outside the living room window, and I feel my world loosening, beginning to come apart.

Gram does call my mother. I hear another round of fighting, which I know is my fault. I go to bed to the sounds of her pleading, her tears and her rage my lullaby. Finally, a blessed silence as I fall asleep.

The next morning is even worse. Gram's eyes look haunted. In a trying-to-be-cheerful voice she says, "Good morning, Sugar Pie." I steel myself to do without this sweet greeting, a sob threatening to break loose.

She pours her coffee and my milk. Her hand shakes as she spoons coffee into my glass. I ask her what Mother said, already knowing the answer.

Gram's eyes are pools of grief. "I'm so sorry, honey, but Vera and Charlie are coming for you tonight."

So soon? I don't know what to do, how to feel. I am a piece of flotsam bobbing along at the whim of the adults. My stomach swims in despair. Every time I look at Gram, we both start crying.

Gram gets out the suitcase and opens it on the bed. She sorts through my clothes, washes my underwear and socks, and hangs them to dry on the clothesline next to the morning glories. I go out to look at the brilliant blue flowers, which comfort me somehow with their pretty faces and bobbing heads. I walk through the house, fingering my pink bedspread and hugging my bear. I decide to leave it with Gram rather than risk the boys killing it. She packs my satin ribbons, one for each dress, and tells me to put on my new shorts outfit. As she ties the matching ribbon in my hair she stifles her tears.

The June day is endless, yet too short. The sun has made long shadows on the grass when the green Ford pulls into the driveway. The kids pile out and gather in a jittery herd, as if they've been told to behave or else. Vera comes in wearing her wide white smile, and plants an onion-breath kiss on my cheek, surrounding me in a cape of possession. Gram's face is crumpled like a Kleenex. She hands Charlie the suitcase, then leans on the counter clutching her side. A fluttery panic rises in my chest and I feel the urge to run, but the adult forces are stronger than I am. I paste a smile on my face, knowing that it will help Gram. She stands at the front door, holding a Kleenex and waving.

Vera takes my arm and leads me to the car, like the witch leading Hansel and Gretel to her cage. The boys and I are stuffed into the backseat, Betsy up front with her parents. As we drive away from Gram's house, a black curtain comes down over the sky, making for a very dark night. Bruce and Terry fall asleep, their heads lolling against my shoulders, their elbows poking my ribs. The moon spills its light on the lonely ribbon of road leading to Wheatland and my new home.

That night, Vera shows me to my room—a huge upstairs bedroom around the corner from the boys' rooms. I lay awake for a long time, listening to each creak in the boards, worried that the boys will sneak up on me.

Bright sun pouring in a large window awakens me. The boys' feet pound on the floor on the way to breakfast. Downstairs I find out that there are a lot of rules: Eat everything on your plate; no snacking without permission. The boys tease and throw food when Vera leaves the room. Betsy whines. Charlie leaves early for work, wearing a suit and carrying a briefcase. The house is so large there's an echo. The roomy kitchen has linoleum floors and a gray Formica table, a pantry, a back porch, a basement at the bottom of a rickety wooden staircase. After breakfast, Vera and the kids show me a rabbit in a cage in the backyard. Everyone is nice, playing and joking around. I begin to think that things might be all right.

That first evening cicadas are murmuring. Soft evening light filters through the sycamores and elms lining a street made of brick. Vera tells me to come to the front porch so she can talk to me alone. She hands me a brown paper bag containing blue jeans and a toothbrush. I like the way the jeans smell and the orange stitching on the legs.

She nods, "The clothes your grandmother gave us are too fancy. We all wear jeans. We have rules here, and you must obey them. Every night we brush our teeth. Every night, mind you. I will treat you as I treat the other children."

I mumble and say thank you, but there's something in her speech that chills me.

"You must remember—brush your teeth every night. Repeat it after me."

"Brush my teeth every night."

She nods, a hank of hair falls out of her bobby pin. Her eyes shine in a ghostly way. She leans back on her heels and crosses her arms. "Another thing. Now that you live here, I am your mother. You must call me Mother. Say it."

I stare at her. Teeth and eyes swirl into an out-of-focus jumble.

"Say it now. Linda, call me Mother."

My tongue sticks to the roof of my mouth. My heart pounds. I can't call this woman Mother. She looks to me now like the wicked stepmother in Snow White, with her straight black hair, her narrowing eyes.

"Say it—call me Mother. Come on." Her voice is hard in her throat.

The sound of a train whistle in the distance makes me yearn for my real mother. I can see her lovely face and tender eyes in my mind. Sycamore trees rustle in the evening breeze. Fireflies flicker on and off, suspended in the liquid green dusk. A dog barks next door. Vera's eyes seem to glow. My body aches.

"If you call me Mother, you can go in. Come on, say it." She gestures for me to hurry up.

She folds her arms over her chest and plops in a wicker rocking chair. "You are going to stand there until you call me Mother. I can wait all night, if that's what you want." The porch creaks as she rocks back and forth, back and forth for a long time. Only the porch speaks; there's no sound from me. One thought darts in and out of my mind—what would Mommy say to this? The trees sink into invisibility. The street-lights are glowing orbs hanging in darkness. A baby cries down the street; children play noisily next door. Vera's eyes are gleaming slits in the thick darkness. Another dog barks; a screen door slams.

"Say it. Say it now!"

My mother's face hovers in my mind, beautiful with her dark wavy hair, her brown eyes soft and sweet, the way they are when she tucks me in. She'd be so hurt by this, but I sink under the weight of Vera's will. I know that she'll never let me go to bed if I don't give in.

I say the word.

It's just a word, but words create whole worlds, and I know this, even at five. My old world ends that very moment.

The next morning Vera leads me down the basement stairs. There are spider webs everywhere. A small twin bed sits under a window, a ping-pong table with paddles in another room. Vera thrusts a paddle toward me. "Feel this."

I stare at her, starting to shiver.

"I said to feel it." She mashes my fingers over the bumps on the paddle. "This is what I'll use when you don't mind me."

I squeeze my arms against my ribs, trying not to let her see my fear.

"If you don't obey, I'll use this on you. You're expected to follow our rules. I'll treat you like the other kids, understand?"

Gram and Mommy hardly ever swatted me. The basement grows dark, as if the sun has fallen from the sky.

A week after I start kindergarten, Vera makes good her promise. I go to kindergarten in the morning. The school is a few blocks from the house. Crayons, chalk, and books are cheerful smells to me. The kids are nice and the teacher is patient, showing us how to write and draw. Vera told me to come home right after school, so I obey, shuffling along, kicking leaves, watching a squirrel scamper up a tree. The scent of fresh grass and earth make me feel pretty good compared to what I find at Vera's. Vera stands sentry by the back door. As soon as she sees me, she shouts, "What took you so long? Do you know what time it is?"

Her eyes are fiery and her teeth seem sharp and pointy. Vera drags me into the kitchen and points to the clock. "See. What took you so long? What did you do all this time?"

"I was just walking." I stare at the clock hands, confused. I don't know how to tell time yet.

"It doesn't take anyone that long to walk home. Where did you go? What were you doing?"

What's wrong? I was just enjoying my walk with the squirrels, the crackly leaves, the autumn day. I just look at her, not knowing what to say.

"Get in here." She yanks me by the arm to the closet. She takes out a ping-pong paddle. I catch my breath. "I didn't do anything, honest. I just walked home."

"You're a liar. Now pull down your pants."

I don't move. She can't mean it, it doesn't make any sense.

"Mind me! I told you to pull down your pants."

I can't fight her. The other night on the porch I learned that she'll always win. My body throbs with shame as I slip down my underpants. She bends me over and at first hits me lightly. The sound of slaps on bare skin echo in the room. I figure that I should muster up a cry so she'll stop. By the end of the spanking, my tears are real, and I hate myself for giving in and crying. She stands me upright. My tears make the room and Vera's face look blurry. I am burning from the pain and from embarrassment. No one has ever humiliated me like that.

"That'll teach you to come home on time and not lie to me. I can tell, you know, when kids lie." She waves the paddle. "This is what you'll get for it every time."

Triumphant, she turns her attention to pie making. Betsy peeks out from behind the dining room door and giggles.

A bare light bulb hangs over the kitchen table. Charlie is at work; the boys are having a food fight. Vera is in another room with Betsy. Bacon and eggs wait on a platter for me. Gram never made me eat eggs once she found out that I was allergic to them. Just looking at the runny whites makes me feel like throwing up. Vera comes in and tells me to eat the eggs. I ask for cereal instead, and even say please. Furious, she stands over me. "What do I have to do to get you to eat your eggs— pound it into you?" She taps my head with her fists.

I realize that, again, she has to win. I dip a small piece of toast into the eggs. The boys turn their curious eyes toward me. I stop chewing in mid-bite, feeling sick. Vera leaves the room again. Terry and Bruce come over to pound their fists on my head, chanting, "Bacon and eggs, bacon and eggs, you've got to eat your bacon and eggs." I sink down, trying to escape, but they keep it up, cackling and making fun of me. I manage to keep from crying.

When she comes back, Vera tells them to sit down. "Get busy

and eat those eggs. We can sit here all day." She spoons the eggs in front of me.

"Open your mouth. Hurry up."

She sticks the spoon in my mouth. My throat closes and I start to gag.

"Don't you dare throw that up! I'll whale you a good one."

I think of Gram's face, her smile, how she called me "Sugar Pie." Somehow the food goes down.

At school a few weeks later, the room swims in a cottony fog. I blink to clear the fog, trying to stay upright. Suddenly the teacher's face is a few inches away, and she insists that I come with her to the nurse's office to take my temperature. The office seems far away in a mist. The nurse takes my temperature, tells me I have a fever and have to go home. If I go home early, Vera will kill me. I'd be ruining her routine. These smiling ladies would never believe what goes on in that house, or that my "mother" would be angry at me for being sick. I decide that if I walk very slowly, I'll get home close to the time that school gets out, and she'll never know I left early. The nice teacher and nurse put a stop to my fantasy of making it work out for myself by offering me a ride. I keep saying no, but they rush me into my coat and send me out to the car.

Each step brings me closer to Vera and her rage. She does not like outsiders. I know these ladies are trying to be nice, but they have no idea how much trouble they are getting me into. The nurse knocks on the door. Vera acts nice and friendly, smiles her thanks. No one would ever guess what she's really like.

When the car's gone, she hisses. "So, you managed to come home early, did you? I had a little surprise planned for you and Betsy—riding sleds and making a snowman, but no, you have to get sick. Go to your room and stay there. You won't be coming with us." She looks triumphant for some reason, with a glint of pleasure in her eyes.

I'd rather play and have fun, but the world is fuzzy and I'm so tired. I look out my bedroom window to see Vera and Betsy playing in the snow. My breath frosts the window glass. Gram would have made me soup and tucked me into bed. Where are the people who care for me? Do they remember me?

Everyone plays the happy-face game when company comes for parties. Being with other people in a normal way cheers me up. One family has a sixteen-year-old boy named Freddie. He's always paying attention to me, reading and playing games. He's nicer than the boys I live with. After hamburgers, when the adults are playing card games, he kneels down and says, "Hey, show me the ping-pong table in the basement. Let's go!"

He's big and leads me protectively into the murky basement. He tells me that we're going to play the tickle game, that I should get on the bed. I am not sure about this, but I lie down and he lies beside me. He says to close my eyes. I feel his fingers moving along my ribs, and I break into a giggle. Then I feel a brush of air on my leg. I open my eyes and yank down my dress.

"This game is about the alphabet letters on your underpants." He grins as he pulls up my dress again. "This is part of the game; it won't hurt. Just let me see them. Oh, they're cute. Here's a red 'B' and a yellow 'A'. Do you know your letters?"

Of course I do. Does he think I'm stupid? I try to squirm away from him and sit up.

"It's okay, just lie back." He keeps playing the lift-up-my-dress game. Part of my mind watches us, another part is thinking about Vera. If she sees this, she'll beat me for sure. Freddie wedges me against the wall and unfastens his pants, releasing a pink thing. I don't see it clearly because I squeeze my eyes shut. I know this is all very bad.

"Do you want to touch it?" he whispers.

I shake my head. I think fast—how can I get him up without making him mad? Vera might find us at any moment.

"I won't hurt you." He climbs on top of me. "Just let me put it between your legs." He's breathing hard. He pulls at my underpants, but I push against him. I have to get away. Now.

I start babbling, "Freddie, I have to go to the bathroom bad, really. Please let me get up. Pretty please."

Freddie blinks and gets off me. I dart up the stairs and he follows, fastening his pants.

"You won't tell anyone?" he whispers.

I shake my head no, but I'm terrified that Vera will see inside my brain and know anyway.

When we burst through the door into the bright lights of the kitchen, I have a smile plastered on my face to cover up any other feelings that might be there. The others ask us what we were doing. "Playing." I feel dirty and confused, terrified that Vera will read my mind about Freddie in the basement, but she doesn't seem to sense anything about it.

❧

One day she accuses me of sneaking food between meals. I am always hungry, and mealtimes are so unpleasant that I can't eat much for fear of being teased. It's true that I did take some sugar bread, but how does she know? Vera's eyes are even smaller than usual. She'll spank me whether I tell the truth or lie, but the truth is worse. I shake my head. She grabs me by the arm and drags me to the closet for the paddle.

"Pull down your pants," she yells. I wonder how I can stall her, get her to change her mind.

"Pull them down, I tell you!" She yanks down my pants and bends me over, spanking me hard, screaming, "You no-good liar. How dare you? You're nothing."

I cry in spite of myself. I hate myself for breaking down, giving her that power over me. She points at me, her face twisted. "Look at you, you're a mess. No wonder your mother and father . . ." She starts hitting me again. "Repeat after me, my mother doesn't love me, my father doesn't love me, only you love me, Vera."

They don't love me? She is voicing my worst fear—that they have forgotten me, that they don't really love me. If they did, why would they leave me here? My stomach sinks in misery and dread. Inside my head I try to fight what she says: no, they do love me, they must love me.

"Come on—repeat after me." Her glittering eyes bore into my brain, my very soul. Her terrible words bang around in my head. For a long time, I cry, refusing to say the awful words that seem too true. Finally I have to give in because she won't stop unless I do. I say the terrible words; darkness falls inside me. I feel like a piece of lint on the floor, to be swept away. I must be a terrible, bad person just as Vera says. I drag myself to my room, my mind flying around frantically, trying to reassemble the pieces.

❧

One day Vera announces that Mommy is coming to visit. I try to remember my mother—her face, her wavy dark hair falling to her shoulders. I want to remember her soft voice and her touch, but now there's just a blurry picture. At the train station in Wheatland, Mother steps out of the mist in all her loveliness. She bends down to kiss my face, and I put my arms around her, inhaling her musky, sweet scent. I want to tell her everything, but Vera stands behind me like a sentry. I know that if I tell Mother, she'll have to take me away now or Vera will make everything much worse.

They drink coffee by the hour, chatting and giggling. Mother clicks her knitting needles, talking on and on, punctuating the air with her wild laughs, kicking her legs in the air. I peek around the doorways, watching them have a fine time. Vera smiles as she always does with strangers, saving her sour face for us kids.

I begin to understand that Mother loves her single life in Chicago. I keep listening to her, checking to see if I'm right. Deep in my bones I know that my mother won't rescue me. Heavy with disappointment, I just watch her, wondering what I've done wrong to make her not want me. At the train station, Mother's soft cheek against mine, I want to tell her everything and run onto the train with her, but I know I can't. She steps onto the train and waves cheerily while I stare miserably at her, trying not to cry.

Instantly, Vera's face returns to its usual scowl. She puts her hand on my shoulder and squeezes hard. "Big girls don't cry."

The train is a trembling silver beauty, yellow and red stripes wrapping around the engine. The Santa Fe Super Chief has come from the west with a real Indian wrapped in a blanket. He stands beside the engine, silent and imposing, his eyes dark and mysterious. The train gathers itself and whistles, shattering the evening, and then speeds off with an earthshaking rumble. In the silence that follows, I realize that I'm on my own forever.

⁂

I get a second chance to be rescued when my father visits. It's been a long time since I've seen him. I can't exactly remember his face, but at the train station he recognizes me and scoops me up in his strong arms, whirling me and spinning the world. He smells like spicy aftershave and makes me giggle when his beard scrapes my face. Daddy talks with a drawl and has good Southern manners. He shakes Vera's hand heartily and introduces his wife, Hazel. She smiles shyly and speaks in a soft voice. I am disappointed that he is with her. I wanted to see him alone so I could tell him about Vera.

Vera serves coffee and cookies, acting every bit like the polite person she appears to be to the world. They'd never guess what she's like with kids, especially me. Right in front of her, Daddy asks me if I'm happy. I fix a smile on my face and say yes, oh yes, so happy, feeling sick inside. All afternoon I watch the adults laugh and chat. Daddy puts his arm around Hazel and talks about his life in Chicago, how happy he is in his railroad work. I realize that Daddy likes his Chicago life, his shiny suits, the diamond ring on his left pinky, and his new wife. A little girl would mess all that up. The morning they leave, Vera takes a photograph of the three of us. I stand in front of my kneeling father, his arm around me. The little girl in the picture looks lost, with sad eyes and not even a hint of a smile.

⊷⊶⊷⊶

I have a series of illnesses, from colds to bronchitis to flu and more colds. When I'm lying in bed, Charlie sometimes brings me soup, and the kids come by to say hello. They are not always mean, but I can't trust them. They'll be nice and then suddenly lash out, making fun of me. I have grown used to Vera's spankings, but I hate it that I cry for each one. I can't seem to keep the tears away anymore. I often see scary monsters in the closet at night, but one night I have a different vision, one that stays with me for a long time.

A lady wearing a red gown and a blue headdress appears in the window across from my bed. I blink, but she does not disappear. I get out of bed and check in the hall to see if someone is standing there, but there's no one. Her dark hair falls to her shoulders, and she looks at me with kindness. She tells me not to worry, that everything will be all right. I feel peace and relaxation as I look at her, and eventually I fall asleep. She isn't there in the morning, and I never see her again, but I return often to the feeling of comfort she gave me, as if she had taken me into her arms like a mother. Later, I discover that she looked just like paintings of Mary, the mother of Jesus.

On my sixth birthday in March, Vera makes a cake for me and everyone sings Happy Birthday. I try to imagine my next birthday, but I can't. My life stretches out like the plains, empty all the way to the horizon. I blow out the candles, my skin crawling with awful feelings: ugly, unwanted, and alone. I know that despite their smiles and singing, these people don't really care for me. I blow out the candles, missing Mommy and Gram, seeing their beautiful faces in my mind. I wonder if they know it's my birthday.

Just after school is out, I get sick again and have to stay in bed. Vera tells me that the family is going on vacation, so I'm going to stay with Gram, and they'll get me after they come back. I should be ecstatic, but I'm too sick to care. They bundle me up with my suitcase and drive to Wichita. Suddenly we are at Gram's house, and she's smiling and wrapping her arms around me. "Sugar Pie, poor sick Sugar Pie," she croons.

Gram folds me into a soft bed with clean white sheets. She tries to hide her alarm at my deflated condition and high fever, but I can see she's worried. The doctor takes my temperature and gives me a shot. I huddle under the quilt, feeling protected and safe. Gram is a kind nurse, waiting on me day and night with juice, pills, and soup, putting warm washcloths against my forehead and a hot water bottle on my feet. Sometimes her tenderness makes me cry, but I don't let her see that. She yells at my mother and father on the phone, "She has rickets and malnutrition!" I don't know what that means, but she says it's their fault for not noticing.

I rock for hours in my mother's childhood rocking chair holding my doll. I rock and rock, grateful for the peace in the house. Gram watches me carefully, puts her face close. "Tell me, what it was like at Vera's? How did she treat you?"

I want to tell her the truth. The words gather in my mouth, but before I can speak, I remember that words are dangerous. When they come back, Gram will pass on everything I say, and Vera will beat me harder than ever. At night I cry, feeling desperately worried, waiting for them to come take me away from Gram. I know that they will be mean again and that I will be unhappy. There's nothing I can do about it, so I just wait, shaking and worrying.

One morning Gram decides to boil an egg for me for breakfast. She bounces around her sunny kitchen, happy, I can tell, because she's going to get me to eat, which I don't do much. Eggs—doesn't she remember I can't eat them? Already I feel like throwing up. She spreads apple butter on toast and pours a glass of milk. I stare at the runny egg whites, not touching them, shaking. Gram kneels on the kitchen floor. It makes me sad to see her like that, begging me to talk to her. I don't want to make her mad, but I'm scared to talk. Movie-like images run across my mind: Vera's spankings, her scary eyes, the boys' cruel teasing. It all gathers up like a steam engine and comes out in a rush of tears and sentence fragments. She smoothes my hair and listens, with tears rolling down her face. I don't dare tell her what happened with Freddie. Her face is sad, then angry, and then sad again. She pats me and strokes my hair, saying, "Poor little Sugar Pie. It's all right."

When I am through talking, she declares: "That's it! You're not going back."

"But they'll get mad. They'll make me go."

"You're not going back with them, and that's final!" Her eyes are fierce. I've never seen her like this before. She calls my parents, screaming that they forced me to go and didn't see that I was suffering. She tells them again that I have rickets and anemia. "I will not give that child back to them. She just sits in a chair and won't talk. She's skinny as a rail. She's not the same little girl."

After many loud phone conversations over the next few days, Gram announces that my parents have agreed to let me stay with her. Gram finally looks happy, and I feel hopeful for the first time in a long while. Still, I wait for Vera's return, rocking in the rocking chair. Will Gram really keep me? I don't trust any of these adults; they change their minds all the time. I keep asking her if she means it. She insists that she will be what is called my guardian from now on.

Finally the day arrives when my tormentors are supposed to come back. All day, my stomach's knotted with anxiety. They all burst into the living room acting as if they are glad to see me, Vera with her white teeth and her phony smile that sends chills down my back. I hide in the bathroom. The adults chat a little, and then Gram tells them. She says that I'm not well and she's my guardian now, with my parents' permission. I come out just to say good-bye, standing close to Gram.

Vera looks genuinely disappointed. I think, sure you are, you won't have me to yell at and hit any more. They make a show of kissing me good-bye as if they cared. I stay close to Gram as we wave good-bye, terrified that they will come back and snatch me away. But the car disappears down the street. Gram, my savior, keeps her arm around me as we stand there waving. Now I belong to her.

Enid and Aunt Helen

GRAM MOVES US to Enid, Oklahoma, a few months after I come back to her from Vera's. The grand sweep of the prairie and the huge blue sky go on forever, knitting into a silvery horizon. Across the street from our little house on Park Street, an ancient cottonwood reaches its branches to the sky, the undersides of its leaves gleaming in the sun. Cows graze and moo contentedly. Everything is so peaceful. I can imagine Indians sitting under that cottonwood tree, horses' hooves and thick clouds of dust, bows and arrows. Evidence that this place was Indian Territory less than one hundred years ago is everywhere: Red Chief Motel, Cheyenne Café, the Cherokee Theatre.

Wheat fields surround the town, their graceful stalks wafting in the wind all spring, changing gradually from baby green to deep amber. I come to love these beautiful landscapes—the wheat, the wide deep-blue sky with great thunderheads building, the clouds that show you the shining underside of heaven.

⁂

One afternoon not long after moving to Enid, Gram tells me to get dressed. We are going to visit her best friends, Aunt Helen and Uncle Maj, who live across town.

"Which aunt is Aunt Helen?" I ask.

"She's not a real aunt; she's my best friend. 'Aunt' is what you call someone who's such a good friend, they're like family."

"Why is the man called Uncle Maj?"

"He was a major in the army during the war, so we call him Maj. His real name is Russell Claire, and we call him RC for short."

Gram puts on a good blue dress and white sandals, glosses on red lipstick, and fluffs on her powder. She always makes herself look nice. As we get in the car, I say hi to the cows grazing under the cottonwood. I'm still amazed to actually be living with Gram. I worry about Vera, sometimes wondering if she'll figure out a way to burst my bubble of happiness, but I trust now that Gram plans to keep me.

Off we go, bumping along on dusty Market Street with its red dirt blowing around us in great gusts all the way through the "Negro section." The street changes from dirt to concrete when we hit the white part of town. The road crosses Highway 81, the route of the old Chisholm Trail. Gram tells me, "The Chisholm Trail is named after

Jesse Chisholm. He drove cattle from Texas north into Kansas before the trains. It was the most famous trail in the west." Gram loves history; her books are piled up all over the house. She likes to tell me about the past and says what happened then is a part of us now.

Eventually Gram stops in front of a green-shingled house with a red front porch and an emerald-green yard set off by bushes of furling red roses. A smiling, red-faced woman wearing a pink striped dress bounces down the stairs, her arms out, her soft belly jiggling with laughter. "Oh, let me get my hands on that pretty little thing. God love ya, darlin'." She squeezes me against her body and my nose is pressed so hard into her soft stomach that I can't breathe for a moment. I don't understand who she is or how she seems to know me. Her blonde hair is a curly mass around her head; her round cheeks blush with rouge or excitement—I don't know which. "Ahh, lovey, look how you've grown. You weren't no bigger'n a grasshopper the last time I laid eyes on you."

"You remember Aunt Helen, don't you?" Gram beams at me. A ruddy-faced man with thick white hair bounces down the steps. "Great balls of sheet iron," he says, clamping a hand on my shoulder, his blue eyes sparkling. He asks me to hold out my hand, where he places a beautiful red rose. I cup the rose in my hand and inhale its delicious scent. The adults start to chatter, Aunt Helen in her drawling Southern accent. Gram's more relaxed and happy than I've ever seen her. We clatter into the house, and the smells of fresh coffee and homemade bread just out of the oven enfold us in cozy comfort.

The house is a delight—a damask tablecloth on the dining room table, a pink rose in a silver vase, lace curtains being sucked against the screen by a gentle breeze. The back yard is like a painting, with roses in all colors—red, pink, yellow, and white—shimmering in the light. I gaze at the photographs in the bookcase: Aunt Helen when she was younger with a smooth face, Uncle Maj in his military uniform. I look at Aunt Helen, then back at the photo, comparing. She sees this and says, "Land sakes, girl, don't be looking like that at me. We're all older now, but the Duchess here," she gestures toward Gram, "looks the same as she always did."

"Duchess," Gram whispers, settling herself with cigarettes and ashtray at the dining room table. I can see that she loves that name. I have never heard her called that, so I ask what it means.

Uncle Maj leans back against the chair and tamps down his pipe. "The Duchess—oh yes, oh yes. She was the Duchess from the first time we met her. At the hotel in San Antone she breezed in looking like a million dollars, dressed to the nines with ostrich boa, silk dresses, velvet shoes."

"Like a movie star. You shoulda seen her," Aunt Helen huffs admiringly.

"No one could hold a candle to Frances," said Maj, puffing his pipe.

"Frances? Who's Frances?" I ask.

Gram grins, gray smoke swirling above her head. "Frances is my middle name. Lulu Frances Hurlbut is my whole name. My second husband's name was Hurlbut, but he died."

So much happened before I was born. "What was your name when you were young like me?"

"I was born Lulu Frances Garrett. I married your grandfather Blaine, your mother's father, and then I was Lulu Hawkins. When I moved to Chicago in the twenties, I preferred the name Frances. Lulu sounds so . . . well, so old-fashioned."

Aunt Helen arches an eyebrow and says, "That's what your mama calls you—Lulu."

"Don't call me that!" Gram says. She seems upset all of a sudden. "I'm Frances to you. To everyone." Gram sashays to the window, carrying her cigarette aloft as if she's posing for a picture.

Helen continues the story. "She glided like a movie star through the dining room at the hotel. It was wartime. Maj was stationed there, a major. Soldiers were everywhere and, oh, a handsome lot they were. Always lookin' at Frances. She was a looker, no doubt about it. What with her silks and satins, that cigarette holder, she looked like Greta Garbo."

Gram comes back to the table. We eat the hot bread, and they sip coffee with cream. Gram spoons coffee into my milk, so I can taste it. I keep looking at her, seeing her in a new way. It never occurred to me before that my grandmother had lived a long time before I was born, that she had her own history. I can't wait to know more about her, and about my mother.

Aunt Helen's house is sunny and open to the air. The sound of children playing and the who-whoing of doves filters through the rooms. I wander off from the adults to explore the layout of the house. Uncle Maj's bedroom is simple, plain, and neat. Aunt Helen's has lace curtains swaying over her bed, which is covered with a white chenille bedspread. I perch at her dressing table, looking at myself in its oval mirror, trying out the various perfumes and powders. Earrings, necklaces, and bracelets spill from her jewelry box. I put some on and spray Evening in Paris on my wrists, enjoying how much I look like a fancy grown-up lady in the mirror. Aunt Helen comes in and puts her hands on her hips. I put down the bottle, afraid she'll be mad.

"Oh darlin', go ahead. You can have anything you want at Aunt Helen's, you sweet thing." She enfolds me in her arms again, and again I'm smothered against her. In her arms I feel safe and happy. For a time, all previous bad things melt away.

***

Gram and I now spend most weekends at Aunt Helen's house, where she feeds us her tasty Southern food—fried chicken and gravy; beef stew; hamburgers; and "glop" made of hamburger, canned tomatoes, and frozen mixed vegetables. On Fridays she makes homemade bread. Another weekly ritual is the bridge game with their neighbors Bob and Willie Jean. The grown-ups spend long evenings playing cards and talking about the war. Aunt Helen always serves coffee and homemade dessert. Uncle Maj doesn't play cards, so he just sits in his chair and reads, wearing his specs, lamplight falling on his silver hair. At night, I fall asleep in Aunt Helen's wonderful bed that smells of sun. In the mornings, warm summer breezes come in the window and caress my skin.

Gram is always in a good mood at Aunt Helen and Uncle Maj's house, and I learn so much about the life they lived before I was born—all about the war, the soldiers who went off to fight, some never coming back. I learn they are all in their fifties, and they say often, "Life begins at forty." That seems so very old to me, a long time away for life to begin, and I wonder what they could mean.

During the week, Uncle Maj walks ten blocks to his office. We see him walking down Broadway on our way to Aunt Helen's on Friday afternoons, looking regal and determined, trustworthy and solid. In the spring, Uncle Maj introduces me to his roses and shows me how to take care of them: clipping, pruning, watering. He shows me all his flowers. "Look at lovely Miss Clematis. See, her flowers are like skirts fluttering in the breeze." He cradles the flowers, with their delicate leaves and petals. Bees buzz and hummingbirds hover like helicopters. He introduces me to his mimosa with her frilly pink flowers. "They're like ballerinas, leaves opening and closing." All summer, I look forward to these weekly evenings with Uncle Maj, where I learn about the living world of plants and the particular delights of roses.

Through Aunt Helen and Uncle Maj, I find a different world than the one my family inhabits. Unlike Gram, Aunt Helen and Uncle Maj are church goers, the First Christian every Sunday morning and evening. She's a regular at the Wednesday night prayer meetings, and each week she takes care of sick old ladies, spreading her warmth with food and her big Texas smile. She tells me that she loves these old, lonely ladies. She has all kinds of sayings—"land sakes," "well, I'll be danged," and "tickle me pink." Aunt Helen is the sun, and the rest of us are planets that spin around her. She makes our world happy with food, her belly laugh, and her jolly Southern sayings.

Gram leaves her English accent at home when we are with Aunt Helen and Uncle Maj. With them, I am Gram's Sugar Pie, and we are all happy.

Night

DARK NIGHT HAS fallen in the house on Park Street. There is no
light, no sound. I am crouched low in the dining room, so the
monsters outside won't see me and I won't whet their appetites. Gram
is silent over on the couch behind a long table that separates the dining room and living room. I can't see her, and I'm worried. She always
closes the blinds and turns on the lights sooner than this, long before
it's so dark. She's never fallen asleep—I hope she's just asleep—like
this before, slumbering through the afternoon and into the night.

I curl up as small as I can. Fear frosts over my arms and legs, as if I'm
being slowly dipped in ice water. She's not breathing; I know she's not,
or she'd be awake. I can't cross the dining room into the living room
to find out because the monsters will smell me. They lie in wait tucked
under the window ledge outside, holding their breath, just waiting to
come in and eat me.

The wind blows against the creaking house. Its walls groan as if they
will fly away, leaving me exposed in the bare air. I curl up even tighter
on the floor, shivering. I can barely make out the imposing dark shape
of the desk beside me, but I catch the smell of its polished wood. Across
the room there is the half-moon of the mahogany dining table and beyond that the long table that separates the two rooms. Gram is so still,
I am sure she is dead. I can't hear her breathing.

What will happen to me if she dies? I would cause my parents a lot of
trouble by being alive if Gram is dead. An abyss opens in my stomach,
a flap in time and space. I tumble into it, at the same time feeling the
solidity of the cool hardwood floor. My mind ticks through what would
happen: If Gram is dead, and Mother and Daddy don't take me in,
then some other adult somewhere would have to. It could even be Vera
again. I know there's nothing I could do about this, and now I'm really
scared. The abyss is total for a few minutes, swirling me in black terror,
but then I get my courage up and begin crawling, one hand and then
one knee on the cool hard floor, my knee bones crunching, making my
way like a prehistoric creature across the desert of that floor, keeping my
head down, alert for movement at the window. If she's dead, I'll have to
figure out what to do. What do you do when a grown-up dies?

At last I turn the corner and see her body lying on the couch in the
glow of the streetlight, her hands over her chest, her mouth agape. Is this
death? Her face looks pale and empty, and she is so still. I crawl quickly,

the only sound now my heart beating against my chest. Trembling with dread, I lay my head on her chest and hold my breath.

Gram's chest is moving up and down, up and down. I am safe; she is alive. The flap to that dark world closes, but the edges of myself are ragged, torn like a piece of paper. I need to hear her voice. I need her to wake up and talk to me, but I don't want to make her mad. Gently I stroke her arm and chest. She gasps a little and flutters open her eyelids. "Sugar Pie." She smiles and holds out her arms. I climb up and hold on tight, her warm body against my own, her breath against my neck.

Liebestraum

THE GREAT PLAINS is an inland sea. I am a speck in that sea, brought to the copper dirt of this place by a migration, as were fish now fossilized in the red rocks. The landscape is dotted with derricks whose steel arms pump oil up through layers of time. The whole town smells of oil. I stand outside to listen to the wind blowing the spirit of the past against my pale body. Dirt from some ancient era blowing against me, I bow my head to the power of the land, the wind lifting my hair and tickling my skin with pinpricks of bone too small to see with the naked eye.

⌑

I lift my head at the sound of a train whistle from across town, a familiar ache of longing for my mother spreading under my left rib. Today I get to see Mommy for the first time since coming back to Gram's. I can hardly remember her; even her face is blurry to me. I go back inside to check on Gram's progress getting ready. She sits at her dressing table, smoking and staring in the mirror, her face drawn into an unhappy scowl. I can't understand why she isn't happy. After all, her daughter is arriving today in Perry, a two-hour trip by car. Gram pulls her face taut with her fingers, muttering about getting older. I try to get her to hurry. When she finally takes out her lipstick, I sigh with relief. I ask her why Mommy doesn't visit very often.

"She's busy."

"Don't you miss her?" I wonder if Gram misses her daughter the way I miss my mother. Gram doesn't answer. Instead she asks me what dress to wear. I choose the one with the red collar. She plops on the bed and lights another cigarette. Gold dust motes and gray smoke filter through the Venetian blinds in the morning light. "You know, I still have a mother. My mama lives in Iowa. Mothers and daughters—they don't always get along."

I have forgotten that Gram has a mother, assuming she is too old to have one. I nod, hoping she'll go on.

"And things happen that nobody—well, almost nobody—can help. And then one thing leads to another. Hell. I don't know. Your mama, she ought to marry again, that would make her happy."

I remember my father and his new wife, but I never think about my mother getting married again. Then she might forget about me entirely.

Secretly, I want my mother and father to be together again and have me with them, but I can never tell anyone this. It feels like an unspoken rule not to talk about it. I can't wait to see Mommy. Still, I worry about her visit. I suppose that she'll fight with Gram the way they did in Wichita. I yearn for her throaty voice and her fingers on my skin. Most of all, I can't wait to find out if she's happy to see me, if she misses me too.

The road is long and straight across the open land. Dry grasses are pressed flat by the strong winds that blow day in and day out. We drive through small towns littered with broken-down cars and dilapidated buildings. Skinny dogs wander alone with haunted eyes.

Perry is whispery quiet, its downtown built around a square with maple trees and a gazebo. A sign announces the Cherokee Strip. Gram tells me the land was stolen from the Indians. In a land run, some settlers stole a claim early, which is why Oklahoma is called the Sooner state. At the station, people wait impatiently for the train—it's three hours late. Gram sashays to the office to ask about the schedule. The train man's glasses slip to the end of his nose. "Ma'am, the train will be here in thirty minutes. It was late out of Chicago and had engine trouble in Kansas City."

Putting on her fake English accent, Gram asks for a light. Her "English woman" routine makes me squirm. The man comes out of his booth and flicks a match against her cigarette. She leans toward him, her eyes meeting his for an electrifying moment. I don't understand the looks on their faces, but there's something in Gram's I don't see at home. Aunt Helen says Gram is eccentric. I'm not sure what this means, but it can't be good.

Everyone gathers on the platform. I stand at the edge of the tracks for a moment before Gram hisses me away, gazing to the silvery place at the horizon where they meet, trying to imagine what is beyond. The whole day is magic—my mommy will be here soon and all will be well. People mill around, some women wearing housedresses, their hair in rollers covered by scarves. Both of my mothers always look beautiful in their stylish dresses and great shoes. A boy kneels down by the tracks to grasp the rails and cries, "It's coming. I can feel the vibrations!"

A beam of light hovers far off down the track. The train seems suspended for a moment as in a mirage, not moving; then the earth begins to tremble, and the whistle splits the air. The power of the onrushing train shocks me, makes my heart pound hard. People scatter as the steel beast roars in so fast I'm sure it will never stop. When the brakes finally take hold, the train keeps going for a few moments, metal screeching on metal. I put my hands over my ears. Finally, amazingly, the huge train shudders to a stop. Regular life begins for me again when men in blue uniforms throw down steel steps and help the passengers descend.

I wonder if I will recognize my mother. I watch a heart-stoppingly beautiful woman step down. She wears open-toed shoes, carries a paper bag and a small suitcase, and walks purposefully toward Gram. I watch them watch each other, and then I know it's her. I break into a run, patent leather shoes tap tap tapping on the bricks. "Mommy, Mommy." I fling myself at her, grabbing her legs, looking up into beauty itself, my mother's soft eyes, her dark wavy hair. She smiles and kneels down so I can kiss her cheek. I can hardly believe that she is real.

"Hi, Mommy. Do you think I've grown?"

"Hi, Linda Joy," Mommy says casually, as if we've been apart only a few hours. She kisses my cheek lightly, stiffens, and gets up.

"Hello, Josephine," my grandmother says in her cool voice.

"Hello, Mother."

The great silver train growls and coughs under the wide blue sky.

⸙

Mother's musky scent fills the car as we roll home. I am suspended in a dream, watching her every move, trying to make up for all the missed time. I feel like crying. I didn't cry for her while she was gone, knowing that if I started I might never stop. Somehow I can control it all when she's away. Now that she's here, I'm desperate for her, but I have to sit back while Mommy tells Gram about her job in Chicago. Gram misses Chicago. She still acts as if it's her real home, even though we live in Enid.

I track my mother through the house, trying to uncover her mystery. I question her about each brush and tube of makeup she put on the hall table, the mascara she brushes on her eyelashes. I reach out to touch the fine hairs on her face. She smiles at me absentmindedly, as if she has just realized I'm here. I drink her in with an unquenchable thirst.

Gram seems a little upset or mad, her dark eyes shadowed with feelings. Mother gets coffee and an ashtray, then sits in the burgundy chair, her knitting needles clicking away. The silent air between them heats up like a hot wire. I watch my beautiful mothers, each of them with a part of the other inside. Unsaid words build up all that day and into the night. Finally, from my bed, I hear them fighting in the cadence I remember from Wichita. Later, Mommy slips between the sheets next to me. Her delicious aroma wafts over me as her dark hair flows across my pillow. I fall asleep wrapped in cottony dreams, breathing in the scent of my mother.

⌁⌁⌁⌁⌁⌁

The next morning, Gram is up early, smoking and pacing. I can tell that it will not be a good day. In the living room, the maroon ceiling presses down into the burgundy rug; smoke swirls in thick gray ropes. Mother saunters out from the bedroom and demands coffee.

"It's in the kitchen," Gram rasps.

"That's a fine how-do-you-do. No way to treat a guest."

"Guest? Just how long do you plan to stay, since you lost your job? You're a grown woman and . . ."

"Look here, Mother . . ." Mommy's eyes flash dangerously.

"Mommy, I'll pour your coffee," I say, desperate to break the tension.

"No you won't; you're too little. Mother, you don't let her handle hot things on the stove, do you?"

"Now what the hell is that supposed to mean?"

Their mad storm of smoke and words travels inside me, words like, "I'm taking care of your kid, you're irresponsible, you're mean and cruel." It is clear that I am a difficult burden. I go to my bedroom and sit by the window, my eyes on puffy white clouds in the azure sky. The outdoors is always lovely and peaceful. For a long time, I watch the wind blowing against a cottonwood tree.

After a while, the storm inside the house passes. Gram begs Mother to play the piano. Mother resists, then sighs and puts down her knitting. A whole new mother appears at the piano bench. As her fingers move across the keys unraveling a haunting melody, I think of the rising full moon, the loneliness of the train whistle at night. An ancient heartache thrums in my chest. The music seems to tell me a story about my mother, about her sadness and her mystery. I watch her skillful fingers run up and down the keyboard.

When she stops, Mother returns to earth, no longer magical, no longer weaving a beautiful world where we all could be together in peace. She returns instantly to her smoking and furrowed brow.

"Does that music have a name?" I ask.

"'Liebestraum.' It means 'Song of Love.'"

All day long, the song weaves through my body, filling in places that have been empty since Mother first left me, easing the ache with a sweetness that gives a lilt to my step.

⸻

Aunt Helen has invited us for dinner. When we arrive, I am surprised that she hugs Mother tight the same way she does me, calling her darlin'. They start talking easily, as if they'd just seen each other last week.

"Did you know my mommy before?" I ask Aunt Helen later. She stands at the stove stirring the glop, adding onion and tomatoes.

She says, "Land sakes, girl, I was there when you were born. I was with Frances that day and . . ." She starts to say something but then falls quiet. I ask her what, and she just shakes her head.

Out in the living room, Gram and Mother start in, their voices rising and falling. Aunt Helen struts out and shakes her finger at them. "Now look here . . ." Uncle Maj stands up like a military man and barks, "I'll have none of that in my house. Talk nice to each other or you'll have to go home."

Mother and Gram both fix their dark eyes on Helen and Maj. I brace for more trouble. To my surprise, they sit down and light cigarettes, the room filling with smoke and tension but no angry words. Maj gets them to talk about more neutral things like the weather, President Eisenhower, how America should have joined in the last war to rescue England sooner. Aunt Helen and I return to the kitchen, where the fun is.

⸻

One night back at our house, I am in my room painting a watercolor of Bethlehem and Jesus and the bright star. In the living room, voices run up and down the scale, high-pitched screeches. And I hear dishes crashing. I want to stop them, but I'm afraid to. I listen for clues, hearing only more crashing and screaming. Finally, I rush out of my bedroom to find our good china in pieces on the floor. Mommy's curls are loose around her face, and Gram is howling. My mother is ranting about something, her voice rising and falling in a tone that is too familiar. I shout at them to stop, grabbing Mother around the legs, trying to get her attention. Suddenly the screaming stops. Gram looks at me with guilt in her eyes. I pick up some broken shards, but Mother takes them out of my hand and tells me in a soft, fractured voice that she'll take care of it. I watch my two mothers crawl on their knees, picking up the china pieces. The rest of what is broken remains hidden from sight for a long time to come.

∙━━━━∙

Despite the horrible battles, my mother's visit is a dream come true. I get used to her being with us, almost get used to the fighting again, again, again. One night as I eavesdrop, I hear the dreaded words: a new job. Chicago. I ask Mother if she is leaving, and she says, "Soon." I start to shake, terrified of losing her for good.

The next morning Mother stumbles out of the bedroom looking sleepy, her hair tangled. When she passes me to sit in the chair and smoke, I clench my jaw, wishing very hard I could get her to stay. But I know that what I want doesn't count in her decisions. Mother smokes, still sleepy, legs curled up under her, looking almost like a little girl. Gram hunches on the couch, relief all over her face that Mother will be leaving.

Mother gestures for me to come to her. She draws me close and puts her arm around me. It is almost more than I can bear without crying. When it is time to leave, she always touches me more. My skin burns with a desperate need, more hungry for her than ever.

"Mama has to leave today," she murmurs. "I have to start my new job."

"Can't you stay?" I say mournfully, touching the curls in her hair.

"Mama has a new job," she says about herself. "Aren't you happy for her?"

I say that yes, I'm happy for her. I have to say the right thing no matter what I'm feeling. But there is one thing I can't resist asking her for.

"Mama?" I twist her hair over my fingers.

"What?" She blows a puff of smoke into the air.

"Can you play 'Liebestraum' for me before you go? Please." She pauses, frowning. I know she doesn't want to, but I keep begging, knowing that she feels guilty about leaving and is likely to give in.

Finally she gets up and arranges herself at the piano bench. I cuddle next to her as she unravels the melody that runs up and down the keyboard. I see colors—yellow and amber, orange and brown, blue and red, greens, shimmering in the waterfalls of notes she plays. The notes fill the room and rise to the sky, filling me with my mother in ways that nothing else can. I soak up all she has to give, folding this moment into my mind so I can bring it back when she's gone.

When she is finished playing, she gets up and goes off to bathe, dress, and pack her things. I follow her around like a duckling, watching her fold her sweaters, smoothing them with her hands. I wish it was me she was caressing like that, but I seem invisible to her. She frowns and smokes, gathering her make-up from the table. I remember the day she put it there. I was so happy then, and now grief fills my body. I ache as if I have been beaten, but it's inside where Mommy and Gram can't see it. I make sure they don't, because it will just upset them.

I ride in the back of the car with my mother, praying that time will reverse, wishing that the train will never come. Gram's mood is lighter, which makes me more upset. If they got along better, Mommy might stay.

The lights are bright at the Perry station. Families gather, whispering and talking. I dread seeing the eye of the train as it comes around the curve, but there it is, a monster that will take away my mother. The whistle tears through me.

Mother kisses Gram on the cheek. Their voices and eyes are soft, as if leaving is the only time they can feel this. Mother kneels down. "You be a good girl. Mind your gram."

Her scent mixes with the air that is laced with diesel and the promise of rain. She slips into the train car and soon reappears at a window. I watch her wave with a gloved hand, remembering our cozy train ride of so long ago. The whistle blows again, and the train disappears with my mother. I stand by the tracks, focused again on the place where they meet at the horizon, the point where time and space come together.

The wind whispers its ancient knowledge, stirring up remnants of the history buried in this copper-red dirt. All that went before is in the past now, both the good and the bad. I resign myself again to life without my mother, but can hardly breathe for the pain in my chest. Particles of bone and dust blow against my legs.

Daddy Is Magic

DADDY IS MAGIC. Daddy is a dream. Daddy is coming this morning! Gram and I wait by the shuddering train, the steel animal that trembles and snorts, pawing the tracks at the Perry station under a brilliant blue sky. I jump up and down on the concrete, the sun warm on my hair. The morning is sweet, full of birdsong and promise. Not a cloud in the sky. Men in suits and long coats sweep from train cars. All the men look like him, almost, the brims of their fedoras shadowing their faces. Under one of those shadows might be my daddy.

I scan the faces of all the men dismounting from the train, my stomach beginning to sink. Did he change his mind? Will he remember me? I know I've grown. Now that I'm seven, I'm much smarter. I was in second place in a spelling bee, and I can read beyond my grade. I can't wait for Daddy's good cheer, his brimming-over energy, his bristling whiskers, the rough nap of his coat, the feel of his strong arms lifting me into the air.

I want to spend time with him alone, to get to know him better, to see his arms without a starched shirt, his dark silky hairs lying against his skin. Other girls talk about their fathers at school. A girlfriend tells me she watches her father mow the lawn wearing no shirt, that she accidentally saw him pee. I can see in her eyes the thrill of it—so naughty, yet so exciting—a secret glimpse of a mysterious part of life that is hidden from children.

I feel cheated without a father in my house, without any contact with men in general. My grandmother doesn't even let the neighbor guy who mows our lawn use the toilet. The Father, with his big body and those illicit private parts, is exciting and dangerous. There is something about the power of men that changes women, though we kids don't have words for it, exactly. But we can feel it, we can hear it in the women's talk about not displeasing a man. We hear the way they chat about their husbands; it's the same way they talk about God—with awe, a little gasp at the end of the sentence. There is much left unsaid, like between moments of a prayer. The only way to hear in between what people say is to learn to listen to the wheat, the land, the wind. You can only hear these things out in the plains, by a wheat field, say, in the spring.

Feet tap-tap-tap on the bricks of the station platform. He's coming for me, for me! Now the heavy breath of his deep voice, "Linda, Linda."

Colors and shapes swirl—the brick train station, the steel train, the conductors' blue suits—around and around. My ribs are squeezed so tight I can barely breathe. His cashmere coat swings around him, and he laughs from deep in his throat. His Old Spice envelops my face and sinks into my bones, and I am happy all the way through.

"I've missed you, my girl, my girl." He whirls me until I'm dizzy with joy, then sets me down and faces Gram.

I'd rather leave out the next part, how Gram leans toward him, her hand cocked with an unlit cigarette, hovering close to him as he flicks open the lighter. She touches his hand with hers; a sizzle, then the tobacco burns orange. She looks into his eyes and he meets her gaze briefly before they break apart.

It's been so long since I've heard Daddy's voice that I've forgotten what he sounds like. Even his face has dimmed in my memory. The picture of him in my mind is not him, not really, and my photograph of him doesn't capture him either. A daddy can't be folded flat in black and white. Sometimes I steal the picture out of its hiding place, but not too often. If you get a good feeling and hold on to it too much, you have to pay for it later.

The Nash Rambler glides down the blacktop. The car overflows with all of us, Daddy taking up more than his share of room, his coat thick with Chicago threads, the white of his starched shirt so bright. His huge hands sculpt the air as he talks excitedly about his work on the L & N railroad, his stock investments, making more money than ever, belonging to fancy clubs. I tug his arm—Daddy, Daddy. He turns back to enfold me in his scratchiness and Old Spice. My happiness knows no bounds. Daddy is a burst of cymbals in my quiet life with Gram.

<hr/>

Daddy and I ride in the elevator of the Oxford Hotel. Looking out the window in his hotel room, I can see all around town—spidery trees, Randolph Street, Broadway, Main Street, and the granite courthouse on the square. We can even hear the train whistles from the Frisco and the Santa Fe, a lonely sound that has always made me think of him and my mother. The spot under my left rib aches even though Daddy is right here and I can feel his warm hands on my shoulders as we look out the window. I don't know why a train whistle always makes me feel sad.

I'm surprised that Gram is letting me spend the night with him here. I love being alone with him, like other girls who have a father spending time with them at night, at bedtime. Tomorrow we'll go to Aunt Helen's for one of her fried chicken dinners. Gram will be there, continuing the silent conversation between them. When they are together, I can sense the events of the past. I don't know exactly what happened between Daddy and Gram, but I can feel it in the dropped words and glances between them.

All I know about Daddy and "the old days" is that he married my mother when she was twenty-nine and he was forty, and they had me the first year they were married. They divorced when I was eight months old. I know it in my stomach and heart. I have no memories of him from before the age of four. No feeling of his clothes or body on my skin. Only a blank space. I'm seven, and we're alone together for the first time. When the man at the hotel counter took too long, I tapped my foot. He was stealing time from Daddy and me. I have only two days and a night to make up for the whole year, 363 days when Daddy lives only in my imagination.

❧

The bathroom at the Oxford has a floor made of tiny black-and-white tiles, a pedestal sink, and a gleaming bathtub. If I can get Daddy and me into that tub, I'll understand what makes him different from me. I'll know what other girls know. I want to be in their club, not left out the way I am at school games—the skinny one, knock-kneed, pigeon toed, always dropping things.

I want to be like the other girls, whose lives are enriched somehow by the thick voices and grime of the males in their lives. They have daddies who fix faucets, repair cars, and mow lawns; wash the car and take out the garbage; come home every night to smooth out the bumps of life. They drive up in white shirts with rolled-up cuffs. The neighbor daddies grin and put their arms around their wives and kiss them on the cheek. The other girls' daddies give them baths or even take baths with them, so I want that, too—to have the mystery of daddies revealed.

He has taken off his jacket and loosened his tie. The bedspread, with its little chenille bumps, is rumpled. My stomach hurts from so much giggling, and my face is raw from his beard. I feel the imprint of his big arms and hands on my body. I feel his strength in me and ask him if we can take a bath. He seems surprised but rustles down the hall to check the tub. It's even bigger than the tub at my house, with feet and great curved edges and long silver spigots like swans' necks. I wonder if I was wrong to ask him, but all I want is wet hair and giggles with my father in the bath. The top of Daddy's bald head shines as he bends down to inspect the bathtub, as if the quality of the tub will decide this question.

He murmurs nervously, "I'm not sure if a little girl should take a bath with her father. It's not proper. It's different for a mother, but for a father . . ." His face registers confusion.

"Oh well, if you don't want to . . ." I say, wanting to smooth things out. "But my girlfriends, they see their daddies in the tub, they . . ." My cheeks grow hot with a shame I don't fully understand.

"It's okay," Daddy says with a soft voice. "There's room for you to sit behind me."

My feet are cold on the tile floor as I undress. Daddy has agreed, but I still feel anxious, thinking maybe this is a bad thing.

"You get in first, and then I'll get in," Daddy says.

Bubbling water bursts out into the tub. I fit myself at the back of the tub, leaving room for Daddy. It will all be okay, I tell myself, but something doesn't feel right. Daddy comes in wearing a towel and turns his back to slip in. I close my eyes after sneaking a look, but with a washcloth in a strategic position, he's taking no chances. He is jittery and giggling, and I feel I have crossed some kind of line.

I turn toward the swan spigots, my white legs small and thin beside his long, tanned legs slicked with thick hair. I pretend to be a cheerful, laughing girl, but I feel bad. The bath is brief, and then we get dressed in separate rooms. We go to sleep in the big bed after dinner. He snores, and his body is so huge. I feel small and grateful next to him, but worried. I hope he doesn't think I'm bad because of my curiosity.

The next day, Gram takes us to Aunt Helen's.

"God love ya," she says, giving me a squeeze. Gram, Daddy, Aunt Helen, and Uncle Maj chat as if they've known each other for a long time. Aunt Helen serves up her fried chicken, gravy, and mashed potatoes, bustling around the room with the energy of a pressure cooker. We must all be family now that Daddy is in her fried chicken club. Gram takes slow puffs from her cigarette, her black eyes fastened on me. Can she tell that today I belong to Daddy?

They get along, tilting their heads back and laughing over dinner. Gram is really strict about table manners and gives me "the look" that reminds me to hold my fork correctly. She tells me to cut the fried chicken off the bone.

"Oh, just let her pick it up in her fingers. You're gonna fancy away that little girl to nothing," my father says with a wink in my direction.

Gram's eyes flash. "Nonsense." Gram shows me how to cut the chicken, then tells me to do it myself. My knife slips, and a chicken leg flies onto the tablecloth.

Daddy laughs. "It's okay, just pick it up. She can't be a lady all the time." He winks at Aunt Helen, who winks back.

Gram's voice is harsh now with righteousness. "Of course she can. My granddaughter will have good manners and hold her head up in society. Sit up straight, Linda, and don't chew with your mouth full."

Daddy wipes his mouth and excuses himself from the table, his shoes squeaking as he paces the floor. Around the table, flustered hand movements, eye glances. Then he's out with it.

"Look here, Frances. I appreciate what you're doing with Linda Joy— taking care of her, buying her nice dresses—but she's still a little girl."

Doesn't he know that he shouldn't say things like that to Gram? She tosses her head and gets up from the table, leaving the rest of us hunkered down.

"You look here. I am teaching her things that she should know. How dare you criticize me."

"I'm just saying let her pick up a piece of goddamn chicken in her fingers. Let her be a little girl. She's only seven, for Pete's sake!"

Uncle Maj's chair hits the floor with a bang, he gets up so fast. Aunt Helen bustles into the kitchen. Uncle Maj fits himself between Gram and Daddy, tamping tobacco into his pipe. Gram and Daddy give each other a lingering glance, an unreadable look in their eyes.

Uncle Maj says to Daddy, "Frances took Linda when her mother left, and she raises her just fine." He looks him straight in the eye. He doesn't say, "Because you aren't taking care of her." He doesn't say, "We've got her here now, and we're all looking after her." But he does.

Gram plucks a cigarette from her pack of Kents and saunters over to Daddy, who fishes out his lighter. Daddy and Gram stand close, her hair touching his eyebrows as she sucks in her cheeks. She sits down and swings her leg, staring off as if nothing mattered. Daddy heads to the kitchen to ask Aunt Helen how she made her delicious gravy. The storm has passed.

⚜

After dinner, Gram, Daddy, and Aunt Helen sit chatting and laughing in the living room. I worry about the train coming to Perry too soon, to take away my daddy. I watch the gold balls of a clock covered by a glass dome roll back and forth, stealing minutes from my time with him. After listening to them for a long time, my jealousy rises like mercury in a thermometer. I want him to myself. Don't they realize that I don't get Daddy again until next year? The ache of his leaving fills my body.

To console myself, I follow Uncle Maj outside to putter in the garden. Thick storm clouds gather in the darkening sky. Uncle Maj's white hair sticks up in the wind, and his face is red. A thorn sticks his thumb, and I touch his hand. "You're hurt, Uncle Maj. Let me get a Band-Aid."

"Oh, it happens all the time. I don't mind bleeding once in a while for my beauties. Here, put these gloves on. You can help me."

He teaches me how to loosen the soil from the roots, and how to angle the cuts as he trims the roses. "If you cut the roses back hard, they'll burst into a fuller bloom in spring. Sometimes cutting things back is a way to make them bloom better."

I yearn for the spring, the yellow daffodils and the roses. I sense that there is a right time for everything, but never for Daddy leaving.

We all ride in Aunt Helen's car for the drive to the station. Daddy smiles at me, patting my shoulder, but I can see that his mind is already on Chicago and his exciting life there. I get out of the car at Perry, the wind pushing against my back, blowing me toward my father. I grab his thick, warm hand and brush the hair on his knuckles with the tip of my finger. His Old Spice makes me want to cry and grab at him, begging him to stay, but I just watch the train get bigger as it comes into the station, steeling myself for what I know comes next. The whistle haunts me, warning me to get ready.

"You be a good girl for your gram," he says, then turns his back, his shoes tapping on the bricks as he strides to the train.

The train roars and trembles. The hard wind reminds me how small I am, and that there is nothing I can do about people leaving. I watch every detail of the leaving ritual, trying to take the ache away. The train men bring in the steel steps, and the conductors wave and whistle. The doors snap shut. My father waves—oh, so happily—from his square window. I memorize him, his wide smile, the gleam of his bald head. I'm ready to live on another year of memories.

I watch until the train is lost in mist and smoke.

Liberace

THE ROOFLINE OF our neighbor's house creates a triangle of yellow sun on my rug. During a full moon, the triangle is milk-blue but so bright you can read by its light. The Great Plains is like that, heat and light everywhere. Even the storms are exciting, making my blood swell and rush like the wind and the clouds and the boughs of the great trees.

The neighbors in the house next door are a real family with a mother, a father, a little girl, and even a dog. Sometimes I wish I lived in that bustling house with a real mom and a dad. George comes home every night after working at Sears. Ruth is always sweet, and she's tender toward Cherie, who is two years younger than me. The dog's name is Pudgy, a yipping miniature boxer that I've grown to love despite the fact that I was bitten by a dog once.

Ruth and George's house vaulted to mansion status after they got a television. They're one of the first families in town to have a TV. Once in a while Ruth invites Gram and me over on a Saturday night to watch Liberace. All our neighbors have variations of the same house—white walls, beige couch, plastic sheets covering pale carpets. The neighbors' houses are neat, with no newspapers, books, or forgotten bills piled up. Our house is wallpapered with dark green and burgundy flowers, a French design, Gram said. The maroon ceiling seems to press me into the hot wool of our Oriental rug. Sometimes I can hardly breathe.

Tonight is Liberace time. A smiling Ruth wears an organdy apron and bears a plate of chocolate-chip oatmeal cookies. All of us are entranced by the small, mahogany box and the black-and-white picture: Liberace's hands swoop up and down the piano; the silver candelabra sparkles. We all know that Gram is nuts about Liberace, with his super-white teeth, his wrists as graceful as a cat's tail. "Oh, look at those lovely hands. See how he lifts his fingers up and down like pistons," Gram croons. While Liberace plays, Gram sips her coffee, on her face a look of such wonder and pleasure that I stare at her more than at the TV. The notes of the music make waterfalls of color In my mind, sweeping me into an unfamiliar, beautiful world.

* ~ ·

The next week, on a day so windy that the house creaks, I find Gram tinkering at the piano, trying to play runs like Liberace, lifting her hands high into the air.

Her dark eyes fasten on me. "Sugar Pie, how would you like to learn piano?"

The piano entices me with its amber keys, the magic waiting beneath them. Playing the piano will make Gram happy. I wonder if I could play like my mother does. I tell her yes, I want to learn. Gram takes out sheet music with a silver cover. A curvy lady with dark hair leans back against a slick-suited man with a tiny mustache. He meets her sultry look.

"This is the music for the 'Third Man Theme,'" Gram says wistfully. "Oh, how I'd love it if you'd play this for me someday."

My grandmother at fifty-seven is as glamorous to me as any movie star. She poses, a hand on her hip, her dark hair flowing around her face. She has a faraway look, as if she's listening to a distant melody. "Ah, this is the music I loved." She gets up to dance, one hand on her stomach, the other hand on the shoulder of an imaginary dance partner. She takes a few turns around the living room, humming the "Third Man Theme," cast back into memory.

"You have no idea, when I lived in Chicago, the kind of life I had, men falling all over each other to dance with me. In those days we danced all night. I wore the most magnificent dresses and shoes with little straps. Ostrich boa over my shoulder . . . oh. I was escorted home properly, of course, with no funny business. Quite a life. I took ships every year to England. You have no idea . . ."

She drifts off, seeing herself before she was a grandmother. I squint my eyes to see that Gram better, trying to imagine her wearing the clothes that hang in her closet—long satin gowns, fancy shoes with ribbons, the ostrich boa I love to stroke. She turns to me, luminous. "If you learn to play the piano, you'll be very popular. People will invite you to parties; they'll ask you to play so they can sing and dance. You'll see."

The future spins before my eyes. I want to be the lady on the sheet music, or Gram with a boa flung over her shoulder. I try to imagine the time before I was born and the person I will become, but it's hazy, like fog on winter wheat fields.

On Saturday, I meet my new piano teacher, Crystal. She flows through the door of her studio, a white caftan covering her full body, necklaces sparkling on her generous chest. Crystal seats me at a white piano with sticky keys and shows me how to position my hands, while

Gram takes notes. Crystal says that musical notes look like black flowers with stems. She shows me the mysterious signs of music—treble and bass clef, half notes and whole notes, the repeat sign, middle C. A world opens up, with its own secret runes.

After that Gram and I have a new routine: She drives me to lessons each Saturday afternoon; I practice twenty to thirty minutes after school. Each week Gram reminds me what the teacher says from her notes.

"Lift your wrists like Liberace," she says, laughing. "What a guy. Wouldn't it be romantic to have him play just for us?" Her eyes glow with delight.

In the beginning, it's fun. The piano, left over from her Chicago days, stands like a proud dowager in our small dining room. The wood is worn; the ivories are discolored. I press keys, listening to the notes and how they create songs. Gram smiles a lot. After a few months, she tells me that we are getting a new piano. A shiny new Baldwin Acrosonic piano, with its shiny polished wood and bright new white keys, is delivered. It smells good, like lemons.

Then, as the practice sessions grow longer, the piano gets boring. The neighborhood kids play outside, the sound of their laughter drifting in. I want to play games and run in the grass with them, but Gram makes me practice almost all day long. At night after they have gone inside, sometimes I stand in the yard inhaling the sweet smell of the grass, watching the grand sky overhead with all its millions of stars, listening to the chirping of crickets. The huge moon rises overhead, painting the world silver. Alone in this landscape, I forget about the pressure in the house, and about Gram's strict rules. I'm part of the night, the land that surrounds us in dust and light.

The Plains Is Our Mother

It's June and school is out. Gram tells me that we are going to see her mama. With tears in her eyes, she says that her mother and brothers and sisters live in Iowa, and she misses them. She loads the car with cigarette cartons and suitcases, and puts the down comforter on the floor of the back seat, to protect me if we have an accident.

The Great Plains is an amber dream, the blue sky a canopy over the flat land that stretches to the far horizon. The wheat fields are ever-undulating seas. It is harvest time for the wheat. Combines lumber up and down the fields spewing golden dust into the air as they cut the long wheat stalks, capturing wheat heads that will be stored in monolithic grain elevators rising from the emptiness of the plains. Every afternoon small clouds grow into huge thunderheads, and the air smells of sulfur. Rain drums the roof of the Rambler, and the windshield wipers bang frantically back and forth. Burma-Shave signs mark our way north.

The car weaves through Kansas towns like Sedan and Arkansas City. We stop at small cafés, where Gram speaks with her English accent, acting like a world traveler. We order milkshakes or hot fudge sundaes and perch at picnic tables.

Gram likes to stop at historical monuments on the roadside, where I learn about the Osage Indians and the tall plains grasses, about outlaws and the Civil War. In Coffeyville, where the Dalton gang was captured, we stay at a fancy hotel with high ceilings and crystal chandeliers. I can imagine an hombre swaggering in, ordering a beer at the bar, then shooting out the brass-framed mirrors. Gram tells me that the Missouri River starts out in Montana, where Lewis and Clark found its source. She tells me about Sacajawea and about the pioneer women in wagon trains that came across here, when the plains hadn't been settled yet.

"My mama, Blanche, was born a pioneer woman, in 1873." I wonder about Gram's mama—what she looks like, if I resemble her. I squeeze my eyes shut and imagine horses running, dust swirling around their flanks. On the way to Iowa, I play with my dolls and imaginary companions, a fairy mother and daughter. The mother never lets the girl out of sight, and I play for hours with the lucky daughter who gets to have her mother with her all the time.

On the third day of our trip, Gram's eyes light up and she points eastward. "We're almost there! Fifty miles to the Mississippi River, the greatest river in the United States. Our family has been living near that river since before your great-great-grandmother was born. That's where my mama and her mama were born and where I was born."

A mist settles over her eyes. I don't understand her moodiness, but I want to know all about these women and the place that made them.

The Mississippi Valley Cradle

O N THE EISELY Hill that overlooks the bottomlands of the Mississippi, a road curves across a wide plain of cornfields and rumbles past roadside fruit and vegetable stands. Gram starts to tell me about the family I am going to meet. "You'll see—it's a big family—all the kids that Mama had when I was older." We turn into a driveway with the sign "Wilson's Mink Farm." When Gram toots the horn, people rush down the porch stairs, smiling and waving.

"That woman with the glasses is Edith, my sister," Gram tells me in a wavery voice, "and the older one is my mama. Oh, Mama." Gram opens the door and flings herself into her mama's arms, tears running down her face. I don't recognize anyone, but they seem to know me. They hug me one by one, murmuring, "Oh, lookit how she's grown." I'm dizzy from so many hugs and the feeling of automatically being part of them.

A woman with white hair caught under a hairnet wipes tears from her eyes. She's the oldest person I've ever seen, with a hump on her back and wrinkles that crisscross her face. Everyone talks at once. "Lulu's here. Linda's here." They pronounce Gram's name "Lula." Aunt Edith wears pink plastic glasses and has dark, tightly curled hair. Willard, her husband, wears a plaid shirt. A pipe dangles from his stained teeth. He pats me on the head. "How're ya doin', squirt? Sure have grown."

Their son, Fred, looks like his father, with the same face and plaid shirt. I've never received so many friendly pats in all my life. The threads of family intertwine around me, making me feel that I belong here even though I have no memory of this place or these people. They keep saying, "Remember Blanche, remember Edith?" I just smile and nod politely.

Blanche puts a bony arm around my shoulders. She smells like an old washcloth and seems strange, with her wrinkles and thick bones all visible under papery skin. She fixes her watery eyes on me. "Linda Joy! Linda Joy, you're the pride of your great-grandmother. I named you Joy, you know, because you were my first great-grandchild."

I don't know what to say, but I feel nice and warm, like I'm home.

Edith leads everyone up the front stairs and into the grand kitchen. The electric stove is new, she tells us. Edith fixes what she calls "a little lunch," which seems like a huge meal to me—baloney sandwiches, red Jell-O with fruit cocktail, homemade pickles, home-canned peaches, and chocolate cake. Everyone talks all over each other as we sit at the Formica table in the middle of the room. Gram is clearly the star by rights of our trip across the Great Plains.

"As a woman alone, I go where the truckers go. You can always trust truckers. They eat in the best places along the way, and they would help me if I needed it."

Nods of agreement.

"Humph," Blanche gnaws on her baloney sandwich. "Good thing you're not traveling in a covered wagon. Never fergit the time one pulled up in front of the house. The people was goin' to Kansas." She pauses to chew. "They came back, though. I was about twelve."

"When were you born, Grandma?" I ask. Gram told me to call her mother Grandma.

"Shh. Don't ask nosy questions," Gram hisses.

"I'm eighty years old, and I don't care who knows it." Blanche fishes peaches from the bowl. "These the peaches we canned last year?"

"Two years ago, Mama, remember?" says Aunt Edith. "Canned two bushel baskets and made four pies for Grace's birthday."

"Damn good peaches. Fill 'er up." Willard holds out his plate with the rind from the baloney sandwich on it. Edith puts the peaches into a separate sauce dish.

"We have to be a good example for Linda," says Edith with a wink.

Fred slops peaches onto his plate despite his mother's sour face. "Oh, Papa, just got to be yerself, don't ya?"

"Can't do nothin' else. Yourself is who y'are. None of this fancying up will do any good," Blanche chimes in.

"Well, if you ask me, getting a good education and teaching a person good grammar isn't too fancy." Gram sounds angry. She scoots her chair out and lights her cigarette from the gas stove.

"Well, just so ya know where ya came from. Can't fergit that." Blanche solemnly eats her peaches.

"Now, Mama," says Gram. They banter for a while until Blanche says, "Did you fergit your old mother, livin' your fancy life?"

"Mama, how can you say that?" Gram, tears in her eyes, puts her arms around her mother. Blanche wipes away a tear, too. Is it possible that this mother and daughter don't get along either? I am disturbed somehow by this possibility.

Uncle Willard starts telling stories, tamping down the tobacco in his pipe. "When you was little, you'd say, 'You want to sit on my lap, Uncle Willard?' Remember?"

Fred chimes in. "We'd have fun pretending for him to sit down on you, and you'd say, 'No, no. I mean sit on my yap!'" Everyone laughs hard at this; I don't remember it, but it feels good to hear stories about me, and to find out that I have a history here.

After lunch, Blanche sits in the rocker by the window, embroidering a pillowcase. She shows me how to push the needle in and how to loop it around to make leaves and stems.

"Just as long as I don't lose my eyes," she says. "Can't hear too well, but if my eyes goes . . ." She chews off the end of her thread.

I watch while she embroiders and Edith irons cotton shirts. She sprinkles the cloth with water from a soda pop bottle, making steam rise from the cloth. Edith lets me iron handkerchiefs, teaching me how to smooth the fabric. How different their lives are from Gram's and Mommy's. They enjoy these daily tasks, it seems. I follow them around from room to room, eager to be included in all they do, feeling the comforting mantle of family settle around my shoulders like a shawl. I am especially curious about Blanche and attach myself to her like a small, happy shadow.

Blanche and the Garden

THAT AFTERNOON, BLANCHE leads me to the garden. She bends over, bowed like a water witch's wand, skirts gathering around her ankles in front, exposing cotton hose rolled under her knees in the back. She gnashes her teeth and yanks, muttering about the weeds. Glossy leaves the size of small umbrellas spread across the sandy earth.

"See this sand—it's part of the Island, and it's why we have the best melons in the world. The Island used to be cut off from the rest of the area by the old slough and the river. That's how it got named."

Blanche is so old that she knows everything. The heat of the July day rises up from the land. Everything smells like fresh air and earth, black and loamy. The strawberries are ripening, like red buttons beneath green leaves. Blanche snaps off a strawberry and bites into it. Juice runs down her chin. Her deep-set eyes gaze at me from behind gold-rimmed spectacles.

"Mmm," she mutters, gesturing for me to pick one for myself. Everything is too raw and close to the earth. I am awe-stricken and a little scared. Bugs and dirt are everywhere, flies are buzzing, ants crawling. Gnats fly into my mouth and stick in the corners of my eyes. Blanche tells me to go ahead and pick a strawberry, and I pluck one with a satisfying snap. Gram would definitely discourage me from eating something without washing it, afraid I would die young in her care and she'd be blamed for it, but Blanche is a pioneer woman and she tells me to eat it.

"Come on, bite down hard."

"But it's dirty."

"Come on. Try it. It's good for ya. Nothin' like the fruit of the earth."

I stare at the dirt in the crevices of the strawberry, still worried.

"You got to eat a peck o' dirt afore you die."

She smears juice across her chin with her sleeve. Finally I bite down on the strawberry and it bursts in my mouth. I choke, surprised, my senses flooded with the sweet strawberry juice, the sun beating down, the smell of earth. Blanche's eyes laugh behind her glasses.

"Good, ain't it?" She turns around to hoe savagely at the weeds trying to take over her vegetables. It doesn't matter that this is Edith's garden, not her own. Here, everyone shares in the work. I grab a hoe and copy her ways.

"See that you get that weed out, root and all. Pull 'em all the way out or they'll take over. Just like some people I know." She chuckles deep in her throat.

"Who, Grandma?"

"Now never you mind. It's a sin to gossip."

I want to know more about everything. "Did you have a mother?"

"Land sakes, girl, 'course I did. That's how we come into this world. My mother was Josephine, and she was born on the Island just like the rest of us."

"My mama's named Josephine." The name Josephine gives me the tingles.

"Your mama was named after my mama." She wipes the sweat from her face with a handkerchief. Her bony, crooked fingers with black dirt under nails are thick like a man's, her forearms tanned and wrinkly. Everything about Blanche is interesting to me, as if she's the only remaining exhibit of an extinct species.

"Tell me about your mama."

"Oh, there's not much to tell. Hard-workin' woman. Delivered babies for half the county. Best blackberry jam in the world." She pauses, leaning on her hoe. "Life was different then." She turns to me, her eyebrows fierce and thick. "You got no idea, young lady. People's lazy now, think the world owes 'em a livin'. Times was hard. But no matter what, we always had enough to eat. Yes sirree, we always had food on the table. And my papa would give his right arm to help a neighbor."

"Where is your mama now?"

Blanche glances at me sharply. She doesn't answer right away. Hardens her jaw and clamps her teeth against her lower lip. "She died near to when you was born." Blanche stands up and rubs her lower back. "Everyone loved my mama."

I watch roly-polys curling up and ants marching in straight rows up and down their earth mounds. Millions of bugs are living full lives out here. I ask, "Did my mama know your mama?"

She grunts as she hoes a patch of weeds that have gained ground. "Oh Lord, yes. When your mama was a little girl, she'd visit my mama in Muscatine. Your mama, Jo'tine—that's what we called her—would come to see me at the farm where Edith and the rest was growin' up. Such a pretty little girl she was, with those big, brown eyes. Poor little thing."

I wonder what she means. "She don't do right by you, I tell ya. At least Lula has the sense to take care 'a you. But this business 'tween Lula and Josephine . . . well, you're too young to understand. I don't know about those two." She stomps on a beetle that had been working its way toward a tomato plant. "Got to get them before they get you," she says, winking at me and wiping her brow with a handkerchief.

I try to imagine all these mothers. Our history, my history, reaches so far back. Blanche, Gram, Mother, and me—we all come from here. Next to Blanche I feel very small and young. I look up at her, the mother of the mother of the mother. She knows everything. I decide to stick to her to find out things. When we go into the house, the dirt caked under my fingernails seems like a badge of honor.

❦

The rest of the day has its rhythm. The men come in and take showers. Edith fixes a chicken dinner with mashed potatoes, gravy, corn on the cob, sliced tomatoes, rolls, red Jell-O with banana, and apple pie. On the hour and half hour, seven clocks chime, a beautiful music that goes with the laughter and conversation. I am part of all this. I sense the threads of our common history and like the way these good people look at me with happiness in their eyes.

After dinner, everyone sits outside in chairs under the elm trees, murmuring in the darkness about family, the weather, the cost of food, and how much better things used to be. Fireflies hover, giving off pieces of light in the velvet night. I swoop smoke into Uncle Willard's empty tobacco can. He lets me sit on his lap, his big paw hands holding me up. Gram seems different here. Lula, as they call her, is not the same as the Frances who lives in Enid. She is her plain self, yet different from everyone else, with her fake accent and haughty ways. But this is family, and she is Blanche's daughter and Edith's sister.

At ten o'clock, as if with one mind, everyone rises and goes into the house, muttering about the mosquitoes and looking forward to ice cream. The men get out the ice cream and chocolate sauce while Edith puts plates of homemade cookies on the table. The room fills with the clink of spoons and the sounds of pleasure. When all the clocks chime eleven, everyone yawns.

Edith tells me that I will be sleeping with Blanche upstairs in the room across from Fred. I feel special, getting to sleep with her, and glance in her direction. She merely gives me a little nod. Smiles do not rest easily on her thin lips. Clump, clump, clump go Blanche's black shoes with their thick heels up the wooden stairs to the bedroom. The fluffy, high bed seems to rise halfway to the ceiling. The air is thick with heat and the smell of the past. Faded dresses hang on hangers, rifles lean against the flowered wallpaper. Blanche peels away her clothes, her ample flesh rippling and swinging.

I turn away, blushing. Seeing all that flesh is not something I'm used to, but she doesn't seem to mind. How can she be so free with all this? She turns her body as she pulls on the white cotton nightgown, exposing round lumps hanging at her waist. I have never seen breasts like that. My mother's are soft and round; Gram's are pouchy and hanging. Blanche's feet have thick, yellowed toenails. Her skin is puckered with thick blue veins.

When she's got her nightgown on she turns to me. "You gonna sleep standin' up?" she asks, pulling back the chenille bedspread.

"The bed is so high." It reaches to the top of my shoulders.

"It's a feather bed."

"Feathers? What kind of feathers?"

"Duck, goose. Nothin' like a feather bed. Been sleepin' in 'em all my life." She pounds the thick mattress with her fist.

"Feathers?" My finger pokes at the softness of the bed.

She hauls her body into the high bed and lays back, her nose pointed at the ceiling. I pause, not wanting to get undressed in front of her. "Well, gonna sleep in your clothes?"

"Can I turn off the light?" I mutter, shyly.

"Wiped a lot of baby's butts in my life. Skin don't mean nothin' to me."

I snap off the light. Her casual attitude about bodies amazes me. I slip on my summer nightie, and clamber over her bony shins to tuck myself along the wall. The idea of sleeping with Blanche seemed wonderful at first, but now this large ship of a woman—her hips curving high, her bony shoulders sticking up, her eighty-year-old smells—seems too real.

Then the cadence of her voice lulls me as she tells stories that will stay imbedded in me for the whole of my life. She tells stories about life on the farm—getting up in the morning before dawn, slopping the pigs, milking the cows; how the men had their chores, and the women had theirs. She baked bread several times a week, gathered firewood, and cooked three meals a day for a family of eight. In the summers she fed ten or more hired men, too. She tended a huge garden all summer, and in August she canned the vegetables and fruit to put in the cellar for winter.

She always did the washing on Mondays. "The big black iron kettle sat in the front yard. We fired up the wood, got it to boilin', and threw in them clothes, stirred the boiling pot with the washin' stick. We used lye soap I made myself, and the washboard to get everythin' clean. No self-respectin' person puts a wash on the line for the neighbors to see that's not clean. After the washin'—then the rinch water." (She says it that way: "rinch.")

"Before them new-fangled washin' machines, we wrung the clothes out and pinned them on the clothesline. Did the wash for eight workin' men and six kids. You don't know dirt until you live on a farm. It took all day. God help ya if it rained." She shakes her head, her gray curls rasping against the pillowcase. I can see it all—Blanche in the yard, children scampering. Dirt and dust, pigs and cows. Pillows of fresh-baked bread with churned butter. I want to be there, too.

"Did Gram live there then?"

"Lula? Gosh sakes no. That girl—always one for gallivantin'. A lot of the time she lived with Josephine, my mother, in town, went to high school there 'cause the country school only went to eighth grade. Things was far away then. You walked or rode your horse, or you didn't go. We was poor people, lived seven miles from town on the Island. I drove the wagon into Muscatine to deliver milk and eggs to the rich folks." Blanche takes a deep breath.

"That Lula always was so different. A dreamer. She had a different papa, Lewis. After he died, I married Mr. Thomas and had your great-aunts and uncles." Blanche pauses for a long time. I wonder if she's gone to sleep.

Soon she begins again in a changed voice, picking up speed. "You know, life is full of sorrow. I'll never figure out some things, no matter how hard I try." She sighs. "I delivered the neighbors' babies. Never fergit the night one died. Two days of labor. Nowadays, that baby would have lived. But there's no way to outsmart God."

"Why did Lewis die?"

"He breathed his last right 'side me. One day he was fine. The next, dead of twenty-four-hour pneumonia. Seems like yesterday. Can't believe I'm eighty. Life goes so fast. Don't you fergit that. Don't you miss a minute."

"He was Gram's daddy?" I feel sorry for Gram. I know what it's like to miss your daddy.

Blanche turns over onto her back. "Lewis was only twenty-two. I can't never fergit it, no matter how much time is passed. Too much dyin'. Always too much dyin'." She sighs and turns her head in my direction. "You're too young to understand."

Her breathing keeps me awake. I'm more awake now than ever before in my whole life, cast back in time, into the nineteenth century. Looming large in my mind is Lewis, who died so young and left my grandmother without a father.

I picture Blanche back then, old, the way she is now, but then I realize that she was young then, at the beginning of her life. By now she is marked so much by time, she is different for having lived it. The history she just told me happened sixty years ago, so far back I can't grasp it, but it pulls at me.

The headlights from the highway make light and dark patterns across the ceiling. Blanche's great white form snores beside me. I am catapulted beyond my child self and perceptions. The past seems to expand and loosen up, trailing behind me, enticing me to follow its threads and find out more about these people and this place, the bones and the land that I'm descended from.

Ghosts of the Past

THE NEXT MORNING I ask Edith if we can look at family pictures. "After lunch," she tells me. At noon we have cheese sandwiches and cottage cheese and the applesauce she canned last year, and then Edith hauls out the cardboard boxes. Hundreds of black-and-white and sepia photographs spill onto the table. She names the ghostly faces in the pictures, people who wear funny clothes and stare at the camera in stiff poses. The women wear long dresses, the men overalls. In one picture, my mother is about seven years old, standing by a car with Josephine, Blanche's mother. Blanche stands nearby, at that time a dark-haired woman in her fifties who was still raising children on the farm. Chickens strut through the crowd in the picture.

Now everyone gathers around and talks at once, lifting out a picture, telling a memory to anyone who wants to listen. Blanche lifts out a piece of paper with a handwritten poem on it:

> Preserving children
>
> Take one large grassy field, one half dozen children, all sizes, three small dogs, one long narrow strip of brook, pebbly if possible.
>
> Mix the children with the dogs and empty them into the field, stirring continually.
>
> Sprinkle with field flowers, pour brook gently over pebbles; cover with a deep blue sky and bake in a hot sun.
>
> When the children are well browned they may be removed.
>
> Will be found right and ready for settling away to cool in the bathtub.
>
> JOSEPHINE DICKERSON STINEMAN

Suddenly the dogs start barking. Everyone goes to the window to see who is visiting. Two cars drive up, honking, spilling out two large ladies and two men. Hellos and laughter clatter into the room, the screen door flapping behind them. One beefy man with a big stomach bellows,

"Hello, Mama. What're ya doin' sittin' round on your can?"

"Oh, pshaw, you know better'n to talk like that," Blanche says, a smile coming to her lips.

"Hal, how're ya doin'?" Edith says, then whispers to me, "This's Hal, my brother."

"Just about great," he answers Edith, then his eyes find me. "And don't you forget it, little lady. Lookit you, you've grow'd up." Hal wraps his beefy arms around me and squeezes.

"This is Grace and Stan, remember? Grace is our sis."

"Call me Aunt Grace. Hi there, little Linda." Her face is wreathed in smiles and her eyes beam warmly at me. Her large body envelops me for a moment. She smells like flowers.

"Lula, what the hell have ya been doin'. Haven't seen ya for a while." As Hal towers over her, Gram puts her head on his shoulder. "Any more trips on them boats? Any new husbands?"

Color rises in Gram's cheeks. "I'm taking care of Linda, making sure she gets a good education."

"Book learnin's all right, long as ya don't fergit how to act," Blanche says as she lays out plates and silverware.

The dogs bark again, and the screen door flaps. In comes a very round woman, her stomach jutting out in front of her, a cigarette hanging in the corner of her mouth. She wears a plaid dress and flat, floppy shoes. Her big grin makes me like her right away.

"Lula, how the hell are ya?" She grabs Gram's neck in the crook of her elbow.

"Delia, you're a sight for sore eyes." Gram's voice sounds more like theirs now; her fancy self is fading.

"Is this the little tyke, Linda? Get over here and give your old aunt a hug. Lula, you don't fancy her up too much, do ya?"

"Sure she does." Grace flicks Delia with the dish towel.

Delia wraps her arms around me tight, pats me, and leans down to look in my face. "Yeah, you're Josephine's all right. How is that girl anyway?"

"Lula could pass for Linda's mom instead of her grandmother," says Grace.

"What about Jo'tine, Lula?" asks Margaret, putting out homemade bread-and-butter pickles.

"They had a fight on the phone last week," I chime in.

"Get over here," Gram hisses between her teeth, grabbing my arm and hauling me into the living room. Sparks seems to fly from her eyes and her fingers grip my arm hard.

"Don't you dare talk about our business in front of strangers."

"They're your brothers and sisters . . ." I protest meekly.

"What happens in our house is not for anyone else to know. Do you understand?" I don't understand, but I nod, wanting to hide in shame. I slink back to the kitchen, my cheeks burning. Grace gives me a friendly look and tells me to follow her. She gestures toward a bushel of apples and two wooden chairs in the room off the kitchen. "Sit down and help me peel these apples." She hands me a paring knife.

"I have grandchildren, too," Grace says. Her brown eyes are huge behind her thick glasses. "You put the blade of the knife into the skin like this." She rotates the apple so the peel comes off in a single long curl.

"I can't do it," I mutter. My apple is in pieces. Gram's recent scolding has me burning with shame.

Grace's voice is soothing. "That's all right. Just watch me. It's nice when the peel comes off in one curl, but don't worry. You'll learn." Her eyes tell me more than her words. After a little practice, I learn to peel two apples her way, with a whole peeling curling into the bowl. She tells me that I'm a quick learner.

At the table, they all joke and talk about the weather, the price of hogs on the market, the rain. I love the easy flow of conversation, elbows poked in ribs. All the adults defer respectfully to Blanche. After dinner, my aunts and Blanche stay in the kitchen, flicking each other with dish towels and telling dirty jokes out of the sides of their mouths. I love the fresh smell of soap, the slow, soft way they talk, the comfortable way they touch each other. Here I can be a kid, with more than enough mothers to teach me the ways of the farm that Gram left so long ago.

❦

After a week at Edith's, Blanche wants to go to her own house. "Here's the castle," Blanche says, as Gram pulls The Nash Rambler in front of a small house covered in fake brown brick. Her house is small, old, and musty. It has two bedrooms, no bathroom, a kitchen with a wood cookstove and a tilted floor. She tells us to sleep In her room, the one with a fluffy featherbed just like at Edith's. An old organ with cloth pedals is on one side of the room, decorated with dozens of family pictures. In one of them, Blanche, her mother and father, and all her brothers and sisters stare sternly into the camera. Blanche looks younger, but still serious.

That night, we go to bed just after dark because Blanche says she doesn't want to burn lights and waste money. The next morning I wake up to footsteps pounding in the kitchen. I get up and wander in, excited to be here in this new place and eager to explore. Blanche is stuffing newspapers into the stove, poking at the stubborn fire. "You sleepyhead, what are ya doin' sleepin' your life away? And Lula, that lazy good-for-nothin'." To Blanche, sleeping past dawn is a mortal sin.

She uses firewood from her back-lot wood pile to feed the crackling fire, then wrestles her iron skillet onto the stove and throws in thick slices of bacon. After a pan of water starts boiling, Blanche tosses in coffee grounds to make coffee.

Blanche seems to have five pairs of hands. When she clanks open the stove to feed it more wood, I watch the fire snap and crackle as if it's alive. I love this kitchen coziness. As she works, Blanche tells me more about the old days: how cows would freeze in the terrible icy winters. "But we had food in our stomachs, we did," she says. "Never had to beg for a dime. People don't know the meanin' of work these days. You just need your garden, your kids, and your pride."

A sleepy-looking Gram comes in. She and Blanche sip coffee, sitting in peaceful harmony together. I watch this mother and daughter, thinking of my own mother. Why can't she and Gram have mornings like this? Why is it better with Blanche and Gram?

I know one thing: Here, in this town by the Mississippi, I'm rooted in our family. I taste the flavor of the past in my breakfast and see it in the coffee grounds as they make patterns on top of the water in the saucepan. The fire crackles a message to me, telling me that I am home, home, home.

Grandpa, the Prayer Man

THE NASH RAMBLER scoots us down narrow highways, bisecting oceans of corn that stretch as far as the eye can see across the rolling landscape. Gram talks about my grandfather, Blaine, whom she's taking me to visit in Wapello.

"We were married when we were very young. We were so in love. Ha!" Gram laughs.

"Why did you get divorced?"

"Oh, just one of those things." She pauses. "He was young and hot-headed . . . Let's just say I was unhappy. But that was a long time ago. He's a nice enough man." She taps her cigarette against the ashtray.

"Did Mommy see her daddy when she was little?"

"Sure. He married Bernie after we divorced, and they had a little girl, Jean, who lives here in Wapello. Her children are your cousins." Gram keeps lighting cigarettes, looking into the rearview mirror to smooth her hair and check her lipstick.

When we pull into a driveway, a bald man with a round stomach and a woman with white hair come to the car. He smiles and greets Gram. The woman says hello, too, but I sense words underneath that aren't being said.

"Linda Joy, how nice to see you again. How you've grown, young lady." They pat my head. I'm surprised at the sweetness of their greetings.

Grandpa's lower teeth jut out of a large jaw, and his voice booms with certainty. Gram stands slightly apart, with her elbow tucked in the crook of her waist, waving a cigarette.

Bernie asks me to come inside to help her make lemonade. Gram and Grandpa chat out by the hollyhocks, Bernie watches them from her kitchen window. She asks about my music lessons. "Your Grandpa is a great piano player. He played all over Iowa and even New York. Last time we saw you, you were a tiny little thing. Remember, you came here with your mother?"

As always, I say yes, even though I have no such memory. Gram stands close to Blaine, speaking in her English accent, but moves away when she sees us coming with the lemonade. They all stand around as if there's an elephant in the garden everyone's determined to ignore. Bernie stands back, her dark eyes flicking back and forth. Gram finally says she has to leave. I don't want to let her go—I've never been away from her since Vera—but I pretend to be brave and don't hug her too long.

After Gram leaves, Bernie seems more relaxed. She takes me to my bedroom, a room full of sun, and helps me unpack my suitcase. Grandpa says really long prayers at meals, his head bowed and eyes closed. The fat on the hamburgers turns yellow, and the mashed potatoes stiffen as he drones on. He asks for help with his temptations and asks God to bless the garden, the fish in the river, and the corn growing in the fields.

"Thank you, Lord, for sending Linda Joy to us. We've missed her. And please bless her mother, Josephine. Thank you, Lord, that Linda Joy has such a nice home with her grandmother."

I'm surprised that Grandpa knows so much about us. As I sit eating at their table that first night, I realize that I have found another strand of family here in Wapello.

<hr/>

I enjoy playing with my cousins, Joanie, a bouncy five-year-old, and nine-year-old Kenny. That week I giggle more than I have in my whole life. We run through the sprinkler, and play hide and seek, Old Maid, dolls, cowboys and Indians.

Grandpa says that not too long ago he bought a black-and-white teddy bear for Joanie and a truck for Kenny. He tells me that when I leave, I can have a toy, too. I decide to get a doll buggy. My doll buggy disappeared when I went to Vera's and I want to have another, thinking it will help erase what happened. Secretly, I really want the teddy bear, but Grandpa might get mad if I ask for the same thing as Joanie. Gram would want me to choose the buggy and not be such a baby.

On the last day at Grandpa's, I feel shaky inside, already missing them. We have had such a good time, and I really don't want to leave. Grandpa takes me to the toy store where he asks for the doll buggy. He hands it to me proudly, but I take it with a heavy heart. I want the wonderful black-and-white bear with the big red bow so badly it makes my chest ache, but I just can't bring myself to speak my feelings.

Big blotches of rain fall on Grandpa's windshield on the way back to his house and the wind swirls the green leaves of the roadside trees. I've had such a wonderful time. I have a lump in my throat as Bernie helps me pack the tiny doll clothes she made for me. Finally, I can't help it and start crying. Bernie puts her arm around me. "What's the matter? Did we hurt your feelings?" Grandpa kneels down before me, his blue eyes full of concern; Bernie kneels down with him. I want them to get up and leave me to my misery like most adults do, but they reach for me, pat me, and keep asking me what's wrong.

Bernie and Grandpa hover, kindly asking me again and again what's the matter. Finally, just to get this agonizing moment to end, I blurt out, "I'm sorry, I don't want to cause any trouble, but . . . could I please have the bear instead?" They sigh with relief.

Grandpa stands up and announces, "We'll take the buggy back and trade it in for the bear. Let's go." Bernie pats my back. They are clearly not upset by my request, and I am amazed.

Bernie cuddles me in the back seat on the way to the toy store. I'm exhausted from so much worrying and crying. They are unbelievably casual about making the exchange. Grandpa says to the storekeeper, without a hint of annoyance, "Could we please exchange the buggy for the bear?" The storekeeper smiles and lifts the huge bear down into my arms. I'm so relieved and happy. I hug him to me, but I'm still embarrassed for making such a fuss. Grandpa and Bernie have seen a part of me I never let anyone know about. Usually I'm careful to keep my fear and my worry, and especially my need, covered up, hidden even from myself.

On the way back to Edith's, I wrap myself around the beautiful bear and stroke his shiny red ribbon. I hold him close, basking in the warmth and ease of this rare drama-free experience.

When we get to Edith's, I gratefully sink into Gram's open arms. The adults talk for a few minutes, but Grandpa doesn't mention our two trips to the toy store. He seems to sense that Gram would disapprove. Everyone gathers around me and my precious bear as we wave goodbye to Grandpa and Bernie.

We tramp into the kitchen, where Aunt Edith boils milk for hot cocoa. She sits me down at the table, my bear by my side, with a cup of cocoa and cookies. I feel wrapped in soft cotton, loved and safe, allowed to be just a little girl.

Spare the Rod

Back in Enid now, I have begun to feel safe, finally believing that Vera won't steal me away again. Gram and I are together, a two-some against the world. Gram especially likes it when I play piano without a mistake at a recital, or when I play more advanced pieces than the other kids. She wants me to be the best at everything and constantly compares me to other children. "They got 100 percent—why didn't you? They are in the highest math group—why aren't you?"

It's a Saturday afternoon and Gram has me doing chores. I'm washing dishes and playing with bubbles, enjoying the warmth and the rainbows in the dishwater. I pick up a plate, but it slips from my hands, shattering into pieces.

Gram yells, "What happened?" I say, "Nothing," but her heels pound the floor toward me. I know she'll be upset, but I figure that she'll hug me anyway and tell me it's all right.

"Sweep it up into the dust pan." Her voice is stern. She goes on, "You need to be taught a lesson. Turn around and pull down your pants."

I stare at her. All the trust I felt with Gram has disappeared in one sentence; she changes into Vera before my eyes. I stand frozen.

"You have to learn your lesson," she says. "Come here." She jerks me toward her and starts whacking my bottom. A jumble of images flash by as I stare at the floor—her kind hands when I had the measles, the love in her eyes when she says "Sugar Pie." I have to make sure that nothing like this happens again.

I have no chance to devise a strategy. Only a few days later she slaps my face for being impudent. A face slap is worse than a spanking. It hurts more and leaves me feeling even more humiliated than a spanking does. A few weeks after that, Gram decides to use a walnut yardstick on me, making a show of the weapon she intends to use the same way Vera did. "See this? It's very hard," she says. Gram warns me about her abilities as a sleuth against lies, tricks, and all the devious ways that children, apparently me in particular, will use to put one over on her. "Don't think you can get away with anything," she says.

I'm extra careful washing the dishes. I practice the piano as much as she tells me to. At school I try to make her proud of me with my grades and deportment, doing my best to be perfect. If I'm not perfect, Gram—the closest thing to a mother I've got—will punish me.

It is evening in late fall. Outside, the plains wind tugs and pulls at the house. The living room lamps are lit, but shadows hide deep in the corners of the room. Gram is on the couch and I am in the chair reading Treasure Island out loud. Each night she has me read to her to be sure I test above my grade level.

"You are my granddaughter. You are not like those other kids. You are smarter. Don't you understand? You have to be educated; you have to get the best grades. You have to become something. You don't want to live like common people, do you?" She waves her hand dismissively. "Get busy and read that passage again."

She mutters her endless instructions in a monotone of criticism that sets my teeth on edge: "Speak up. Read that with expression. What do you mean, you don't want to read? I would have given my right arm to have my grandmother do this for me. You're so ungrateful. I spend my time doing this when no one would take you. You have the nerve to tell me you don't like it. Who the hell do you think you are?"

I mutter something back and make a face. Suddenly my face is stinging, she's screaming, and my hair is being yanked by the roots. My scalp is on fire as she drags me across the room to the bathroom, screaming that she's going to wash my mouth out with soap. This can't be happening. What happened to my regular Gram? She grabs the Ivory soap and forces my head back, pressing the soap between my teeth. I choke and try to spit out the bitter pieces that bring tears to my eyes.

"That'll teach you to mouth off at me. You are not to talk to me like that; you are to obey me, understand?" Her fingers are still entwined in my hair, so I can't move. She yanks my head back hard until I say yes. I'll say anything to get her to stop.

Afterwards, she goes into the kitchen and makes coffee. When she comes back with her cup, she is the picture of serenity. Shaking, I pick up the book and begin to read. I write her a note before bed that night.

> Dear Gram, I love you very much. I'm sorry I was bad.
> I love the watercolor set, and I will paint you some pictures.
> I'll try harder to learn lots of new words so we can read books.
> I love you. You sure do make good coffee.

I hope the note will make her like me again.

The next day my sore scalp tells me that it wasn't all a bad dream. I ease down the hall and slip around the table to spy on her. I need to know who she will be today—the good grandmother or the bad one. Last night my real grandmother was gone. Gram looks up at me now and lifts her arms. "Sugar Pie," she whispers with a smile. I take a breath. All is well. She goes to the kitchen and pours fresh-perked coffee into our best cups and saucers. She adds real cream and sugar. This wonderful ritual means we are friends again. The good Gram lifts her cup for a toast.

Lemon Meringue Pie

A FEW MONTHS later, we're back at Aunt Edith's house in Iowa on a hot June afternoon. The wind flaps the sheets and towels that Edith pinned to the clothesline in the morning. Chocolate chip cookies that I helped to make are baking in the oven. Edith announces, "Now we're going to make a lemon meringue pie!"

She measures the flour and the Crisco into a bowl, mixes it into crumbly pieces, and pours in just enough cold water to gather it into a ball. She shows me how to roll it into a circle with the rolling pin. She smoothes it one way, then another, turns it over, sprinkles it with flour, then shifts it again to keep its shape even and round. Once the crust is a big circle, she slides it into a pie pan. We crimp the edges, pinching the dough between our fingers until the fluted crust is high and proud.

While the crust bakes, we make lemon pudding to fill it with, and then make the meringue. Edith teaches me how to break the eggs so not a speck of yolk gets into the bowl. With the mixer, I whip the egg whites into high, white peaks. We fill the baked crust with pudding, mounding the meringue nice and high on top. It goes into the oven to brown for a few minutes. Through the oven window we watch the peaks turn a golden color. With great ceremony, Edith and I take the pie out of the oven and place it in the middle of the table. Everyone gathers around to admire it.

"See, you can make pie. This is your first pie!" I'm so thrilled that I grab Edith, hug her, and do a little dance. She blushes a little and turns away, but there's a sweet smile on her face.

I love learning to cook with Edith. Her working-woman hands are always busy, just like Blanche's and all the Iowa women's hands. She's always making some delicious dessert: cookies of all kinds, pies like lemon meringue, apple, peach, and banana cream. She makes cakes from scratch. I love licking the bowl and making frosting with powdered sugar and butter. And Edith cooks delicious suppers: fried chicken and mashed potatoes, roast, stew, homemade potato salad. Edith and her sisters do the canning in August, sharing recipes, tomatoes, peppers for relish, and peaches. The only female person out of the food-preparing loop is my grandmother—she sees herself as too much of a lady to take part. She sits alone, reading and smoking, while everyone else bustles happily in the kitchen.

I love being more like Blanche and her kids than Mommy or Gram.

Neither of them knows how to cook, but all my great-aunts are home-makers. Food is the hub around which the wheel of family moves. Fresh coffee is started whenever a car drives up. Every visitor is offered a homemade dessert. The unspoken rule is that when people come, you feed them out of what you have, even if it's not very much or very fancy. These Iowa women are always apologizing for their offerings: This gravy is lumpy, this cake wasn't baked today. No one could ever come into the house, not even for a few short minutes, without being fed. How different Blanche and Edith and the rest are from Gram, who doesn't want people to come to our house, who acts put upon if she has to be a hostess. My Iowa family knows true hospitality. It's hard to believe that the same blood flows in Gram's veins, but she smiles when she lifts the fork to her mouth, just the way all of us do. Lemon meringue pie is the way you make a great summer's day even better.

Mother's Shadow

At Aunt Edith's, there is a time for everything and a rhythm that drives the day. The family knows this rhythm, which begins with the chiming of seven clocks at six in the morning. I burrow into the featherbed, Blanche's warm body rousing beside me. I hear the clink of her false teeth against the glass and peek out from under the sheet, seeing the folds and ripples of her flesh, the hump on her back stretched thin, like pie crust over the bumpy backs of apples. It's strange that her body seems both young and old, wrinkles everywhere along with smooth, white skin. The rooster next door announces the beginning of the day. Thin necklaces of sunlight shine on the elm trees outside, making leafy shadows on the flowered wallpaper of the bedroom.

As I watch Blanche, I think about my mother's body and Gram's— the three of them, the bodies of the mothers of each generation. Seeing them as older women gives me a glimpse of how I will look one day. I can't imagine getting that old, yet getting old doesn't seem so bad when I see that Blanche still works hard and does everything she wants to do. The rooster crows again.

"You hear that rooster?" Blanche says cheerily. "It means get up, get the fire started, the milkin' started. In winter it means when you first get up, you have to break the ice in the water barrel. Oh, shut up, you red devil," she says to the rooster, the hint of a smile on her lips. "I'm already up." She turns back in my direction, holding her waist with one hand, bending over and clutching the bed railing with the other.

"Are you all right, Grandma?"

"Oh, don't worry 'bout me. I'm just catchin' my breath."

I lie back in the feather mattress, hugging the whole bed. The aroma of fresh-perked coffee filters upstairs. I don't know it yet, but today my mother will sweep across this peaceful landscape like a wildfire.

※

She calls just after breakfast, while all of us are still sitting around the kitchen table. Willard is lighting his first pipe of the day. Edith grabs the phone on the third ring. All eyes go to her and the phone.

"Josephine? Where?"

"She's at the bus stop in town," Edith whispers to the rest of us, holding her hand over the receiver.

"Let me talk to her," I say, grabbing at the phone. She is my mother. I can see by her face that Gram is already irritated. "Mommy?"

Mother's voice is all business. "Who's coming to get me?"

"I don't know," I say. A spark of anxiety fires in my stomach.

Mother's imperious voice shouts over the line, "Well, get someone over here to pick me up right now!"

I hand the phone to Fred, who placates her by agreeing to pick her up in a few minutes. Wincing, he holds the phone away from his ear. We can all hear Mother's rage: "What's the matter with you? Why aren't you leaving right now? Get over here!"

Edith giggles and shrugs. Gram mutters something under her breath, and Blanche shakes her head. Fred, winking at me, tells Mother he'll be there as soon as he puts on his pants.

I beg Gram to let me go. I'll jump out of my skin if I have to wait an extra minute.

Willard says, "I'll drive ya. Come on, Fred, let's go get her before she bites somebody's head off." He brushes pipe tobacco off his shirt.

"That Jo'tine. Haven't laid eyes on her for a while," Blanche murmurs. She sounds almost sad, but her face doesn't give any clues as she continues her embroidery work.

Gram has a familiar look on her face, the oh-hell-my-difficult-daughter-has-arrived look. I wave bye and rush through the screen door before she can change her mind about letting me go.

———————

Mother stands beside what serves as the bus stop: an abandoned gas station with a drooping sign and chipping, mustard-colored paint. She looks fresh and beautiful in a beige suit, open-toed shoes, dark hose, and red lipstick. My heart beats faster at the sight of her. Gravel spits as Willard pulls the car to a stop.

"Watch out, for God's sake," Mother cries, stepping back.

Willard stays at the wheel. I am first to approach my mother, suddenly shy, drawn to her despite her shrill voice. I wrap my arms around her waist, waiting for her to squeeze me back, but she only touches my shoulder and pats my head, looking over at Uncle Willard.

"Uncle!" she laughs. "Aren't you going to get out of the car?"

"What for? I'm just the chauffeur."

Fred gets out though, and gives a little bow.

Mother smiles. "Well, Fred, you look just like your papa."

"That's what they say. Let's not stand around jawing. Get in the jalopy."

Mother holds her cigarette holder aloft and says, "Aren't you a gentleman?"

"Hell, not any more'n I can help it."

"I'm sure Edith taught you to open the door for a lady."

Fred puts his hands on his hips and looks around. "Lady? I don't see no lady. Oh, excuse me. Linda, you get on in." He bows and opens the door, gesturing toward the back seat. I know he's kidding, but Mother looks irritated.

"Mommy, you're the lady." I want her to feel happy, so I stand aside to let my mother, the uncrowned queen of the day, into the back seat. I feel unsettled by her act-like-a-lady routine that echoes Gram's haughty attitude. Nevertheless, all the cells of my body are switched on. My mother is next to me; it's like a miracle.

"When are you leaving?" I ask, worried already about when she's going to leave.

"You mean how long am I staying?" Mother teases, with a smile. She doesn't answer my question.

At the house, Edith has already laid out lunch. Blanche is at the head of the table, as always.

Mother chats on about being a legal secretary in Chicago, about how wonderful Chicago is, the best city in the world. Around the table we pass the baloney, liverwurst, and Velveeta cheese. Edith has put Wonder Bread, coleslaw, and sliced tomatoes on the table. A variation on this menu is served every day during the summer. It will be the same for forty years.

Mother talks on about antiques before launching into her inevitable topic, men. This is the part that always gets Gram mad—Mother's hour-long monologues about the men in her life. I watch Gram's anger rising on her face.

Mother turns to Willard and Fred as the male experts in the room. "You're men, so you know how men are. After all, you're all alike. If this man comes by my desk every morning and talks to me—talking about himself, personally—don't you think it means something? Listen, listen, he even took me to lunch! At an expensive restaurant! The lights were low—very romantic. Now why else would he be giving me all this attention?"

"Is he married?" Gram asks.

"What the hell does that have to do with anything? If he's unhappy with his wife, it's no business of mine."

"Look, Josephine, what are you doing? We've been through this." Gram paces and smokes.

"Oh, Mother, you're so old-fashioned. You don't understand."

"Nonsense. I worked in Chicago. I've been to England."

"Lula has been around the world," Blanche says, the sting of irony in her voice.

"Oh, Mama," Gram says with annoyance, "you know better than that. I was only in Europe."

"Anyway, as I was saying . . ." Mother goes on about the man. Finally, she pauses in her monologue to ask Willard, "Well, what do you think, Uncle?"

"Hell, Josephine, I don't know nothin'. Been married to Edith here all these years, and that's it."

"You need to pay attention to money," Gram says, pulling out another cigarette.

"Money? Ha. Money's not important," Mother says dismissively. "Love is the most important thing in the world."

"Money's not important? As long as I keep sending it to you it's not." Gram's sting is felt around the room. Blanche watches the two of them snipe at each other, lips caught between her teeth in disapproval.

"Well, Mother, you have more than I have. Why shouldn't you help your daughter?"

"Because you aren't going to make anything of yourself! I'm never sending you another red cent as long as you . . ."

"Now, now, you two." Willard stands up decisively. "Let's have dessert and not worry about money right now. We don't got none, and we don't need to hear about it." He gets the cookies, and Edith takes the ice cream out of the freezer. We eat dessert in an uneasy hush.

Afterwards, Mother and Gram talk-fight all afternoon, chain smoking until the room fills with gray. Edith drops a bowl on the floor; Blanche pokes her finger with her embroidery needle. The men try to take refuge in outdoor work, but Mother follows them for a flirtatious tour of the mink pens, a scarf over her nose.

Back in the house, Mother teases, "Gonna give me a mink collar, Uncle?"

"No, 'fraid not."

"Why not? You've got lots of mink out there."

"I don't even have a mink collar. I should get mine first." When Edith jokes, she smiles sidelong and shy, but she means what she says.

"Well, your man will give you one some day, but I don't have a man.

No man, no mink, no diamonds." Mother throws her head back and laughs hard, takes a breath, then keeps laughing, seemingly on the verge of hysterics. Everyone stares at her. "Josephine," Gram commands after a minute or two. "Stop it. Come to your senses."

"I, ya-ha-ha, can't help it . . ."

My face flushes with embarrassment. Other people don't laugh this way, so loud and long.

"Josephine," Fred says, attempting to bring Mother back to earth, "all you need to do is get married again, and you'll get your diamonds."

"Yeah, well," she says, bringing her laughter under control. "Mother thinks I'll never grow up. Mother thinks I'm a child, but I just need someone to take care of me."

"Would you take Linda Joy if you got married?" asks Fred. The room suddenly fills with a hollow silence. Everyone stares at their hands in their laps. Gram is the first to speak. "Linda Joy has her music lessons now."

I know that underneath she is saying that I will be staying with her, and mother won't be taking me away. But I can tell that neither of them is sure of anything regarding where I belong.

Mother goes into the bathroom, the rest of the family heaves a sigh. Everyone leaves to attend to chores. The drama carried by my mother's energy comes to a halt, but the rest of the day I worry. I worry about Gram, wondering what would happen if I wasn't with her. She'd be lonely and sad, but Mother is alone, too. Is she sad? Does she miss me? How can I make them both happy? I follow Mother around, wanting to touch her, wanting her to talk to me, but she is either arguing with Gram or following Willard around like a lost puppy.

*

After dinner that night, we all sit out in lawn chairs in the yard. The sun has set behind the bluffs to the west; a golden haze still hangs over us. The elm trees that surround the yard rustle gently; cicadas and crickets throb in the warm evening. The air smells of the Mississippi River, thick with moisture, making me think of the fish in the river, the herons, squirrels, and raccoons that live near the water. Soon the stars come out, filling the sky with small lights all the way to the horizon. I take the spot next to my mother on the swing, leaning into her warmth. Gram's and Mother's cigarettes glow in the velvet blackness. The fireflies wink on and off. The night is thick with longing and history: the land where Blanche's mother was born only three miles away;

the house where Gram was born just a bit farther, near Grandview, the town where Lewis, Gram's father, was born.

Blanche knows all this history. She keeps her eye on her granddaughter Josephine and on her own daughter, who act more like enemies than kin. They keep picking at each other with small, sharp implements, unconsciously honing the tools that will someday tear them apart.

Birthplace in Wapello

THE NEXT MORNING, I get up early. Mother and Gram have slept in the living room, Gram on the couch, Mommy lying on a mattress on the floor. My mother's eyes are closed, and she seems so peaceful now. I kneel beside her, admiring her beauty even at rest—her dark hair and beautiful skin. Seeming to sense my presence, she blinks and smiles. "Good morning." She stretches out her arms to me. Thrilled with happiness for this closeness, I crawl in beside her. She's softer now, not the tense, terse lady she appears to be during the day. I curl into her and soon persuade her to scratch my back. Her fingernails give my skin goose bumps. I feel so close to her, irrepressibly happy as the smell of fresh morning coffee sails into the living room. She asks me to scratch her back. I love touching her bare skin, looking at each mole and bump, memorizing her. She asks for a massage and shows me how to rub hard.

"You're really good, Linda Joy. You should be a masseuse!" Mother laughs, pleased with me. My real mommy is back.

⁂

Soon the house is bustling with activity. Mother tells me that we are going to Grandpa's house today. Gram is decked out in her maroon silk dress, makeup, and opal rings. On the way to Wapello they fight again, but I keep my attention on the landscape sweeping by—rolling hills of corn, wide patches of blue sky, dollops of white clouds. Later in the day, I know, great mountains of clouds will grow in the sky. I wonder if Gram and Mother will notice. They don't see the Jersey cows grazing or the crows on the fence posts. They are in their own world, noxious smoke pouring from them the way it does from factories along the Mississippi.

When we arrive, Grandpa puts his arms around Mother; she kisses him on the cheek. Gram watches warily, and I wonder if she's sorry she divorced him. Bernie surprises me by hugging my mother.

In the kitchen after Gram leaves, Mother lights one cigarette after another, chatting on about her life and the same man she'd gone on about yesterday. She doesn't tell them she was fired from her job. Bernie and Grandpa politely let her go on for awhile, then Bernie busies herself fixing dinner—bacon grease in the green beans, whipped potatoes, fried chicken. The evening is peaceful, the sounds of cicadas and crickets drifting in from outside. Then suddenly Bernie slams down a bowl.

"Need some help?" Grandpa Blaine asks, interrupting my mother's monologue.

Bernie says, "Well, your daughter isn't offering. All she thinks of is herself."

"Bernie, that's not very nice," Mother huffs. "I haven't seen my father for two years."

"Well, it's hot, and I have a lot to do. Even your daughter knows enough to help out, don't you, Linda?" I smile and keep folding paper napkins, hoping the fight won't escalate.

Grandpa puts the potatoes in a bowl and pours the iced tea while Mother sits and smokes, still talking fast and loud. Questions dart through my mind like bats. Why doesn't she do anything to help? Can't she see that she's making things worse? My mother just does whatever she wants, I conclude, and it's obvious she doesn't want to help Bernie in the kitchen.

At the dinner table Grandpa launches into one of his long prayers. I peek to see if Mother takes the prayer seriously. She sits with her eyes open, staring across the room. Bernie's anger still simmers, and Grandpa talks about forgiveness.

"Bless us, Lord, that we have our family with us—Josephine and Linda Joy. It's been a long time since you've blessed us like this. Help us honor you and remember your commandments to love and forgive. Amen." I glance at Bernie and Mother to see if the prayer makes a difference, but they eat in heavy silence.

After dinner, Grandpa and Mother go outdoors and pace back and forth across the lawn. Grandpa's voice drones, Mother's pierces the air. I help Bernie with the dishes and then play with my dolls, wondering why my mother's presence always provokes disharmony.

<hr />

Later, Grandpa paces up and down the driveway. Bernie shadows him, trying to talk to him, but he keeps pacing. She begs, "Please, Blaine. You've come so far." His face is crumpled up—he's either angry or sad. When Bernie tries to touch him, he jerks away and slams his fist against the car, swearing. What has happened to the holy man? He has turned into a different person, too, just like my mother is wont to do. I start to shake, anticipating disaster. Grandpa gets in the car and sits behind the wheel, his head in his hands.

Bernie comes over and kneels in front of me, looking at me kindly.

"Don't worry, Linda Joy. Your grandfather is all right, but he gets these spells. He's much better than he used to be. He has a sickness called alcoholism; it makes people drink too much and hurt those they love. He was saved by taking the Lord as his savior, but he still feels bad at times. Don't be afraid; he'll feel better soon."

She soothes my nerves and we go into the house to have peach cobbler. She sits me down, cuts into the steaming cobbler, scoops on vanilla ice cream. The light of the day is seeping away, taking with it the clutch of tension in my stomach as Bernie kindly tends to me. Crickets and birds sing.

That night is soft and silent as I lie close to my mother, inhaling her smell, brushing against her in the night. I make a memory package to take away from here with me: the cobbler, Bernie's soft eyes, and Grandpa's prayers. The love I feel all through me.

I will leave behind the parts I don't want to remember.

The Music Man

MRS. ROCKWELL'S FOURTH grade classroom smells of polished wood, chalk dust, and pads of Red Eagle tablets. Twenty-five of us are sitting at our school desks, books and papers tucked neatly—or messily, as mine are—in the well beneath the desktop. The boys are noisy. Some have dirty fingernails, and their hair is cut in a flat top or slicked to the sides with Brylcreem.

I soon notice that there are the "in" kids and the "outs," and that the girls' hierarchies are more complex than the boys'. The most popular girls sit in clumps (if the teacher doesn't keep rearranging them throughout the room), their perfect hair swinging and shiny on their shoulders, wearing saddle shoes and white socks. These girls' fathers own car dealerships, or they are accountants, teachers, or school principals. Their mothers belong to the PTA, drive them to school and pick them up in polished cars, and visit the school dressed nicely, often towing another couple of children.

The most "in" girls are on the honor roll. At recess, they lead the games on the concrete slab behind the brick school, the wind blowing their skirts tight against their legs. All of us kids know that these girls will marry well and live in the best houses on the west side of town. Their muscular husbands will come home at night to barbecue in the backyard with neighbors, wearing a chef's hat. In 1954, that is the best life we can imagine.

The lowest-class boy or girl is easy to spot, with dirty or frayed clothes, yellow teeth, furtive eyes. It is clear that these kids will never get anywhere, and they are ignored at best or sniggered at openly. Their mothers have to work as waitresses or housecleaners. Their tattered houses ruin the perfect look of decent, tree-lined streets. Old cars and disemboweled washing machines lie listlessly in dead grasses around their houses. You don't befriend those kids because their bad luck will rub off on you.

The kids in the ill-defined middle group—despite good enough grades, good enough clothes—demonstrate qualities of lucklessness. Perhaps the family has some taint, as mine does. It's strange when a child lives with an aunt or a grandmother instead of with her parents. Our houses aren't shacks, but they aren't up to snuff. Perhaps the front yard is not a tidy green patch, or the mother is not perky enough. Perhaps she is tight lipped or square shouldered, carrying the family secret of alcoholism or penury or incest in her posture. Perhaps it shows in her hair that isn't just so or her lipstick that's the wrong color and seeps past the well-defined edges of her lips. The town might not know exactly what is wrong, but it will sense a discordant note, and the child will be judged accordingly.

I live with a grandmother who wants me to compete with the girls whose parents own houses with perfect lawns and curtains. She doesn't understand why I shouldn't be accepted as one of them, why I'm not considered their equal simply because of who she is. I know it's because of my hair, my buckteeth, the clothes she makes me wear that are always a little off in design and acceptability. I live with a grandmother who speaks with a fake English accent, wears clothes that are too fancy, uses a cigarette holder, and never sets foot in church.

We are all held to high standards in this small town by our forty churches, all Protestant but one, mostly Baptist, with a few Methodist, Church of Christ, or Nazarene thrown in. The quality of the souls of Mrs. Rockwell's fourth grade class is measured by their Sunday school attendance as well as by their timbre of voice, or whether their eyes are closed or open when they recite the Lord's Prayer each morning. The kids who mumble, recite mockingly, or stare off blankly are considered inferior beings. Also noted and rated is your degree of enthusiasm while singing the national anthem. In this place called Enid, Oklahoma, there are good children and bad children and questionable children, and you know who you are.

It is into this milieu that he comes one morning, the Pied Piper who will change my life. He will save me from the town's obsession with class but also will make me more vulnerable to it.

⌐══╩╧╨═⌐

The day begins as usual: the pledge of allegiance, the Lord's Prayer, a round of spelling. Melodious music wafts into the room. Then a tall, willowy man enters, bright red hair tumbling over his forehead, a violin tucked under his chin. He dips and sways, his enchanting sounds making us stop what we are doing.

His violin sings melodies from heaven. We leave our seats to gather around him and drink in the enchantment. He plays and dances and charms us like a leprechaun. He kneels, grinning, his blue eyes shining. He rips through a toe-tapping "Turkey in the Straw," then an unfamiliar melody that makes me think of clouds and God. My chest hurts. I want more than anything to draw such sweet sounds into the world.

"Hey, folks. This is called a violin. It is one of the stringed instruments in the orchestra. How many of you want to play an instrument?" I am hypnotized by his violin. It speaks in high notes and low sultry tones, silky and intimate. His violin laughs and tells jokes. Magically, his bow flies into the air and comes back down in just the right place.

"My name is Mr. Brauninger. I'm the orchestra teacher. Do you want to join our orchestra? You could play the violin or any other of our stringed instruments. You just have to take a slip home to your parents to be signed."

I am drawn to him by his bright blue eyes and his golden-toned violin. He asks my name.

"Linda Joy."

"What a pretty name you have, Linda Joy," he says, looking directly into my eyes as if I'm a real person. He talks to me as if what I say matters to him. I've never met anyone like him before. He gives me a permission slip and tells me that I have to get my parents to sign it if I want to come to the orchestra next week.

"I don't have parents. I live with my grandmother." He doesn't seem to think there's anything wrong with me because of this, though I know I'm the only kid in the class whose parents are divorced, and I'm sure none of their families fight the way my mother and grandmother do. Mr. Brauninger's smile makes all that go away.

Mrs. Rockwell tells us to sit down in our seats and fold our hands like polite children. Next Mr. Brauninger plays something soft and sweet, his face tender with the music, his lips quivering. His left hand vibrates back and forth. I want to cry. I could sit at his feet all day. I have to be included in his orchestra or I'll die. I begin to plan what I need to say to convince my grandmother.

When I go home that afternoon, my determination to play the violin sits in solid clarity in my chest. I will make any promise, I will do whatever it takes to be with the man with the red hair, the man whose love flows from him in waves.

I tell Gram about the man who came to class with his wonderful violin. I promise her that I'll practice; she won't have to remind me. "Please, please, please let me play the violin." She nods and takes a drag on her cigarette. The room is filled with smoke. I see from her coldly calculating eyes that I need to let her think about it.

I know that Gram wants me to be a famous musician, so my foot is in the door. Later that evening, I try to convince her that the violin is what I am meant to play, but I promise not to neglect my hour of piano practice each day and to finish all my music theory assignments.

I hear her talking to Mr. Brauninger on the phone after I go to bed. She tells him about Vera and about my divorced parents. The next morning I find out that they've decided I should play the cello instead of the violin. Gram tells me, "You'll be more popular with the cello."

I am disappointed, but she says there is a cello waiting for me. I'll play anything just to be near Mr. Brauninger.

❦

The first day of orchestra is on Thursday. My shoes squeak on the polished, walnut-colored cork floors. I run down the stairs to the basement music room. The room smells of oil, wood, and the musty dust that is caked in the thick window curtains. Mr. Brauninger greets me with a sunny smile and shakes my hand.

A group of kids has gathered in the room. I am surprised by who is here—a few of the popular boys, the "guy" kind of boys—Roger, Michael, and Dennis. They talk and laugh among themselves, but then listen when Mr. Brauninger starts to explain about the stringed instruments. "This is a violin. Next to it is a viola, a little bigger." He plays a few notes to demonstrate the deeper range of the viola. Then he picks up a cello.

"Linda Joy, I talked to your grandmother, and we thought maybe the cello would be best for you. It's a special instrument for a special girl like you. I picked out one just your size." He holds up a burnished brown cello, half-sized to fit me.

We gather around him as he shows us how the stringed instruments are constructed: the curves of the ribs, the maple coming together in the back to make a beautiful wavy pattern with a perfect seam, the intricately carved bridge, the nut at the top of the fingerboard, ebony tuning pegs, the graceful scroll, and the strings made of steel and catgut. Curlicue F-holes carved in the top allow the sound to emerge from the belly. The sound post connects the top with the back, creating vibrations along the whole instrument. The bow is made of Pernambuco wood from Brazil. Hair from real horses is strung from an ivory tip covered all the way to the ebony part, where we hold the bow, called the frog.

"Ribbet, ribbet," he says, grinning, his blue eyes shining. We look at him with wonder. He makes us feel important, not like the other teachers who treat us like silly children. I am surprised that the boys take Mr. Brauninger so seriously. I thought all they wanted to do was joke around.

In this very first lesson, he shows us how to drape our hands over the frog. We take turns holding the bow, learning to place it on the strings and pull it smoothly. I notice how the string widens as it vibrates. When I press down on the ebony fingerboard, I can feel the hard tension of the string under each finger pad. It hurts my tender fingertips, but I don't care. I am making music. I am playing the cello.

Finding Beauty

Mr. Brauninger becomes my inspiration and my guide into realms of beauty. In my little girl way, I fall in love with him. I can't wait to practice because his face lights up when I play perfectly. He draws little pictures in my string book to make me laugh: little men with bulbous noses lying over the lines and spaces. He tells me I am special, but it is the look on his face that sustains me, a look that tells me I am a real person as well as a cellist. He sees the music in me and coaxes it out, helping me discover something beyond the dissonance at home. He is a guide to the true harmony inside me.

In my school world I become "the girl with the cello," one of the strange musician kids. Mr. B. invites me to join the Youth Orchestra, where children learn to play symphonic literature. Only the best musicians are selected for it.

The night before I am to join the orchestra, I polish my cello. Gram rolls my hair to make it fluffy. Being asked to join the Youth Orchestra at such a young age means I have talent. They both talk to me about Carnegie Hall, but I don't know what it is, only that it's in a foreign, scary world called New York. Because of Mr. Brauninger, I can imagine accomplishing almost anything with my cello.

The Youth Orchestra meets on Saturday mornings in the basement of the high school music room. When I arrive I notice a clump of kids gathered around Mr. Brauninger, their faces shining with admiration for him. French horns, trumpets, and woodwinds are tuning up in the upper tier of the room. The noise is huge and thrilling. Trying to conquer my shyness, I wander over to the group of kids laughing and grinning around Mr. B. A boy with jet-black hair is laughing in a deep voice. His eyes behind black horn-rimmed glasses are soft brown, and he is full of energy. He dances toward me, hands fiddling with change in his pockets. "There she is, the new girl."

Mr. Brauninger introduces me. "This is Keith. He's first chair cello, a wonderful cellist. Keith, this is Linda Joy."

"Nice to meet you, Linda Joy." Keith's dark eyes are like lassoes, drawing me to him. He shakes my hand, then leans over and whispers in a conspiratorial voice, "Don't worry, you'll get the hang of things. It's nice you could join us. We've heard good things about you."

I'm surprised that they know about me already. Mr. Brauninger comes over, takes my cello, and puts his arm around me. "This is Linda

Joy, a bright new star from Adams Grade School." Another young girl holding a cello, long dark hair flowing down her back, flashes me a quick smile. She seems tall for her age, nearly as tall as Keith. Mr. Brauninger puts his hand on her shoulder. "This is Jodie from Emerson Grade School, another bright star. Do you know that you two started cello at the same time?" Next, I am introduced to redheaded twin boys who look alike except for their haircuts.

"Floyd plays viola, and Lloyd plays violin. They're fine musicians."

They nod at me, grinning. "You can remember us this way—Floyd, flat top; Lloyd, long hair."

Jodie and I are the last two chairs in the cello section. Mr. Brauninger taps his baton. "Good morning. We are here to play the greatest works of music ever written. This is the start of something new—an orchestra for all you talented young musicians in town. We'll get started with Vivaldi, and after that Bach, and a little Mozart. Some of you will not keep up with all the notes, but just do the best you can. Let's have fun."

The music builds up around me, filling the room. Most of the time, the strings are out of tune and the woodwinds squawk. The music rushes over us like a mountain stream. Jodie and I scratch away at our posts, watching Keith and the other cellists play their parts with ease. I wonder if I'll ever be able to play that way. During a rest, Keith looks back and winks. I feel happy that he notices me.

During Vivaldi's "Four Seasons," thousands of notes rush by that I can't seem to play. Jodie and I look at each other helplessly, knowing we missed most of the notes, but I've never had so much fun in my life. Mr. Brauninger stops to demonstrate dynamics, how to crescendo and diminuendo, his fingers opening wide and then coming together like the hieroglyphs on the page. He tells jokes and stories about the composers, and makes wavy pictures with his hands to show how sound vibrates through the wood of our instruments. He singles out each section of the orchestra to play separate passages, teaching us to hear how each person is playing and how the section works together. We learn that we are one body of music makers, not individuals. We must play together, feel together, and listen as one being to the composer's ideas coming alive through us.

The music rises above us, lifting us to a higher plane of knowledge, a realm of experience untouched by the rest of life. Through Mr. Brauninger's conducting—the swoop of his lanky arms, the shining in his eyes, his waving red hair—I am birthed into feelings I never knew possible, into a beauty that has no words, a connectedness I could never imagine. It soothes the sore places within me.

At each week's rehearsal I am transported into this ethereal realm. The music is more than words or ideas or anything the mind can conceive of. It goes straight to my heart, the place under my breastbone where my cello rests.

Mr. Brauninger becomes a family friend. Gram invites him over for dinner one evening. I am overjoyed to have company because we so seldom do. Gram says, "Poor thing. He's a bachelor all alone. He needs friends and a home-cooked meal. Now, you be sure to mind me . . ."

She goes on with a list of rules, but I don't care. I am thinking only of Mr. Brauninger's face when he urges us, "Come on, come on and play with everything you have," gesturing with his whole body, his long arms swinging around wildly. I think of what he told us about Beethoven, that he wrote his music for God. The look of beatific surrender on Mr. B.'s face inspires us to take a leap of faith to this transcendent spirit in ourselves, even as we work so hard to play.

Mr. B. arrives with a present for Gram and a new ball of rosin for me. He brings his records so we can hear wonderful symphonic music. Gram fixes New York steak with mashed potatoes, a salad, and corn on the cob. After dinner, while Gram is still in the kitchen, he sits on the floor spread-eagled and begins to play marbles.

"Come and sit on the floor with me, Linda. We'll have fun. Do you know how to play marbles?"

I tell him I want to learn. I smooth my dress and sit on the rug, careful to still look like a lady. I roll the cool, hard marbles in my hands. Gram comes into the living room with that look on her face. I hope she won't say something bad to Mr. Brauninger. She says to me in a hardened tone, "Get up off that floor. Ladies do not sit on the floor with their legs spread like that."

Mr. Brauninger gently tries to tease her. "Oh, it's my fault. I just thought a little girl would like to play marbles. I loved them when I was a kid. Can't she play with me?"

He looks up at Gram with a sweet, begging look, as innocent as a young boy, but she holds her line, not unfriendly but stern. "I'll have you know that I am raising my grandchild to be a lady, and ladies never, ever sit on the floor wearing a dress. They never sit on the floor in the living room. Period. Get up, Linda Joy."

I watch this exchange with interest, impressed that he does not simply try to please her, but actually stands up for me. After all, I am only ten and I should sometimes be allowed to play like a child. Still, I'm thoroughly conditioned by Gram's insistence that I be a small grown-up, that I always have the best manners of any kid in town. In the state. In the universe. I get up.

Mr. Brauninger takes out his violin, caressing the deep red wood that is marked with beautiful patterns. He says, "There's something I bet you don't know. The wood that goes into making the violin has to come from trees grown at high altitudes, where it is very cold. They're blown around by high winds and live through many years of bad storms before they are cut down for violin wood. If the wood grows where it is warm and where things are easy, it isn't as strong and doesn't make as good a sound. It needs the storm, it needs the cold to be able to make beautiful music."

He pauses for a moment and wipes his violin with a soft cloth. He looks into my eyes and his look goes beyond words. I think he is telling me more than about wood, but I'm not sure what. It gives me a good feeling anyway. Mr. Brauninger is the nicest man I have ever known. Now he takes out a three-record set, recorded at the Prades Music Festival, and wipes each record with a soft cloth.

"Linda Joy, this is a recording by the greatest cellist in the world, Pablo Casals. He is Spanish and was exiled from his own country because of the terrible Franco regime that killed lots of people. He refuses to go back to Spain, as a protest against all the bad things happening there. Each year he conducts this wonderful festival with other great musicians—Isaac Stern, Alexander Schneider, and Dame Myra Hess—because he thinks that great music can help make the world better."

Gram adds from the kitchen, "Dame Myra Hess gave free piano concerts at the National Gallery in London during the war—to cheer people up." I see that Gram thinks this was a good thing. She and Mr. B. both know about wars and bad times, some more of the hidden history I have come to know all adults have inside.

Mr. Brauninger puts the first record on the turntable and carefully lays down the needle. Out pours the most sublime music I have ever heard. It fills the thick dusk of the living room—the burgundy Oriental rug, the maroon ceiling, the stern portrait of Rembrandt staring down at us—with light. Mr. Brauninger sits under the brass floor lamp by the piano, a golden glow all around him. Waves of peace, love, and serenity emanate from him. His face is composed, his usual grin replaced by a smile that suggests heaven. I take his cue and quit worrying about my grandmother.

I relax and let the music create a universe of harmony within me, as it seems to with Mr. Brauninger The hurt I usually feel inside from Gram's scolding, my frustration from being held back and controlled by her, the deep aching for my mother and father, and my shame about my family—all of this is gone. Replacing it is a smooth, silky feeling. Peace and beauty beyond imagining fill me, and I am brought back to myself, the person that I really am. Mr. Brauninger sighs. I fold my hands over my stomach, sighing in perfect synchrony with him. For a time we are held and healed in this music.

When he leaves, and regular life takes hold again, I hold these memories inside me to guard against the darker days.

Who Do You Want More?

ONE FALL DAY during my tenth year, there is a knock at the door. Gram is still wearing her nightgown even though it's one in the afternoon. She's hunched over on the couch, newspapers, books, and letters strewn around her. Two ashtrays holding smashed butts ringed with lipstick overflow onto the stained, glass-topped coffee table. I pause, embarrassed to open the door.

Gram mutters, "Don't answer it," but I have already opened the door a crack. My body knows who it is before my mind absorbs it. An electrical jolt burns through me, leaving me shaky. A woman stands before me. At first she seems like a dream. It's my mother—wearing a black hat and veil, a fine charcoal suit, silk blouse, and high heels. She carries a wrinkled paper shopping bag and a black leather purse with a gold clasp. On her lovely face is a small, wistful smile. "Mommy?" I hear the hiss of Gram's breath. I know what it means. I'm suspended on that thin wire strung between Mother and Gram. Gram is behind me, Mother before me, the screen door another veil between us as Mother waits to be let in. Gram is angry; Mother wants to be welcomed. Already, the battle line has been drawn.

I ask Mother how she got here; it seems to me that she has dropped from heaven, the answer to my prayers. She gestures toward Aunt Helen's car putt-putting in front of the house. Aunt Helen waves at me and takes off, wisely deciding not to enter the lion's den.

Mother waves her ivory cigarette holder as if to say, "Aren't you going to let me in?" I open the screen door, watching while they exchange first glances. Gram seems to paw at the earth, itching for a fight.

Mother steps in and I put my arms around her to prove that she is real, her flesh soft against me, her musky scent a balm. I am overcome with relief, a letting down of tension I didn't know I had; yet at the same time part of me ratchets up, preparing for what I know will come.

❦

Mother's visits all follow the same pattern. She comes in acting sweet, her voice soft and quiet. She unpacks her paper bag, lining up her pots of makeup on the hall table. Gram makes coffee. She and Mother speak to each other like civilized creatures for two or three hours. The details—how long they keep up the friendly fa ade; the precise content of the fight; the exact number of swear words spoken, and by whom;

who cries, how much, and for how long—differ each time, yet I can predict how things will go. The rhythm of their grief, rage, and blame reverberate in my blood.

> Who do you think you are, asking me for money, why do you talk to me like that, don't you dare raise your voice, I'll do what I damned well please, no you won't this is my house, well if you feel that way about it, oh so you're gonna run away, that's what you did, what do you mean, oh never mind.

> You don't understand me, you never did, what's there to understand, you're wasting your life away, what's the matter with you, are you an idiot, stop telling me I'm stupid, you don't know what you're talking about, and you're so smart living here in this hell hole, you don't clean the house, what are you teaching my daughter, well if you can do so much better, take her with you, you know I can't, well don't say anything, don't try to control me, I'll say what I want, not in my house you don't, well then I'm leaving, I've had it, I'm calling Aunt Helen.

Smoke swirls. They circle each other, eyes glittering. The room crackles with their overloaded wires. There's no place for me to go where I'm safe from their sting and burn.

After one bad fight Mother runs into the hall and throws her make-up, all the pots, liners, powder, and lipstick, into her Neiman-Marcus shopping bag. She folds her pink nightgown into a square, its musky scent rising in a cloud and settling over me. My mother's aroma threatens to open the flap in my stomach that leads to an abyss of loneliness and sorrow. I don't want to fall in, so I try to comfort Gram. A tear runs down her cheek, but her mouth is set in an angry sneer. "How dare she talk to me like that, after all I've done for her. She has no sense of other people; she just thinks of herself."

I don't want to hear bad things about my mother, so I make coffee, hastening their usual end-of-the-fight ceremony. I know how to make coffee by now, but I let Gram direct me. "Measure the water, exactly eight cups, and nine spoons of Folgers. Be sure to put the percolator top on."

I dread the next phase, when I'm tormented by questions I don't dare ask. I get water from the tap, making sure it hits the eight-cup line. I breathe in the fragrant coffee and measure it carefully. Meanwhile, my mind reels. What will happen now? Will Mommy go back to Chicago tonight? Can I go to Aunt Helen's to see my mother, or would that be a betrayal of Gram? When will I see Mother again? I want to know the precise size and shape of my time with her, exactly when she'll leave. I don't want surprises. I don't want to feel this aching hole in my stomach.

Soon Aunt Helen's car coughs and mutters in the driveway. She leaves the headlights on and shuffles into the house wearing bedroom slippers. Her dyed blonde hair is in pin curls, and she wears a bathrobe over one of her working dresses. She is smiling, as usual, but doesn't seem happy. "Well, well, well," she says, her eyes taking in the scene: Gram blowing smoke from her chair while Mother smokes and paces, her heels threatening to punch holes in the floor.

"Josephine. Frances. Now look here. Jo, you can come to my house, and you can come too"—she gestures to me and Gram—"but I'll have none of these shenanigans. I'm a Christian woman and believe in the Golden Rule, but Maj and I, we'll have none of this malarkey in our house."

"I just want peace and quiet," Mother whispers as she rolls up her bag. She gathers her cigarettes and cigarette holder. Gram glares. "Peace and quiet," she says sarcastically, implying it was all my mother's fault. "That would be nice."

"I don't know why I come here if this is the way you're going to treat me," Mother says, flouncing toward the dining room to grab a carton of Marlboros.

"I didn't invite you," Gram growls.

Mother faces her, eyes blazing. "Well, that's a fine how-do-you-do. I'm not welcome with my own mother."

Aunt Helen is ready to go out, her hand on the doorknob, but after this outburst Mother grabs her paper bag and her purse and her hat with the veil. She storms through the kitchen and makes her escape out the back door, shrieking about how unwelcome she feels, why does she bother. I hear her open the garage door and know she's already out to the driveway. Panicked, I run after her. Aunt Helen's car sits there idling, and Mother gets in. The car's headlights blaze against the thick black night.

Aunt Helen comes out the front door and pauses beside me on her way to her car. "Are you coming or staying here?" she asks, tapping her foot. I stare at her in a panic. How can I decide that? I love both of them.

She repeats the question. "Are you coming with your mother or staying with your grandmother?" I just stare at her, speechless.

She gives up. "Call me," she says, and gets in the driver's seat. The car backs out of the driveway. My mother is huddled in the back seat illuminated only by the orange glow of her cigarette. The car climbs the hill and disappears into the night.

I go back inside the house, knowing that somehow I've made my decision, that I belong with Gram now. She sucks on a cigarette, slumping into the couch. The aroma of fresh coffee mixes with the stench of smoke and grief. I pour coffee into china cups, place them with the sugar bowl and creamer on the silver tray. I carry the tray into the dark living room with a smile on my face. Gram's eyes glitter, as if with anticipation. I begin to pour.

Hate Letters and Harrison

GRAM TEARS OPEN my letters before I get home. It doesn't matter to her that the letters are for me. It's her house, so the mail belongs to her.

"Why can't I open my own mail? It's addressed to me, see?" I wave the envelope at her. She grabs it and lifts her hand, threatening to slap me, her eyes flashing. Her lips are gray, with flecks of old lipstick. I don't like her right now.

"Yours? Excuse me, miss, did you say 'your' mail? For your information, nothing in this house is yours. You are my guest. You live here because I am kind enough to invite you. Everything here is mine, do you understand? This house is mine; everything having to do with you is mine. So shut your mouth."

A dark wave of energy emanates from the green brocade couch where she's plunked herself down in the usual mess, glowering over the orange tip of her cigarette. The new mail bears my father's handwriting. I'm afraid to ask her what he says, so I start to play my cello, but as usual she yells at me, telling me that I'm doing it all wrong. "Why can't you follow what Mr. B. says. You'll embarrass me at the next concert."

After a while, I put down the cello and go to the bathroom with my book, forgetting about time. She comes to get me. "Get out here. We have things to do."

I put the book away, a fine Nancy Drew mystery. I can feel the storm brewing, the way you feel a slight charge in the air as a rainstorm builds up. The clouds go from gray to green and then turn an ominous purple. She is at the purple stage now, her face twisted, her eyes dark. She pours herself a cup of coffee and tells me to sit down.

"You're going to write to your father."

"But I just wrote . . ."

"It doesn't matter. It's time for you to understand who he is."

"But . . ."

"Shut up!" She waves his letter at me. "He says that he's not going to pay for any of your lessons. Do you have any idea how much I spend on you? You're old enough to tell him what you think. Now write this . . ."

"But these are your thoughts, not mine."

"You shut up and mind me unless you want me to get the yardstick. Listen to this." She pushes her glasses up on her nose and reads: "Your grandmother wants things for you that you don't need. You need to be a child, to play and have fun. Forget all those music lessons and concerts and privileges. Fit them into the budget with the money I send . . ."

She looks at me and says, "See that? He's a selfish, stingy son of a bitch, and it's time you knew it. Pick up your pen and get ready."

A rock sits in the pit of my stomach. I pick up the pen and the paper she shoves toward me. I know what she'll do if I resist.

"Dear Daddy," she dictates. "How dare you tell Gram you won't pay for my cello lessons. Don't you understand—I mean to make something of myself . . ."

My hand lies still. "That doesn't sound very nice," I whisper.

"You shut up! Just write what I tell you. Say, 'If you cared about me, you would help with my expenses. I take music lessons and need to have nice clothes for the recitals. I am good in school, and . . . '"

"I'm not that good."

"Now you stop that. You are going to write what I tell you! Get busy." She threatens me with the yardstick, and my breath gets shallow. She sits back down with it across her legs.

She dictates a nasty letter to my father, saying he's low class and doesn't know anything. She doesn't have enough money and takes care of me because no one else will. He owes her money. And so on.

None of this is what I think, and I would never say it. I object.

She continues with a diatribe about how stingy and mean he is. She's said this before, but not with this much rage. She paces, smoking and gesturing, thumping the floor with the yardstick. Smoke swirls around her head, and the room is gray and dark. She won't open the blinds. She forces me to address the envelope and sign the letter "Love, Your daughter, Linda Joy." I put a stamp on the letter and fasten it with a clothespin on the mailbox.

That week I go to school, practice, and take my lessons, all the while worrying about Daddy. Will he be mad? Will he hate me?

Two weeks later when she picks me up after school, a letter is lying on the front seat. She barely stops the car long enough for me to get in. As she whirls away, she starts in. "That son of a bitch. He's the most horrible man I've ever known. And to think that he doesn't care about his own daughter. That damn father of yours is a selfish man who doesn't care about you. If he did, he'd help take care of you."

"He does too care about me!" I want him to come and see me. He's the most fun of my three parents.

"You think he's so great because he comes around once a year? Well, other girls' fathers make sacrifices for their daughters. What's so great about him? Tell me what's so great?" Her voice rises. I know she wants me to say some particular thing, but what? I'd say almost anything to get her to be quiet.

"He works. He works very hard, he told me." We drive by some of the girls from school playing jump rope in their front yard. I wish I could join them.

"Ha! Sure, he works hard. Him and Hazel, all cozy up there in Chicago. He could come more often. He would if he cared. He could give you more money. Believe you me, he has it. He's selfish. When we get home you'll write him another letter."

❦

Every two weeks she forces me to write my father a hate letter, and he writes back. When his letters come, Gram flies into a rage, pacing up and down the living room, smoke billowing from her nostrils.

She reads aloud: "I work damn hard. Young lady, when you grow up, you'll need to know the value of a dollar. You can't just expect me to dole it out. I have a budget. I see that you're getting some bad habits, like Frances. You'll be an unhappy person if you continue. Just spend what is in your budget and no more. After all, I came up from nothing to earn my money. I decide where it will go and how much."

She argues as if he were there with us in the room. "Came up from nothin'! You're damn right he came from nothin', and he is nothin'. How dare he tell me to watch my money!" Her voice rises to a hysterical pitch.

"He said it to me. See, it's addressed to me." I point to the salutation, "Dear Linda," at the top of lined L& N Railroad parchment.

"You know damn well he's talking to me. How dare he! He's a son of a bitch, and I won't have him taking advantage of me."

The dining room grows dark and she doesn't think to turn on the lights. I'm stuck on the chair next to her. I can't leave the room. If I move, she yells. I try to become invisible, thinking of more pleasant things. I think about Keith, his warm dark eyes, how he seems to like me. I think about the curve of my mother's cheek, and how nice it feels when she scratches my back. I wish I could be with Blanche in her garden right now. I'd like to transport myself to Aunt Helen's house, where she'd make us some nice homemade bread and Gram would calm down. But I'm stuck here with this hateful version of Gram. She doesn't make dinner and seems to forget that I have to practice and have homework to do. For six hours she reads and rereads his letters, examining each sentence, memorizing his angry replies as night falls.

Finally, I whisper, "Can I make us some soup, Gram?" She nods yes, and I slink from the room. I hear the snap as she turns on the lights. I get out a can of Campbell's chicken noodle soup and heat it on the stove. I pour it into a chipped bowl, add crackers, and bring it to her on the silver tray with fresh coffee. She folds the letters, puts them in a copper jar near the couch, and begins sipping her soup and coffee.

The next day, without explanation, she goes back to being the nice, sweet Gram who rescued me.

❧

One night that winter, the wind rattles the house and sleet plays a staccato melody on the windows. Gram starts reading me "Annabelle Lee" by Edgar Allen Poe. I've never heard such a beautiful poem. As she reads, the wind seems to match the poem's rhythm. The wind accents the ends of the verses with hearty gusts. Afterwards, Gram's eyes grow misty and her face wistful as she talks about her life.

"I understand that you miss your father. I didn't have any father. I used to wonder how my life would have been different if he had lived."

I ask her about herself, hoping she'll tell me the stories that Blanche has already told me, wondering how her version will be different.

"I was born in 1894, and my father died a few months before I was born. You have no idea how much I think about him, and my little son. He was stillborn, the cord wrapped around his neck." She sobs quietly. "I wonder, if he had lived . . . I might not have had another child." She pulls out a Kleenex. I pat her arm, worried. If she hadn't had another child, she would not have had my mother. Then where would I be?

She goes on, wiping her eyes. "He was born in 1914. I didn't understand anything. Let me tell you this, young lady, you be careful around men. They'll tell you all kinds of things that make you want to, you know, get close to them, but it's just an act. They'll tell you they love you and all that. They just want one thing, and if you give them what they want, they'll leave you."

She's always telling me about bad things I should watch out for, but I don't really know what she means. She pauses, sips her coffee, lights another cigarette, and goes on with her story.

"Things got bad with your grandfather after your mother was born. He was an alcoholic. I hate men who drink. Eventually I left and worked in Chicago. Through my job at the glove factory, I went to England on ocean liners. Such a life—dining at the captain's table. People back then knew how to act and what to wear. The trunk in my bedroom, remember all those stickers on it? What a life! I'd give anything to be able to do it again. Promise me when you grow up you'll take a ship across the ocean. Of course, everything's changed now. That was before the war. I tell you, if only Americans knew what they did to England by being pacifists. Thank God that damn Roosevelt finally got us into the war. It was a crime to let the Brits fight alone."

"What was the baby's name?"

"What?"

"What was your baby boy's name?"

"Harrison. Harrison Hawkins. I wish he'd lived. Just think how wonderful it would be to have a son. To have a man to take care of me. That mother of yours—so irresponsible."

"How old was Mother when you left for Europe?"

"That father of hers. His family, they had their noses up in the air, I tell you. Always looked down on me. But who were they anyway—people living in a little one-horse town, nobody really. Just because they owned the newspaper didn't make them special."

"He took care of Mommy?"

"Your mother lived with my grandmother. Your mother is named after her, Josephine. When I was still young, and before I married Blaine, I lived with her so I could graduate from high school. You will graduate from high school, I'll see to that. Most of my brothers and sisters just got to fourth or fifth grade. Education makes a difference. It used to be that girls couldn't even go to school. You will go to college, read, and learn history and art. You'll find out—life will be better for you. There's nothing like culture; not many people appreciate that."

Gram tells me more about her life tonight than she ever has before, and for the first time I see her as a complicated person with many different emotions. I feel sorry for her. I climb up to lie in front of her on the couch, stretching my body along the length of hers. She puts her arms around me, her breath ruffling my hair. Without her, I think, I would have no one. I feel her heart beating next to mine.

Sex and Beethoven

ONE DAY AFTER penmanship and before recess, a girl named Cheryl who's in Mrs. Collins's fifth grade class with us, rushes to the teacher, crying. After the school nurse takes her away, everyone whispers at recess about her having a "period," a term most of us haven't heard before. Mrs. Collins tells us in a business-like tone that Cheryl is sick, but she'll be back to school soon. I don't understand what all the buzzing means, but the girls in the in-group start talking about monthly bleeding so you can have a baby. They say it will happen to all of us. Some girls seem to know what is going on, but the rest of us view the information about bleeding with horror and disbelief. Surely they are wrong about this. It must be some kind of terrible rumor just to upset everyone.

That afternoon, I tell Gram the story. She reacts with wide-open eyes and goes into action. When she calls the school, she finds out that Cheryl is from a poor family and ruined her only dress. Gram gathers clothes from several of my friends, makes up a box for Cheryl, and takes it to the school nurse, who delivers it. When we get home, Gram sits on the couch, lights a cigarette, and tells me to sit down on the piano bench for a talk.

I have a feeling I won't like this. I'm already worried and nervous, and Gram has a gleam in her eye I don't trust.

"Has your mother already told you about monthly bleeding like Cheryl's? Do you know it will happen to you?"

I want to tell her that the girls have told me enough, but I shake my head. Gram's eyes are the black points of obsidian they turn into when she's lit up. I sit on my trembling hands. My armpits are damp.

She goes on to tell me about eggs inside a woman's body, that every month the body prepares for a baby, and when the woman doesn't get pregnant, there is a flow of blood. She uses a word I don't understand and don't remember. When she was young, rags caught the blood, but now we have Kotex. She describes the pad and belt in one embarrassed second. She doesn't like this talk any more than I do.

Smoke comes out the side of her mouth. "You know about sex, don't you? It's pretty disgusting; the only reason to have to do it is to give your husband a baby, and after that you don't have to be bothered with it. I don't know what's the matter with women who think otherwise. Must be oversexed." Gram blows a stream of smoke high into the air.

"You know how a baby is made? I was so shocked when I was young and all. The man's organ . . ."—she accentuates "organ" with a grimace—"sticks straight up in the air. Imagine! It's for marriage, but even then . . ." She makes another face, and laughs.

I'm confused. "But how is the baby made?"

"It goes straight inside you and shoots out sperm. It unites with the egg and makes a baby. I don't want to hear of any such goings on with you until you're married. These low-class sluts that just let any man have them, they aren't worth the powder it would take to blast them to hell, and to hell is where they're going, believe you me."

Gram goes on and on: sex is revolting; it hurts. Men are evil and selfish. "Just tell them no, and only let them do it once, just enough to have one baby someday. Then you'll be done with the whole damn misery. Remember this; it's for your own good."

I stare at my grandmother, her face distorted with disgust, and I vow to never let any of this happen to me, wondering how I can have a baby and avoid all the scary stuff.

⁕

The boys I know are nice, and would never do mean things to a girl. Keith, for instance. A few weeks ago after Youth Symphony, Gram and I saw him hauling his cello on his back far from home. He was scurrying down the sidewalk with the energy of three men. Gram asked him if he wanted a ride.

He smiled, thanked us, and got in the car. We drove him to his house on 20th Street, where we met his family. His sister and two brothers were all bundles of energy, racing through the yard, laughing and teasing. I want a family like that: a mother who stays home and makes cookies; a father who laughs and jokes, a twinkle in his eye.

Keith is polite to my grandmother, and he treats me like a real person instead of a silly child. He shakes my hand when I come to orchestra and pats me on the shoulder when I do a good job. His eyes are always glistening with good humor and fun.

⁕

That week, Eva, the passionate new conductor joined Mr. Brauninger to conduct the Youth Orchestra. She makes the orchestra even more fun. She's enthusiastic and energetic; she waves her arms and shouts at the top of her lungs, "Come on, don't hold back, give it all you've got!" She seems so powerful, I'm a little scared of her. I've never seen a woman like her in my life, so sure of herself.

We kids joke that they are like Mutt and Jeff, because Mr. B. towers over her at six feet. It doesn't take long for us to notice the way they walk together, heads close, holding hands. That year, they become our musical mother and father, touching us with their hands, their voices, their hearts as the music opens up new horizons. They are wildly enthusiastic about Bach, Handel, and Vivaldi. Then they introduce us to Beethoven.

At first Beethoven is too hard to play—so many notes making intricate layers of sound. We learn his First Symphony, whose brilliant notes of the violins and deep sonorities of the brass transport me into realms of glory. I forget about my parents and my grandmother. I forget about the hollow place inside me that is cold, dark, and unreachable. In the music I am alive, at one with a greater universe. And Keith is there with me.

⁂

This afternoon after school I wait under the swaying green trees for Gram to pick me up. I've been uneasy for days now, wondering if I've done something wrong, waiting for Gram to get mad at me.

What will it be tonight, I worry. Will she make me practice for three hours or study for two hours? Perhaps she'll insist that I read David Copperfield for an hour.

The Nash Rambler swirls around the corner. I try to figure out what kind of mood Gram's in by the look on her face or the gesture of her hands. Uh oh. I don't like what I see today. Her hair is frizzy and her eyes look wild. Jittery, I open the door.

"Get in," she hisses and we speed back home. Standing in the kitchen door with her hands on her hips and her elbows sticking out in two V shapes, she orders me to wash a pile of dishes. "Your room needs dusting. And you have to vacuum."

"I have lots of homework."

"Just get cracking and you'll have enough time. You kids today, you have no idea how easy things are. In my time we had to do chores all day long. We were lucky to get any schoolwork done at all. You ought to be grateful."

"I am grateful. But . . ."

A flash of her rings, my lip burning, my hand jumping to my face. "Why did you hit me?"

"I didn't like your tone of voice. Shape up or ship out, young lady. I don't have to put up with your back talk."

She dictates what I can say; it's not a democracy. If she wants to shout and scream insults, I'm supposed to be silent, to just take it. Later, when I sit down to practice a new Mozart sonata, she tells me the rhythm is wrong, the position of my hands is off. She hovers too close to me, the full strength of her cigarette smoke drifting into my face. I cough, but she doesn't move back. I can hardly see the music through the noxious cloud.

"You'll never make anything of yourself this way," Gram snarls. "What's the matter with you?"

I know I shouldn't say it, but I've had enough. "Then you do it." I get up from the piano and try to get away before she can hit me again, but I'm not fast enough and feel her sting on my cheeks.

"Don't you dare talk to me like that. Who do you think pays for your lessons?"

"I just thought if you knew how to play, you should . . ." I know I'm on dangerous ground, but I can't stop myself.

"You're mocking me, you little brat." Her hands are out of control around my face, flailing and slapping, pulling at my hair. I shout for her to stop and she yells, "Sit down there and get busy. You have a recital next week, and I will not be humiliated. Mind me."

I slink back to the piano, hating it, hating her, trying to read the notes though my tears. My hands throb where her rings hit my finger bones as I tried to fend off her blows. Then the music reaches up and takes me, the melody and chords flowing through my body. The colors of the music present themselves, rich gold and burgundy, pale yellow and chartreuse green. Soon there is nothing but sound and color, only the music and me.

The Facts of Life and Death

IN THE SUMMER of my eleventh year, Gram and I visit Iowa again. Mother takes the train from Chicago and picks me up to spend a few days in Wapello. Blaine is out in the garden on this warm afternoon, wearing his battered straw hat and whistling between his teeth, weeding, cutting flowers, trimming the grass. Grandma Bernie scurries around the kitchen, putting away groceries and banging bowls on the counter as she gets ready to cook. So far, it's been a good day, the adults getting along. I can detect none of the usual fault lines; still, I know that at any moment an invisible seam could part, tumbling all of us into darkness.

Mother calls out to me, "Linda Joy, come in here."

I can tell by the tone of her voice that she wants to talk to me about something serious. I follow her into our bedroom, my stomach edgy. Mother tells me to sit on the bed. I hide my worry behind a good-girl face. Her brows furrow. "Have you ever heard the word 'menstruation'?"

It doesn't sound familiar, it sounds like a disease.

"It means the monthly cycle your body goes through to prepare you to have a baby."

Then I remember the school lecture, but not that word. I recall vividly the scary description Gram gave me last year of "the act." I can't tell Mother about that. It would only cause a fight.

Mother smoothes the sheets, takes a long puff from her cigarette, and says. "Each month an egg comes down to your womb, where a baby will grow when it is the right time, after you're married. A lining builds up, but when there's no baby, it comes out." She pauses. "It comes out down there," she says, indicating the area between my legs, "and it looks like blood. Each month you bleed. It's perfectly natural and nothing to get excited about. Some women complain, but that's nonsense. It's the way God made us, and there's nothing to worry about. Understand?"

Mother is matter of fact. She pulls down the waistband of her shorts and snaps an elastic belt. "Go home and tell Gram to buy these for you. I didn't need them until I was fifteen. You should not be embarrassed or think that you're sick. It is just part of life; it's not bad at all." She looks up at me. "And don't listen if your grandmother says negative things. She came from another era. Just remember what your mama says. She has your best interests at heart." Mother refers to herself in the third person, as usual.

I know she must be wrong. It is incomprehensible that this could happen to me, this serious and messy event, however normal it may be. I want to run back to my dolls. Blood, eggs, this mystery awaiting some particular moment to burst forth within my skinny body, make me feel off balance. Around the tables of my Iowa relatives, the mention of childbirth or any suggestion of sex—a bastard child, a girl who "had" to get married—causes shivers of electricity. I don't want to experience this dangerous thing that makes adults act weird.

Mother has revealed to me the mystery of women, as Gram did in her way. I look at my mother through new eyes, respecting her for taking on the job of telling me what a daughter should be told. At least Mother thinks it's all natural and good. She doesn't hate men, and I love her for that.

❦

As we finish our conversation, Grandma Bernie calls out, "Hey you, want some chocolate chip cookies?" Smiling, her silver hair shining from a recent trip to the beauty shop, she carries them to the dining room table, filling the room with a delicious aroma. Mother cackles with delight. I realize that what she has just told me connects me like a river of blood and creation to all the women in my family, and especially to her.

After cookies and milk, Grandma Bernie opens a suitcase hidden in the closet. It holds a wonderful array of miniature doll clothes. "Your little dolls need some new outfits," she smiles. I scoop them up, marveling at their snaps and buttons, pinked edges, and perfect proportions. I run to show my mother.

"Nice," she nods absentmindedly, furling a lock of hair round and round her finger. Tiny curls, made from her nervous twirling, circle her face. She looks up again. "Well, at least someone does that for you. Grandma Bernie is really good to you!"

I spend a happy afternoon dressing and undressing my dolls. They remind me that I'm still a little girl. I play and play, imagining balls and fancy dates with handsome men. Being grown up is far, far away.

The next day we all get in the car for a drive. Part of any visit to Iowa includes driving on the back roads, looking at houses, picking up fruit at the roadside stands. Grandpa says that he wants to stop by the Wapello Cemetery. Bernie nods her approval.

"I don't want to go there," Mother says in the cadence of a spoiled child. "Let me get out."

"Nonsense, we're almost there." He drives between high rows of green cornfields.

"I hate cemeteries," Mother mutters between puffs of smoke.

Blaine turns into the cemetery and stops at a square white stone with the name Hawkins carved on it. I am used to trampling through grass and looking at headstones. All my Iowa relatives have already had their gravestones carved, leaving a space for the death date.

Mother stands beside the car, looking disgusted. Grandpa puts flowers on the Hawkins site. There's also a gravestone with Harrison on it. "He was your mother's brother who died at birth."

"Why do you have to talk about that?" Mother whines. "Linda, get back in the car and stop talking."

"Now Josephine, let her be. Why shouldn't she know about Harrison?" Blaine says. "And over here," he goes on, "is where I'll be buried. Over here, my beloved mother is laid to rest." Grandpa lays flowers on his mother's gravesite. "My father is over here, God bless him." He folds his hands in prayer.

Bernie keeps an eye on Mother, whose face gets meaner each minute. "For God's sake!" She throws her cigarette to the ground. "Let's get the hell out of here. This is so spooky. I hate cemeteries. I don't see why you all have to be so morbid."

"If you believe in God, then you have nothing to fear," Grandpa Blaine lectures.

"Oh, hell. You and your damned religion. Let's go." Mother paces back and forth by the car.

"Is this the Harrison that Gram told me about?" I ask Bernie.

"Yes. He was born and died in 1914, one year before your mother was born. You'll have to ask your grandmother about the details, but I know he died at birth. I'm sure she must have been very sad, but it happens sometimes."

"Stop talking about him," Mother screams. "Why do you have to talk about him?"

We get back in the car. Mother hugs the door, as far away from me as she can get. The gentle connection between us since yesterday's facts-of-life talk has disappeared. The anxious, yelling mother is back. I watch her, wanting desperately to bring back the mother with the soft voice and gentle ways. I touch her arm, and she glances at me as if she has forgotten my presence. Grandpa drives home, talking softly to Bernie.

I can't stop thinking about what this all means. One day, there will be a stone for Mother.

The Wedding Dress and Gram's Secrets

AFTER MOTHER LEAVES us in peace and returns to Chicago, Gram and I stay in Iowa for the rest of the summer. I love being with my down-home farm family, where it's a different world from our house on Park Street. I feel freer, because Gram is less strict with others around. Each morning begins with Blanche slamming around the kitchen, then going outside to do the weeding. I love immersing myself in the cozy world of her cookstove and garden, enveloped in the smells of good cooking, healthy soil, and growing things.

On this summer morning, Blanche and I have already gathered strawberries and made coffee and pancakes by the time Gram straggles out of bed. She stumbles into the kitchen in her glamorous maroon robe with silver and green flowers.

"Lazy bird," Blanche barks. "You're wastin' the day away."

Gram smiles, forcing cheerfulness. "Good morning, Mama." She leans toward Blanche to give her a kiss, but Blanche barely stops moving on her way to the cookstove.

Blanche teaches me how to feed the fire, my face crinkling with the heat, while Gram looks on disapprovingly. Blanche is a whirlwind of productivity—already she's done the garden chores, made a pot of soup that's simmering on the stove, and put breakfast on the table. In her estimation Gram is lazy, "always lying abed." I know that Gram loves her mother, but Blanche's home-and-farm orientation is what Gram escaped long ago, seduced by the fancy clothes and higher society of the big city.

Blanche finally takes a break and sits at the kitchen table, her fingernails caked with dirt, her hair frizzed around her head. Quiet for the first time since 5:30 this morning, she reads the paper. Gram sits back with her cigarette and coffee.

Blanche grunts and reads out loud. "Listen. 'Mrs. Thomas Trent, daughter of the late Mr. Schimmel of Muscatine, is home from Boston to visit her mother, Mrs. Gertrude Schimmel. Mrs. Trent is the former Betsy Schimmel. There's an open house at Mrs. Schimmel's home on Sunday at two in the afternoon.' What do you think of that, Lula? Want to go?"

"I don't know any Trent or Schimmel." Gram's voice is steady, nonchalant.

"Her name is Betsy Schimmel. Are you telling me you don't remember Betsy?" Blanche leans over the paper, glowering at Gram. I sit on the edge of my chair, my heart racing. What is going on?

"Mama, I don't know any Betsy. Never heard of her." Gram is suddenly edgy, though. She shuffles to the cookstove and pours herself another cup of coffee.

"That's a good one. You don't remember Betsy? I can't imagine you ever forgetting her, with what she did for you."

"Mama, I said . . ." Gram stands imperiously, arms akimbo, eyes sparking, glaring at Blanche. Blanche glares back. Gram stomps into the living room. I am too tense to follow. Blanche sits there stiffly, lips pushed together so tight they're almost inside out. Gram comes back into the kitchen and blows a cloud of smoke almost in her face.

"Mama, why are you irritating me like this? I don't know any Betsy."

Blanche stands up and shouts, "You don't remember the girl you borrowed a wedding dress from when you ran off to get married?"

Shocked, I stare at Gram. The look on her face tells me it's true, but she says, "Dammit, I don't remember any Betsy!"

"You're lying through your teeth! You can't forget something like that. Don't play fancy to me. I'm your mother. I'll never forget the shame of it. You never forget the day you can't hold your head up with the neighbors."

"Mama, not in front of Linda. Linda, go . . . go get ready for Aunt Dell's." Aunt Dell is Blanche's sister who lives in a nursing home. I know that Gram is trying to get rid of me so I won't find out anything bad about her. She's always presented such a perfect picture of herself, as if she never did anything wrong in her life.

I leave the room but peer at the two of them from the bedroom door, holding my breath, my pulse racing. This scene reminds me of Gram and Mother. Do all mothers and daughters fight?

"I never borrowed it, Mama. I didn't."

"You did too, and you know it. You lied to me; you told me you were going to a party. How could you do that to us? I never got over it. Never." Blanche starts to cry, something she almost never does. "And look what happened. Serves you right."

Gram cries, too, clinging to Blanche. "I'm sorry, Mama, I'm so sorry. Please don't be mad at me. I can't stand it. Mama, Mama . . ."

I finally understand. When Gram was young, she lied to her family to run off and marry my grandfather Blaine in Wapello. She must have borrowed a dress from Betsy.

Gram's hair is messed up, her face streaked with tears. Blanche stands for a few moments with her hands at her sides, then she puts her arms around Gram and pats her. Soon they wipe their faces and go off to dress for the visit to Aunt Dell. I sit on my bed and pretend to read my Nancy Drew book. Here it is again—more proof that the past is still tripping everyone up.

Looking for Lewis

A N ICE-CREAM MOON hovers over us on this velvet-black night, the voices of the generations murmuring across air laced with moisture from the Mississippi. There is no beginning and no end to this night with its soft, friendly darkness. The wind caresses my skin, whispering its ancient secrets, to me and to the ghosts who hover around us, unmoored from the past.

On a summer night like this one in Aunt Edith's yard, I am keenly aware of the threads of connection that weave everyone here together. The family tapestry includes many others who aren't present. I've heard their stories so often—aunts, uncles, and cousins to Blanche, long dead. I sense that somehow they are with us even now in the soothing darkness. Their names flit around us like fireflies.

❦

The next morning, the adults start talking about Lewis, Gram's daddy who died so long ago. "Let's find him," Gram says. In a flurry, everyone gets dressed and piles into the car. How in the world can we find someone who's dead?

Every summer the Nash Rambler carries my relatives and me down corn-rimmed roads near the Mississippi, behind the hills and byways, to the houses and farms where they all lived in earlier times. Eventually, we find ourselves at some cemetery, where the names of our kin are etched in mossy stones. I used to be scared of walking among the dead, but now I'm used to it. Cemeteries are peaceful, social places, with everyone chattering about who is who, almost as if the dead were still here, living in this stone city amid grass and birdsong.

Now we're tramping the Letts Cemetery, where Blanche, Gram, and Edith peer at the gravestones, muttering the family names and their histories. Blanche has a big frown on her face. I ask Gram what's wrong and she tells me that they can't find Lewis.

I remember Blanche's story of how he died of pneumonia so young, not long after they were married. "Lewis's father was a farmer out of Grandview. That's where we was married."

Memory smoothes out Blanche's face. "Aunt Jessie stood up for me. She lives down the road."

"Maybe she could tell us where he is," Edith says, confirming my sense that the dead are only slightly removed from the living. Aunt

Jessie might know his current address.

Blanche and Gram seem pleased to be on our way to see Aunt Jessie in Grandview. Gram tells me that Jessie is the youngest sister of Josephine, Blanche's mother, and that she lives with her daughter now. As the youngest sister of Blanche's mother, Jessie is a generation above Blanche, but the same age.

Aunt Jessie comes to the door this hot afternoon, her white hair flowing down her back, her crinkled-up eyes happy to see Blanche. Their thin arms cling to each other in a lingering hug.

"Oh, Blanche, it's so good to see you." Jessie cups Blanche's face in her wizened hands. "So much time, so much time," she says, shaking her head.

We come in the house, and Jessie's daughter serves iced tea and tuna sandwiches. Blanche and Jessie lean toward each other on the living room sofa, nodding their white-haired heads as they talk. I'm curled up on the floor out of the way, but close enough to listen.

Their false teeth clack as they tell the old stories. "I'll never forget your wedding to Lewis. New Year's Day, 1894. A beautiful sunshine day, bright with new snow. The horses' bells jingled. There was food from all over the neighborhood. The two of you . . . oh, my." She glances at Blanche, who has tears in her eyes. "Lewis, such a nice boy. The wedding was perfect. Everyone was so young. It's a shame, it is," Jessie says.

"We couldn't find him at the cemetery," Gram says.

Jessie widens her eyes. "Well, he's out there. I saw him buried." She pauses, then picks up the thread of her story. "Blanche sure was strong. And then you was born, Lula . . ." Her voice rises at the end, suggesting that this event, Gram's birth, was the good part of the story.

Sun streams across the living room as they talk, dust motes swirling in golden light. These elders tell about things that happened so long ago there is no clue left, not even a gravestone. Somehow I am no longer a young, stupid girl, but an observer of history. Someday they will die, too. I will visit their graves and have conversations with the dead.

Blanche seems lost in memory as Gram drives us away from Jessie's through narrow dirt roads, passing deserted houses, empty fields. After a few minutes the car pulls up in front of a shabby wooden house tilting slightly in the wind, a silent windmill carving the sky beside it.

"Here's the house you was born in," Blanche says to Gram.

Gram stares and then says in a stricken voice, "Oh no, Mama, where's the orchard?"

"It's gone, all gone," Blanch whispers. She points to an upstairs window. "That room there is where you was born."

Gram and Blanche have entered an invisible world together, faces reflecting their journey of memory. I wish I could click open their minds and see what they see. I can visualize the orchard that used to be over there, the climbing rose bush in front of the house.

Blanche says, "Our wedding was in the living room. Lula was born here. We lived here a few years with my papa and mama."

Gram is speechless and pale. She doesn't even light a cigarette. I've never seen her like this before. She is like the little girl I've seen in photographs, a forlorn-looking girl with long blonde hair. I imagine her playing with her dolls in the orchard.

Later that evening, Edith takes out a big box of photos. The faces of the dead come alive again in black and white, their eyes burning across time. "Here he is. Lewis. Now we've found him."

The face of a young man looks out from the photograph. His hair is cropped short, he looks barely older than a boy. I catch my breath—he looks so much like us, with beautiful soft eyes and full lips. Suddenly, he's a real person to me. I realize in a flash that here—once alive and breathing, once falling in love, getting married, having a child—is my great-grandfather. He's an actual part of our family, not just a ghost from the past. The adults pick over more old photos while I go into the bathroom to stare at my face in the bathroom mirror for a long time, comparing his face to mine. He seems almost alive, shining out from our faces, my mother, grandmother, and me, that boy who died so long ago in the last century, way back in 1894 on a winter day in March.

Saved

Bringing in the Sheaves

Sowing in the morning, sowing seeds of kindness,
Sowing in the noontide and the dewy eve,
Waiting for the harvest and the time of reaping,
We shall come rejoicing,
Bringing in the sheaves.

Bringing in the sheaves,
Bringing in the sheaves,
We shall come rejoicing,
Bringing in the sheaves.

BACK HOME IN Enid, at the Baptist church on Broadway Street, I learn all about the war between God and the Devil. The Sunday School class gathers in a circle in the concrete-block basement classroom. Boys with buzz cuts sneer, slapping their knees and throwing spit wads when the teacher isn't looking. The girls pretend to be listening, but they are mostly interested in writing notes on their palms. I sit with my hands folded in my lap, trying to hide my shaking knees.

We find out that both the Devil and God are dangerous. The devil is evil incarnate—that means evil in a body, the teacher says—a threat to us day and night. God in his omniscience knows everything we're thinking, and the devil is always tempting us, so we can't really trust our own thoughts. The devil is sneaky; he could be anywhere, scheming to set us on the path to hell.

"How do you know it's not the devil whispering in your ear?" the teacher says ominously. She says if God hears a thought the Devil puts in your head, he'll punish you like the Israelites in the desert. Or send a plague of locusts. Terrifying.

The teacher says we're in real danger if we don't come to church and learn to pray and believe in God. The devil is sneaking around at this very moment, tempting us and our families to serve him instead of God. Hell is a place you don't want to go after you die—it's sweltering and tortuous. We must do anything, everything, to avoid it. The devil will try to get us to play cards, to dance, kiss, or go to movies. The devil will tempt us to cheat or lie to our parents. "The devil waits for you, innocent little you," the teacher warns, "just to trip you up." She says he wears a black suit, has a forked tail, and leers with beady black eyes. He lives in a red hell made of fire, and delights in stealing people away from God.

The teacher drones on, scaring us all to death. You have to fight this devil all the time. You have to be on the lookout for him. He wants to possess you; he wants to suck you up into his maw and make you suffer for eternity. He lives in smoke and heat, his breath stinks, and his fingers are claws. He'll talk sweetly to you or he'll yell and scream and scratch you. And when you die, you will never have another chance to be good. You will suffer for eternity.

***

The big church is upstairs, with rows of polished wooden benches and a wooden cross in the front. Bibles and songbooks are tucked into holders on the backs of the pews. The church fills up with noisy families, mostly people who seem to know each other. Gram gave me special permission to attend "real church" with my friend Janille. A thin woman with a bun, glasses perching on the tip of her nose, bangs out hymns on the piano.

The preacher starts off with a very long prayer, like Grandpa's, going on about sin and forgiveness, the temptations of the devil, and God's mercy. During the sermon he's red-faced and shouting, punching the air and yelling about a righteous God. We have to accept Jesus as our savior or we'll go to hell and burn forever in eternal agony. Scary. I want everyone to be happy and things to be good and beautiful.

When the preacher talks about sin, I know it's in my family, in me, in our history. Lying, adultery, anger, and general meanness—it's all there in abundance. I feel hopeless. When they die, my relatives will go to hell for sure. It makes me want to cry, but I mustn't, not here in front of my friends.

"Come up, come on up, and let Jesus in your hearts. He'll take away your pain; he'll soothe your worries. Put your burdens on him. He'll hold them for you. He's the answer. Lord, show these sinners the way." The preacher invites us, his voice silky smooth, the sweet hymns going straight to my heart.

I peek at the others going forward. A limping old woman with tightly curled white hair goes up and leans against the preacher, whispering in his ear. A red-faced, lanky-limbed boy goes up with his mother. Are they telling him their sins? Are they embarrassed? He lifts his arms to pray them into the fold. I watch carefully to see what happens when you give up your life to God. The preacher says, "Let the Lord hold your burdens. He died for you, for you. Bring your sorrows up and lay them at his feet."

The music and the sound of the preacher's voice fill me with a longing I don't understand. Tears run down my face. I wipe them quickly so no one will see. The congregation sings a gentle, lilting invitation. My foot moves forward a little against my will, but I'm too scared and embarrassed to go to the preacher. In slow motion, I pull my foot back, staring straight ahead. The people sing sweetly, swaying to and fro. There is something here that I want so badly, but I can't have it. I can't be like these other people. They seem too happy.

My parents have broken the Ten Commandments by getting divorced. Will they go to hell, too? And there's Gram, perpetually perched on the sagging couch, cursing and smoking and telling me what a bad girl I am. I wonder if the other kids' parents act the way she does. I love Gram. I want her to be happy, and to be saved, too. I want her to think I'm good. If she doesn't think I'm good, does that mean that God doesn't either? I forget to take out the garbage and don't always do all my homework. Occasionally I take money from Gram's purse, a nickel here and a dime there. I only want an occasional candy bar, and Gram won't give me any allowance. After my day at church, I think differently about these things. I am in danger. I have to be careful.

The next time Gram allows me go to church, Janille and I slide onto the pew, our legs squeaking on the polished wood. I look around, noticing the smiling faces of the women wearing cotton dresses, the men in sport shirts and jackets, some in suits even though it's at least 97 degrees outside. Inside, it's like an oven. Perhaps this is what hell is like all the time. Janille grows solemn and silent when her parents join us. "The Old Rugged Cross" makes my chest hurt. Again I have to fight away my tears.

Today the preacher is quietly serious rather than bombastic. I listen to the wages of sin being death and how much we need Jesus to save us. "Just listen to your heart, tune in and hear what it is saying to you. It tells you that you need Jesus, that Jesus is the way, the truth, and the light. Trust in him and he will take away your pain. Come up, come up and give yourself to him." Five people make their way to the front.

The preacher's voice is reassuring, promising peace and calm. They are singing "Bringing in the Sheaves" now, and I understand that I am one of the sheaves of wheat; everyone is.

The minister looks directly at me, and I rise. I blend into the sweet singing and promises as I find myself moving down the aisle. My face is a mess, my nose running, my eyes spilling over. The minister smiles pityingly at my poor self and opens his arms. I lean against him grate-fully, and he murmurs in my ear, "Do you take Jesus as your savior?"

I'm crying almost too hard to speak. I say yes and manage to answer when he asks me my name. I wish he'd come home with me and protect me from Gram. I guess Jesus will do that now. I can't wait for my life to get better; it's going to change starting today. The minister gently turns me around to face the congregation and calls out my name.

I don't want the eyes of the congregation on me, but I stand there obediently. To my surprise, the strangers smile their approval. I try to stop crying and make myself presentable but finally give up, wishing I was invisible.

"Six more souls for the Lord, out of reach of the Devil."

Joyous piano music fills the room; voices rise to the rafters. I hold my breath and paste a smile on my face. When it's over, strangers come up to me, shake my hand, then wander off. Janille waits for me by the door and says nothing, to my relief. I feel as if I'd just stripped off all my clothes in public, but no one seems to have taken much notice.

I arrive at home a new person, with an aching desire to be gathered up into the arms of the minister over and over again. Gram's beady black eyes peer out from her cave on the couch. Her teeth are stained yellow. She hunches over, chain-smoking, the stinky butts piling up on the coffee table.

"So, what did you do at church?"

"I joined the church, I . . ."

"You what? You joined those hellfire and damnation Baptists?"

"Well, they're nice, and they sang and were very friendly. You said I could go."

"I told you to go and sit there and keep your mouth shut. What did you tell them about me?"

All of a sudden she's out of control. I should have lied, but I don't want to be a sinner or a liar.

"How dare you humiliate me like that! Look at you—you're a mess. Go change your clothes." I feel the sting of her opal ring across my cheek. Her eyes are wild. Where is Jesus now? He's supposed to help me. I've given my life over to him. I told the truth just now when a lie might have been better for me. Gram is in a terrifying frenzy. She tears up newspapers and scatters them around the room. "How could you, how could you?"

What does she mean? What have I done to make her so mad? I shiver and huddle down, trying to be very small.

"You're just like your no-good mother and father, doing what you damn well please. You don't deserve all the good things I give you. Where would you be without me? You'd be dead, that's what. You know damn well your mother and father don't want you."

I think about Jesus all the time, praying silently for him to save me.

Over the next two years, I get saved at church several more times, still hoping for a better life. Now and then, in the sunlight dancing on the prairie at dusk, I catch a glimpse of Him, a flicker of His pure white cloak. I know that if I just keep believing, He will someday save me.

Happy Twelfth Birthday

MOMMY IS CURLED into the burgundy velvet chair. Her knitting needles go click click, and a pink sweater trails down her lap. Her hair is newly dyed a warm auburn. The pink yarn, the burgundy chair, Mother's hair, and the sun's golden light create a vision of paradise and peace. At the moment, Mother is calm, even happy, chatting about her magical life in Chicago. She looks so beautiful to me right now. I wish her good mood could last forever, but I know it's only temporary.

Mommy throws back her head to laugh. "The restaurant was perfect—candles on the tables, white tablecloths, and the best silver and china. He bought me the most expensive dinner, and held my hand."

Gram snorts from her murky lair. I tense up, waiting for the usual outburst. She tears down all of Mother's romantic stories piece by piece. It's one of the reasons Mother runs off to Aunt Helen's. She doesn't want Gram's negativity to destroy her perfect fantasy world.

I love just looking at my mother, filling myself up with her beauty. I know I will never be that beautiful, that men could never want me the way they want her. To hear her talk, she is the most desirable person in the world.

I have just turned twelve, old enough to think it's strange that mother hasn't married again, despite all her romantic talk. No one knows my secret wish: that my parents will someday remarry and take me to live with them in Chicago, that city in the clouds. Daddy seems happy with Hazel, but I'm certain that my parents belong together. From time to time I look at the picture of their honeymoon in my mother's scrapbook. She wears a two-piece swimming suit and a huge smile, her head thrown back like a movie star. She sits next to Daddy, her long legs in front of her on the sand, exuding a breezy happiness I have never seen in person. Daddy sits with a long hairy arm around mother, a big smile on his face. I stare at this picture, trying to figure out who they were then and how things got to be the way they are now.

Today I bring out the scrapbook, sit next to Mother, and start turning pages. In one picture she stands huddled in a fur coat in front of a brick building. The caption reads March 18, 1945. Mother tells me that this picture was taken the evening before she went into labor. "Don't worry about giving birth. It's nothing. All these women complain, but for me a few pains, and whoosh, there you were!" She throws back her head and laughs again, her eyes dancing.

My baby bracelet is pasted in the book—little white beads spelling my name. My tiny footprints are there, and a photograph of Mother and me when I was about two months old. She is dressed in black lace and smiles broadly at the camera. The smiling baby with big blue eyes lies in her lap, not cradled in her arms.

"Is that me, really?"

"You were so tiny, I was afraid I'd drop you. I had a baby nurse. You cried a lot, but that was good for your lungs. Once you turned blue and I was so scared, but the nurse got you breathing again."

Moments like this are like hand-blown glass.

Later, Mother is knitting and I am putting on my dress. "Come here and let me see you," she says.

I giggle. "Why?"

"Come on—you're turning into a young lady. I want to see how you've grown!" Mother is in such a great mood. I fold my arms across my chest, knowing I'm too skinny, with bony knobbed elbows and wrists and knees.

I force myself to stand in front of her.

"Oh look." Her laugh rises and bubbles like quicksilver. "You have curves! Mother, she has curves."

"What curves?" The only curves I know of are the slight mounds on my chest that I hope someday will grow. Mother's hands brush along my waist and hips. "These curves—see? You are growing up. You really are."

"I'm twelve now."

"Oh, what nonsense." Gram can't stay out of it. "Childhood—humph. In my day there was no such thing as childhood. You worked and went to school and did chores. Agghh—I hated it!" Gram gets up to spin playfully around the room. "Blanche had such a hard life, but that wasn't for me. Chicago—oooh—that was the ticket."

Mother says softly, "I wish I'd grown up in Chicago. I was stuck in Muscatine with all those old grownups."

"You didn't have it so bad. It was family, and they loved you."

Mother sighs and says, "I was so lonely sometimes. But at least you brought me to Chicago when I was Linda's age."

There is an awkward silence, which I fill by prattling on about my birthday party, the one given by my friend Jewel's mother. It was a surprise, with a cake and candles and wrapped presents. Gram dropped me off for the party, and I enjoyed a few hours of pure crystal happiness in Jewel's breeze-filled house—a grand piano gleaming in their living room, yellow tulips in a vase. Theirs is a beautiful world that I don't belong to but love to visit.

Mother and Gram stay calm and happy for a few days. It is a strange, special time, these two women drawing sustenance from each other. Their faces are tender with feelings, and their voices betray so many layers of emotion and history.

The front door is open on this warm March day. Outdoors and in, peace and good will prevail. I know this will change, that the bitterness will rage again someday, as it always does. But at this moment I am happy, content that we three, who are mothers and daughters to each other, can be at ease together, if only for a time.

I enter my thirteenth year on a tide of love and hope.

Welcome as a Snake

As I come to my senses from sleep, the delicious perfumes of spring—honeysuckle, freshly mown grass—fill me up. I bounce out of bed, excited by the bright, hopeful day, and put on a new dress. Then, as I tiptoe along the hall, I feel a prick of apprehension.

"Gram, what time was Daddy supposed to arrive in Perry?" I know the answer: 7:30. I hope my question will nudge her into action.

"Oh, who cares?" She shakes a shoulder at me, a sardonic look on her face.

Uh-oh. She's making trouble, and she'll blame it on him. Time to shift into fix-it gear.

"What are you going to wear?" I chirp. "I'll pick out a few dresses, then you tell me which one, okay?"

She sneers at me, filling me with dread. It's 8:30 now. Even if we could fly, we'd be two hours late. It will take her an hour to get ready, then another hour to drive to Perry. We'll be three hours late, and Daddy will be furious. I haven't seen my father for over a year, but if I get angry at Gram or try to rush her, she'll slow down even more just to be nasty. So I suppress my irritation and act patient and cajoling.

By the time the Nash Rambler is on the road, it is ten o'clock. I could swear that she's poking along on purpose. Just before the curve that takes us into Perry, she pulls over by a field of cows and forks out a cigarette. She smokes and talks about the cows, how handsome they are. "They are nice to look at, but awful to smell and milk. Be glad you have the life you do." She hates her farm roots and often reminds me how lucky I am to have escaped her fate.

The cows chew their cuds in a slow, circular motion. The day is magnificent, the sun glinting on emerald grasses, but I am consumed by worry. Gram seems intent on ruining any chance for good will between her and my father. The cows watch us while Gram takes her time smoking.

I am shaking by the time we get to Perry. It's like waiting for an execution. The sun is high and hot when we pull up to the station. Instantly, a large shadow blocks out the sun; then Daddy's head is in the car, inches from Gram's face.

"I feel as welcome as a goddamned snake!" he shouts, spit flying from his mouth. "A goddamned snake! How dare you make me wait for almost four hours!"

"How dare you talk to me like that! You have no business yelling at me, you bastard!" They are engaged in a pitched battle within seconds.

I reach out my hand, calling, "Daddy. Hi, Daddy." They're both yelling so loud my voice is drowned out. I crouch low in the back seat, not wanting any passersby to know I'm with these crazy people.

Finally, Daddy opens the car door. He seems to notice me for the first time. "Hi, Linda, honey. I'm sorry, but I'm so damned mad . . ." He tosses his suitcase and a box in the car and climbs in the backseat with me. I suppose I'm too old for the pick-me-up-and-swirl-me-around, but I miss that old giddy feeling of abandonment to joy.

They argue almost all the way home. "Daddy, Daddy." I tug at his sleeve, hoping my little-girl act will distract him. "Daddy, what's in the box? You have a present for me?" I act excited, bouncing in my seat.

"Linda Joy, don't ask for presents. That's rude." Gram's voice is flat.

"Oh, let her be." With a ceremonial gesture he holds out the box. "Happy birthday."

I tear it open to find a Tiny Tears doll that I had begged for a year ago. It doesn't fit me now. I have curves and need Little Lady make-up and bath oil.

"Thank you! I just love it!" I hug the doll to my chest, playacting delight. I start to tell Daddy about school, Mr. Brauninger, and my cello, but then realize those topics are dangerous because of the money fights. I change the subject to the spelling bee, but this chatty interlude is brief.

Daddy and Gram start up again, their loud voices caroming around the car. I try to ignore them, watching through the rearview window as the world streams by. When we pass the pasture where Gram and I stopped on our way to the station, I'm pleased to see the only friendly faces of the day. I blurt out, "Look, Gram, there are our cows. Here's where we stopped for your cigarette!" Gram's narrowed eyes in the rearview mirror and her hiss from the front seat tell me that I have made a terrible mistake.

Daddy's body tenses. "So you stopped, eh?" The fight ratchets up several notches. In the back seat beside Daddy, I put on and take off the doll's diaper and her little pink jacket. I feed her with an empty bottle, pretending that I am her mother, rocking her in my arms. I don't really want her, but she is my only friend right now. I feel guilty about not wanting her. I kiss her plastic face and tell her I'm sorry.

The next morning Gram drops me off at the Youngblood Hotel to meet Daddy. I nestle my face against his suit, breathing in his smell. He buys me lunch, ordering a Coke and all the French fries I want. He tells me that I'm growing up and that he wants to treat me like a young lady. This remark helps ease the disappointment I felt at his choice of the doll for my birthday gift.

There's a strange feeling in my stomach as the elevator door closes. Daddy's large, hairy body fills the elevator car, energy zipping from his arms and legs. He is thrilling, but behind my excitement I worry about Gram's anger, and his. Of course, who could blame him, with Gram making us four hours late.

In the room, Daddy takes off his coat, removes his gold cufflinks, and rolls up the sleeves of his shirt. He asks me to sit next to him on the bed. The room is good sized, with a desk, a hard chair covered in a cream-colored cushion, a fancy mirror. A television is playing Saturday afternoon cowboy movies.

I look at my father, the man Gram has taught me to hate. Words that I have written in the hate letters flood my thoughts—son of a bitch, bastard, skinflint—but I blot them from my mind. His tanned face, with its green eyes and thick eyebrows, is like a magnet to me. He croons that he misses me, that it's wrong for Gram and him to argue, but that he has to take a stand with her.

"I don't want this for you, but it's best that you live with her. I've thought of bringing you to live with me in Chicago, but you have your life here. She's doing a good job with you, too—you are boo'ful, and thweet." Daddy uses his old words for me, making me cuddle closer. His dark eyes fix on me, looking me up and down. "You're getting to be quite a young lady. I've missed you. Come here, I want to show you something."

"What, Daddy?" I giggle as he tickles me under the arms.

"Just come here and sit on Daddy's lap."

I climb on his lap facing the television set. Tonto and Silver are hiding while the Lone Ranger shoots at a bunch of cowboys beside a big boulder. Daddy puts his arms around me and turns me to face him, pecking kisses all over my face. His prickly beard makes me giggle and I start to pull away, but he presses me toward him. "Come on, let me kiss you."

His sweet words keep me in place, though I don't really want to kiss him any more. He gives me a slow kiss. I squirm to get away, but he keeps it up. I don't know what to do. I want him to like me. He leans back. "You have to learn how it is with boys. They like a girl who's not easy but who kisses back."

Boys? I am not going to kiss boys for a long, long time. Gram's voice plays in my head about what a bad person he is. I know she'd be furious if she knew he was kissing me. I finally get him to let me down. Already I'm hiding all this in a secret place inside me. My voice is steady, my tone casual. "Daddy, let's go. Gram will be waiting for us." Daddy and I are normal again, and the kissing never happened.

At Gram's house, they eye each other warily. She's wearing one of her favorite dresses, and her hair is coifed nicely. I wonder why she dresses up so much for Daddy if she doesn't like him. He plans to teach me how to roller-skate on the skates he sent me for Christmas. I put on my jeans—something I rarely wear because Gram thinks they're low class—my chunky oxfords, and a scarf to keep the wind off my ears. I ask Daddy what he's going to wear. He laughs and pinches the lapel of his dark brown suit. "This is all I have. I promise I won't get dirty." He sits tensely across the room from Gram, visibly struggling to keep his anger at her in check.

Outside I am a little girl again, steadying myself on Daddy's arm and giggling. I try to keep my balance, sticking my feet out like a duck as we trudge up the hill. Neighborhood fathers are in their front yards wearing T-shirts or plaid shirts and jeans as they peer into the open hoods of their cars or push lawn mowers. My father has never been seen playing with me on the street, so I feel proud as I cling to his arm. The hill looks steep, and my stomach flips over as we look down it. Daddy senses my anxiety and murmurs, "You can do it. I'll be right here with you. Just let go."

The world is green lawns and pastel houses, bright-colored cars, the sound of mowers, the voices of neighbors. I am rolling along, Daddy's hard leather shoes tapping out a staccato beat beside me. Tap, tap tap, the grind of the skates, Daddy's voice—I hear all this and the whoosh of wind against my body. At the bottom of the hill I skate onto our lawn, laughing so hard that I fall down. Daddy chuckles in his throat, and Gram comes to the door, surprising me with a smile on her face. Twice more Daddy and I trudge up the hill and rush down again. At the end of the third run, Gram comes out with the camera. She points to the front steps and says, "Sit there together. I'll get your picture."

Daddy murmurs to me as we sit facing Gram and the Brownie camera, "Smile; you look thweet." I hold on to the idea that Daddy and I are playing just the way other fathers and daughters do.

⌘

The ride back to Perry is deathly silent. The car passes the field where Gram and I stopped two days ago. The cows are far away in the pasture, and I miss their comical, friendly faces. Daddy's large form is in the back seat with me, a bundle of irritated energy, barely contained. I can see Gram's face reflected in the rearview mirror—a mask of snide superiority. A mist of misery settles over me and I feel a terrible emptiness.

The bricks of the station are dark against a pearl-blue dusk. Daddy comes out of the lobby to tell us that the train is an hour late. My heart leaps. I wish he could stay much longer than an hour. I glance at Gram as I inch toward Daddy. I don't like the kissing lessons, but maybe it's really okay, maybe other girls learn this way too. I already miss him. I grab his arm like a little girl, as if to remind him that I'm still only twelve, skipping beside him as we head toward the Kumback Inn a block away. The neon sign blinks and music blares from the jukebox. Plaid-shirted farmers are served piles of food by the down-home waitresses.

We order chicken fried steak, fried chicken, and mashed potatoes from the blonde waitress. Daddy engulfs his fried chicken; Gram slices her steak with dainty care. All around us is the din of crashing plates, cooks yelling orders. Gram, with her red lipstick and haughty attitude, and Daddy, in his slick Chicago suit, stand out in this crowd, looking like city folks. I wonder what happened in Chicago long ago that led to this hatred they feel for each other. I wish I knew the history, so I could make sense of things.

Eating with Daddy, such an ordinary act, always makes him seem more like my actual father. I look at Gram's face, which suggests that I'll get in trouble later for being disloyal by sitting next to him. I'd rather sit next to this energetic, cheerful man than cranky Gram.

As we leave the café, streetlights give an amber glow to the square. Otherwise there is the deepening black of night. Daddy's long legs gobble a block in a few strides. I fold my arm in his the way ladies in the movies do, skipping to keep up. Gram lingers behind, but I don't care. I treasure my last few moments with Daddy.

The dark night sky is silent as we await the whistle of the train from Texas. Daddy paces back and forth. Gram sits and smokes, with an attitude of weary disgust. The whistle calls out, and people rush over to the track. The bright light grows huge and the ground vibrates as the train sweeps in with a heart-throbbing bass drum beat. Daddy gathers me to him, his rough cheek smearing my face. That wavy liquid feeling I always get when one of my parents leaves comes over me. Gram and Daddy say a tight-lipped good-bye. Then he grabs his suitcase, finds his seat on the train, and turns to wave at me. He's framed in the golden square of the window, my father. Little do I know that it will be a very long time until I see him again.

I'm grateful for the silence in the car as Gram drives us back home. We make our way around shadowy curves, the headlights illuminating the yellow dashes on the road, bushes and trees looming on the shoulder like ghosts. The sky has an eerie glow from the oil derricks burning off gasses in the distance. I watch the orange flames rage like the fires of hell, licking up into the jet-black sky.

Thirteen

GRAM SCURRIES AROUND vacuuming like a demon, cliffs and cre-
vasses distorting her face while she shouts and yells. What is
wrong with her? Why is she yelling and screaming? I can't imagine
what I did to make her act this way. She screams about how she has
given up her life for me, that I'm ungrateful and selfish. Doesn't she
know this is my birthday and that I want to be happy today?

I try hard to stay cheerful, thinking about pleasant things, like Keith
and some of the other cute boys. I think about the symphony practice
room, where the music lifts me away from the darkness, Mr. Brauninger
grinning at me from first chair as Keith, Jodie, Floyd, Lloyd, and I play
Beethoven's Seventh. I reflect on the books I'm reading—Sue Barton,
the nurse, Jim Bridger and Kit Carson, mountain scouts. I dream of my
mother and father. One day they'll get back together, and I'll join them
in Chicago where we'll start a new life together.

Gram screams that no one appreciates her; she could kill herself and
no one would care. I hate her screaming, but I get scared when she talks
about dying. Where would I go? My parents don't really want me to live
with them—it's just an old fantasy of mine that things could be nice
and sweet with them.

The postman comes. There is no birthday card from my mother, but
I see one with unfamiliar handwriting. Gram opens it, as always. It's
a birthday card from Keith, with yellow flowers and a pleasant verse.
Right now it's the best thing that could happen, a reminder that someone cares. I'm smiling and happy, skipping around the room. But out of
the corner of my eye, I catch a glimpse of Gram's grim face.

"Oh, that's a fine how do you do," she snarls. "What the hell do you
think that means, anyway? You know that men are up to no good."

"It's just a birthday card, and he's our friend." How can she say bad
things about him—he's sixteen years old and is always nice.

"Sure, you start there, and then where does it go. You are destined
to be on the stage. You'll be too busy with concerts and traveling to
get involved with men. Do you think I give you all these lessons just
so you can get googly eyed about some boy? I better not ever catch you
with anyone until you're eighteen, and after that you'll be too busy for
such nonsense."

She goes on yelling about her sacrifices, how I'd be dead if it weren't
for her. I can't bear the noise and go to the bathroom, where I get a few

minutes of peace. I feel shaky, but I can't bear the idea of crying today. I cradle the card, holding Keith's signature to my heart. It's all I have to hold on to.

Gram's rage goes on and on. To shut her up, I sit at the piano. Gram has to be quiet when I play. The sweetness of a Chopin nocturne takes me into another world. I see a veranda surrounded by lilies, a full moon rising, a soft breeze riffling through the trees. Chopin gathers me into his embrace, lifts me into a lovelier time and place, and I'm free.

Swan Song

BRIGHT LIGHTS FLOOD the stage and gleam on the graceful curves of the grand piano. Its S-shaped top is open, exposing the wires of its secret inner life. The house lights dim and the ritual begins. Mr. Brauninger, handsome in his black tuxedo, cradles his amber violin as he steps into the light. Petite Eva, her dark hair shining, bounces with energy as she joins him on stage. Mr. B. begins to play. Music streams from his violin, melodies moving gracefully through the air the way a butterfly floats on a spring breeze.

I am most fully alive in the rarefied world of music, where I am surrounded by wonderful sounds and colors. Music paints the world with pale maroon, soft lime green, and a mellow aqua blue, like photos of the sea. Music transports me into a world free of pain and darkness, a world of soothing safety, where hope returns to me.

Mr. Brauninger has told us that he and Eva are getting married and moving soon to their new home. I understand that they must leave and go on with their lives. I'm thrilled with the romantic notion of it, but it also breaks my heart.

I can hardly remember life before him. He awakened me to a world I never could have imagined, offering me the symphony and its magical sounds, along with more tenderness and encouragement than anyone else I've known. He has believed in me without reservation. The sweetest and safest man I've ever known is leaving.

At the recital, he and Eva play together, she on the piano, he with his golden violin under his chin, in perfect synchrony, responding beautifully to each other's gestures, the signals that musicians use—a nod, a glance, the movement of a finger, bow tip, or shoulder. I know this same language, it will always be with me. I am the string, the bow, the piano key. I am the vibration through which Mozart and Beethoven continue to express their inner worlds.

At the end of the performance, Mr. Brauninger bows deeply. I take a picture in my mind of my musical parents—the gleam of light on the instruments, how Eva and Jim shine together, holding hands.

❦

It's an evening in June when they come to the house to say goodbye. I can't imagine my life without them. I take in the love in Mr. B.'s eyes, the graceful movements of his fingers as he talks. My childhood is truly ending now. He has found a full-size cello for Gram to buy for me. "The size of the cello will challenge her, but we know Linda Joy loves a challenge." Mr. B. winks at me and Eva laughs, saying, "That girl will make it, she's a trooper."

He shakes our hands, then says with a grin, "Don't take any wooden nickels." My heart contracts in agony, but I smile and wave at them as they disappear up the street in their blue Dodge. This is a terrible, familiar feeling. The cicadas are humming in the silver evening and a bright moon has risen in the east. The summer air is sweet and warm. I hold in my tears as so many images of Mr. Brauninger flit through my mind—that first day when I was nine years old, tapping his toes as he danced, rosin flying everywhere, the light in his eyes as he kneeled down and asked my name. My memories are like pages of a calendar, tearing off and flying away—Saturday morning Youth Orchestra where I labored joyfully with my friends over Haydn, Bach, and Beethoven.

The mourning doves say who, who, who, as the wind sweeps and swirls away my childhood. Without a word to Gram, I go to my room and take out a Nancy Drew book, losing myself in a world of adventure with a smart girl who always figures things out.

Wasteland

ONE WEEKEND DURING the summer of my fifteenth year, Aunt Helen drives me to her house. Gram hardly leaves the house any more, so every week Aunt Helen and I take care of the chores like laundry and shopping; sometimes I go to church with them on Sunday. I'm always welcomed with homemade food and warm hugs. Uncle Maj takes me out to the garden to cut roses, cupping the flowers in his hands. Today it is warm, the fragrance of roses wafting through the house. I inhale the scent deep into my body, glad to be away from Gram's smoke and caustic ramblings.

After lunch Aunt Helen tells me to sit down, she wants to talk to me. My heart beats a little faster—this phrase usually means I'm in trouble, but Aunt Helen smiles. "Darlin', I just want to talk to you about your father. It's not right what your grandmother is doing, making you write those terrible letters, going on and on about him."

Despite everything, my loyalty to Gram makes me take her side. "She says he doesn't take care of me the way he should. She's right; he doesn't send enough money."

"He does all right, and besides, he deserves respect. He sends money; some fathers send nothing at all. The real problem is Frances. She's not fair to him. He's a darned good man."

"How do you know about him?"

"Land sakes, child, I've known him for years. He's hot headed, but they're two peas in a pod. He deserves to have his daughter's respect. It's a sin, I tell you, a sin not to respect your father."

I'm shocked to hear her talk against my grandmother. Long ago I gave up defending my father. For three years there's been no exchange between us except the hate letters. Until this conversation with Aunt Helen, I had never considered the possibility that Gram's web of hate is woven with lies and her own agenda.

Aunt Helen continues. "He isn't the man your grandmother says he is. If I were you, I'd write my own letters. I'd give him a chance to know me through my own words."

I'm knotted up inside with worry. I begin to cry, partly out of fear, partly from relief. At least I know that someone cares about what is happening. I pace around the living room. "Gram will know. I can't get away with anything. She opens my mail, she reads my mind . . ."

"She won't find out," Aunt Helen tries to reassure me. "You'll write your letters at our house, and he'll send his replies here for you to read. They'll be waiting for you when you come over. She'll dictate the other letters as usual, and he'll answer those at your house."

"What if he gets mixed up?" I grab a Kleenex and blow my nose, trembling with the possibility of Gram finding out. Aunt Helen puts her arm around me.

"Great balls of sheet iron," Maj says in his typical colorful speech. "The Duchess is our good friend, but it isn't right that she's come between you and your father. It's criminal, I tell you!"

I'm excited by the plan but terrified. She's always threatening to send me away to the juvenile authorities. If she finds out about this, she'll have more reasons to beat me senseless with the yardstick. When she's crossed, she's a demon from hell.

———

Nevertheless, on that spring day, Aunt Helen, Uncle Maj, and I make our pact. That afternoon I write to my father, telling him in my own words what I think about school, the symphony, and my friends. It's been years since I wrote him a letter that comes just from me. I seal it and give it to Aunt Helen to mail, feeling triumphant and a little bit freer from Gram's shackles.

She seems to know everything I do or think, as if she's inside me, breathing my air. It frightens me that her attitude toward my father has taken root inside me. Perhaps I am becoming like her, learning from her to be hateful. I embark on this journey to know and be known by my father as a way of saving myself.

Gram and I continue the hate letters, which seem to have become her sole source of enjoyment. She perks up on the couch, more awake and alive than at any other time. I write down her terrible words without guilt now, knowing that Daddy is getting my real letters, too. In those I tell him that he has to be very careful about keeping the letters straight, that Gram still opens my mail before I get home. He assures me that he understands; he will be careful.

The great glacier that has frozen over us for the last several years begins to thaw. With joy I come to Aunt Helen's to find his letters written with affection and excitement. My father is very verbal and always writes several pages in his distinctive loopy handwriting, expressing himself freely. We're finally getting acquainted. Things have been going along well for a few weeks when suddenly the world tilts on its side.

I come home one afternoon in July to find Gram standing at the front door, her hands on her hips, a letter in her hand. The look on her face would turn Moses to stone. Her hair frizzes in all directions and her eyes shoot a dangerous light, the kind of light you could fall into and die. She rattles the letter at me.

"How dare you! You betrayed me. You've been talking to your father behind my back! Don't deny it, or I'll slap you into the next life."

I break into a sweat, frantic with worry about what she'll do to me. I can see that Daddy blew it, writing about something that she didn't dictate.

"Behind my back!" she rages. "You wrote to him behind my back! Who put you up to this?" She goes on and on, screaming, pacing, ranting. For a long time I don't admit to her that Aunt Helen suggested it.

"Fine. I can see you don't care about me any more, for all I've done for you. Call your mother and tell her to come get you. Call your father. You think he's so damned great, let him take care of you. I can't have you living under my roof."

She has threatened to send me away for years now, whenever I express my own opinions or question hers. I fight back, fighting for my life, screaming at her about wanting to know my father, having a right to know my parents; it doesn't mean I don't love her just the same. After several hours, she pummels me into submission until I tell her the truth about Aunt Helen.

On the phone with Aunt Helen her voice crescendos to ever higher peaks. Gram has entered into some new realm of the rounds of hell. After she puts down the phone, her face in a sneer, announces that Aunt Helen told her thatt I'd asked her to help me write to my father. This is the lowest point of the day—Aunt Helen has covered up her own role in this. Now that Gram thinks I am lying, she closes in on me. I protect myself with my hands, but I can't escape Gram's mindless fury. I'm still in shock, stunned that Daddy slipped up and Aunt Helen lied, both of them leaving me to face this Medusa who's trapped me in her lair. My face and arms sting as I slink into bed. I wish I could run away, but I know Gram would beat me even more when I got back.

Gram seals my prison, enforcing her complete control over me. She allows me to complete summer school, but the rest of the time I'm isolated in the dark smoky house with her, my only respites in music and reading. Gram can't allow me to have a speck of autonomy. Accusing me, hating my father, and being angry at Aunt Helen seem to become her reasons for living, yet she constantly threatens to die, saying that with all this stress—which is my fault—she'll die of a heart attack and haunt me for the rest of my life.

I don't want her to die; time and time again I've told her so. After a few weeks of her wailing, I get wise to her and build a shield that protects me from feeling guilty any more. She just wants to scare me and make me do what she wants; she loves having total control over my body and soul. The more she burrows into me, the more I practice hiding from her, making sure she never knows what I'm thinking again, learning how to make my face a mask.

⋆⊱⋅⊱⋅⋆⋅⊰⋅⊰⋆

Summer passes in this way. Every day she threatens to send me away for talking back to her, either to a juvenile hall or to my parents. As much as I want to be away from her, I don't want to leave the only home I've ever had, my friends, and my school. Chicago is a huge city, scary and impersonal. I worry about the future and what bad things might be in store.

She sits on the couch and goes on and on. "You want your damned parents so bad, you can have them. If they'd wanted you all these years, they could have had you. I did them a favor taking care of their brat when they had better things to do. Your father never wanted a child; he was forty years old before you were born. You were an accident. Go on and live with him if that's what you want. Go to bed. I can't stand the sight of you."

I keep telling her it's normal to want to know your own father, and that I love them both, but she doesn't understand. In her eyes, it's one or the other. I can love my mother, of course, but my father, he's in a different category. I wonder if what she says about him not wanting me is true, remembering my time at Vera's—I could tell then that I was inconvenient. Did my father want me? I don't know what to believe.

⋆⊱⋅⊱⋅⋆⋅⊰⋅⊰⋆

One day, several weeks into this madness, Gram sits quietly on the couch, pondering and smoking. She's suddenly so quiet I wonder what she's up to. She says, "I suppose your father could come for a visit."

Is it a trap? She's just testing me; she'll attack me if I agree. Over the next few days, she pursues the idea enough to call my father and arrange it. I still don't trust her, but plans are made for him to pick me up and drive us to Oklahoma City so we can spend time away from Enid, meaning Gram.

As the day draws near, I start to get excited about seeing my father.

The last time I saw him, I was twelve. I wonder what he'll think of me, if he will recognize me. Since I last saw him, I've gotten my period, started wearing a bra, and grown several inches, though I'm still thin as a rail and wear glasses. Will my father like me? After all that has happened, will he think that I'm like Gram or Mother?

He comes to pick me up in a rented, cream-colored Cadillac. He and Gram are civil to each other, nodding and tight lipped. I feel proud that I was strong enough to win him, and convert Gram to my side. His deep voice curls around me like a warm blanket. I try not to show how happy I am, not wanting to make Gram jealous.

❧

We drive to Oklahoma City on highway 81, the Chisholm Trail. The sky is azure blue, with clouds floating above the edge of the horizon. Daddy bubbles over with talk and laughter, his eyes bright with admiration as he looks at me.

"You sure have grown up, such a nice little figure, just like your mother. You have to be careful about boys. They've only got one thing on their minds."

"I don't worry about that," I say.

"I just want you to know that if something were to happen, if you ever got in trouble, you could talk to me. Your gram, she's old-fashioned, but I'm your father. You know you can come to me."

I say all the right things: thank you, I appreciate your concern. At the same time, I'm almost insulted, shocked that he could think such a thing about me. Clearly he does not know me very well at all. Good Baptist girls don't go around getting pregnant. I'm not even sure of the details of the sex act.

Daddy goes on to tell me that boys are wily creatures. "I ought to know. I was a very horny young man myself. Still am, but . . . Hazel and I don't have that kind of relationship any more. Hardly ever did."

I'm surprised and discomfited by this new kind of intimacy, but I'm grateful to know that he'd be there if I needed him. Gram would throw me out of the house if I ever got pregnant, but that will never happen. Gram's scary stories and the Baptist teachings have me thoroughly scared about boys and sex.

Daddy gives me a taste of a new, free way to live, riding in a Cadillac, my hair blowing, a smile on my face. I feel triumphant. My father, in the flesh. Real after all, not just a dream.

He rents us adjoining rooms in a motel in downtown Oklahoma City, with a connecting door. After a few minutes I wander through the open door, surprised to find him naked, his face covered with shaving cream. I back out, apologizing, burning with embarrassment. I'm not used to having men in the house, especially naked ones. I keep my eyes on his face as I leave the room, worried that the encounter might trigger his desire to kiss me.

A few moments later, he comes in the room partially dressed, smelling of aftershave, grinning and telling me in his deep, melodious voice how grown-up I am, how I still need to learn how to kiss. I laugh and push against him playfully. It's been so hard to win him back. How can I reject my own father? I laugh and tell him I'm too young to date, but he keeps up the litany. "Let me teach you. Boys are awkward; you need to know what to do." He pulls me toward him and I can't bear to turn him away. A few kisses demonstrate that things have changed since I was little—it's definitely not all right for my father to do this. I don't want what he's doing, but I want him to love me. Memories of the last few weeks swirl in my mind, the long, smoke-filled nights of Gram's ranting and attacks, everything I went through to get him back into her good graces. Now I'm know that I can't let him do this, but I'm afraid I'll lose him forever if I say no. I want to run away, but he kisses me again. I resort to something that's sure to work—I simply put on my helpless little girl act. "Oh, Daddy, I'm so hungry. Can we go eat now, please? Really, I'm so hungry I can't wait. Please, Daddy."

I stand by the door, making it clear that he has to leave. He shuffles back to his room and I close the door. The silence is so loud I can't hear anything but the pounding in my ears while I try to understand what has happened.

Daddy's wearing his Chicago suit and starched shirt when he takes me to a club for dinner. A live jazz band plays in the smoky basement. Bubbly and ever so cheerful, Daddy orders Manhattans for us, and New York steaks. This adult bar and dinner-dance place is both exciting and frightening to me. The drink burns my throat and all the way down to my stomach. The Baptist voice growls–sin, sin. I feel desperately sad, as if I've lost my father all over again. This is not the way it was supposed to be—kissing, drinking alcohol. He talks on excitedly about his wonderful life in Chicago, unaware of my misery. After we eat our steaks he asks me to dance. Before I would have wanted this attention, but when he takes me in his arms, my face pressed against his diamond tie tack, my throat is full of tears. A voice in my head says, "No one will ever really love you." I want so much to go home.

I play along with Daddy the next day, pretending to have a good time. On the way home, he insists on showing me how to drive by having me sit on his lap at the wheel. For a time, being at the wheel is great fun if I don't think about his lap, but I soon get uncomfortable enough to insist on getting off his lap. I want so much to be happy. I focus on the beautiful sky and the way the land stretches out from horizon to horizon. I imagine the Cherokee Indians on their horses a long time ago on this land before we took it away from them; I look forward to the next season of wheat as Daddy drives me back to Enid, back to Gram and the house on Park Street.

A sea change has happened to me this summer, especially on this trip with my father. On the way back, I think about the girl who traveled the highway in the other direction two days ago, innocent and full of hope. This new girl is wiser, aware of the subtle ways that life plays tricks, giving us what we want but in a form we can't accept. This new and different girl is on her way home to a new kind of darkness. I almost don't mind when he leaves. There is no way to know how long it will be, and how deep the darkness will grow, until I see my father again.

Back at Gram's, I watch her smoke and tell her lies about what a nice time we had and how wonderful Daddy was. I try to persuade her—and myself—that he really is a good father. I watch her face; my lying skills are improving. She accepts what I say and doesn't grill me about it. I feel empowered by my ability to hide the truth from her. Little do I know how adept at lying I will eventually become.

I know one way to smooth the pain in my chest. I sit down at the piano and play a Bach Prelude and Fugue. The clean colors of the music as it unfurls into the thick air of the house, green and red, black and cream, will clear my mind. The logic of Bach braids my mind into ordered bars and measures, contrapuntal melodies weaving so clear that there's no way to get lost in the labyrinth of notes. Not so with the painful puzzle of my family, trapping me in a tangle of feelings. I can see that Gram and I are destined to be together for the long haul, until I graduate from high school. My father is lost to me for good.

God's in His Heaven

Pippa Passes
The year's at the spring
And day's at the morn;
Morning's at seven;
The hill-side's dew-pearled
The lark's on the wing;
The snail's on the thorn;
God's in his Heaven—
All's right with the world!

ROBERT BROWNING

SLUSH DRIPS FROM the windshield of the city bus. A bitter winter wind rolls from the Rocky Mountains across the Great Plains, all the way to Oklahoma. A light dusting of snow covers dull brown grasses, winter's grieving for the green seasons of growth. As soon as the bus pulls up in front of the high school, I jump out and dash into the warmth of the building, trying to outrun the bite of the wind on my thighs. I love the way the snow softens the edges of the world and conceals a bare, lost landscape, but I hate the cold that burrows deep into my bones.

I pull open the door, grateful for the blast of heat in my face. It seems my body constantly shivers from a cold no heat can penetrate, a cold that's settled deep in the crevices of my soul. Gram is the Ice Queen, sitting in her hole in the couch for hours, even days, without speaking to me. Other times she's hot and desperate, as if she must see me cry in order to satisfy her hunger for misery. She runs either too hot or too cold, with fewer of the pleasantly warm times that we used to share.

At school, I'm cast into what I think of as the "real world," a world where people talk and laugh. I'm thrown together with kids from normal families who golf, eat pizza, go bowling, and have friends over for dinner. At home—or, I should say, at Gram's house, since she always insists I'm just a guest—there's none of this kind of activity. Home for me is not a place to be comfortable and let down your guard. My places of safety are away from the house.

I don't know it yet, but it will take much of my adult life to be able to experience home as a place where the cares of the world are released.

At this point in my life, survival is my goal, so I escape Gram's house as much as I can, just as I'll eventually escape Enid to go to college. I love going to school. It's the only place besides symphony where I am with normal people who have seemingly ordinary lives.

Jodie and I always meet every morning at school, joining the stream of kids in the promenade through the halls. As I enter the building, I see her waving at me from the end of the corridor. The slight blush of her lipstick gleams when she smiles, and her beautiful chestnut hair flows down her back. Her ever-ready grin and gentle kidding keep me floating a notch or two above the misery that tugs constantly at my mind, threatening to submerge me in the dark world of Gram's house.

Jodie runs up and starts in with her jokes and good humor. We both know we're outsiders, but we don't care—we have our own world of music and literature. We stroll together, observing the golden girls who wear twin-set sweaters with tiny pearl necklaces or pencil skirts with bobby socks, everyone's hair coiffed in a flip. They are already making good progress in the quest for a secure future—going steady, sporting their boyfriends' class rings, well on their way to the husband, house, and weekend barbecue in the backyard.

Jodie tells me how hard she's been practicing and about the quartet rehearsal she had at her house. I try not to feel envious of her life, but I do. I could never host a group or party of any kind—Gram would just embarrass me. Jodie and I are both serious about music and our futures, though she's a much more dedicated musician than I. She practices the cello every day for five or six hours, and then spends most of her free time immersed somehow in music. At Monday night symphony, I've observed how her technique has developed to a higher level of professionalism, how her sound and approach to the instrument have advanced.

I love watching Jodie when she solos, and lose myself in admiration for her concentration and technique. Every time she finishes, she winks at me and jokes, as if to deflect attention from herself. It helps me more than she knows that my best friend has serious goals and is always there for me. Jodie is my lifeline, helping me survive day to day, but she has no idea of this.

Since we started going to the same school, we've been inseparable. Because of the competition between her mother and Gram, we don't do the normal things girlfriends do, sleep over or go to the movies, but we've shared Mr. Brauninger, the symphony, and our love for the cello since we were ten years old. Now we talk about almost everything, the usual teen concerns of makeup, kissing, and boys, as well as our future. The secrets I carry loom large in my mind, but I don't share them with her, and it will be years before I know that Jodie's life is not so great at home. We are good girls—we follow the rules, work hard, and don't talk about home except in the most general terms.

For first period, Jodie and I rush to Miss Fromholz's French class, where we like to make her say "I love you" in French.

"Je t'aime, je t'aime," she repeats with a wink. During class she shows movies of Paris, narrating in French—the Eiffel Tower, Notre Dame, Impressionist paintings full of light and joy. Jodie and I promise to meet each other one day in a café on the Seine.

"I can't wait to get out of this town," she murmurs behind her hand.

"Me neither," I say, and mean it.

I can't wait to escape, even though I'm scared of the larger world beyond Enid. Paris . . . Now there a girl could live a magical, artistic life—eating fine cuisine, flirting with exotic young men—unhampered by strict Midwestern rules. Thanks to movies in French class and Gram's love of Europe, I can imagine living in a worldly, sophisticated way somewhere else. Jodie and I dream together of that enchanted future someplace far away.

We discuss the books we've read in English class with Miss Young. She's introduced us to the plays of Shakespeare and the worlds of English and American literature through Austen, Longfellow, Dickens, and Melville. Miss Scott, our journalism teacher and a world traveler, demonstrates her philosophical bent by quoting poets, philosophers, and statesmen. One of her favorite quotes is from Alfred Lord Tennyson: "I am a part of all I have met."

This line opens a window for me, telling me that the sorrow I've experienced will weave itself into the tapestry of who I am becoming, that my life will be richer for it, that my fractured childhood isn't for naught. I still wish things could be different for me, but this simple verse casts a glimmer of light on my grim circumstances.

Jodie notices Browning's poem "Pippa Passes" in my wallet. "God's in his heaven, all's right with the world." She smiles as if she understands that a poem can save you. I have memorized it, repeating it silently when Gram spews her hate. Darkness and light weave through my life, but the suck of the negative is so strong it frequently engulfs me. I keep clawing my way back up—thanks to Jodie, music, and books.

Jodie and I say good-bye after our two classes together and make a plan to meet again later. I watch her graceful gait as she walks down the hall and feel such gratitude that she is in my life. I know I'll see her in orchestra later, where Vivaldi or Bach will sweep away the clutter in my mind.

I enjoy orchestra, but the high school group isn't as much of a challenge as Monday night symphony. But it is an opportunity to play, and I need that. My cello technique is not what it should be, because Gram doesn't send me for lessons any more. For a couple of years after Mr. Brauninger left, she took me to study with a wonderful teacher in Oklahoma City, but Gram doesn't go out any more. Still, it's understood that I'm to major in cello in college.

For now, my musical development is focused on the piano, where I'm learning concertos: the Liszt Etudes and Chopin Preludes. Maybe it's Gram's own life-long love affair with the piano that makes her continue those lessons. I am gratified to be seen as a better-than-average pianist, but playing in recitals and concerts is torture for me. I have never admitted to anyone the extent of my stage fright, which for some reason reaches truly terrifying proportions when I'm to play the piano. Each time there's a performance on my schedule, I go through hell as the day approaches, as if I'm waiting to be shot at dawn. Memorizing long pieces means hours of labor, my sweat literally falling on the keys. By the time the recital comes, I have to trust that the music is in my hands, that they will play on even if I do forget the music.

When I'm on the brightly lit stage, my mind can shift into a complete blank. But sometimes it whirls into a panic about what Gram will say if I make a fool of her, as she puts it, by making a mistake in my playing. So far, when this fear takes over, my hands keep running up and down the keyboard as if they had a life of their own. Maybe they do. It's comforting to think that part of me is invulnerable to my bouts of panic and depression.

Sweet Sixteen

Mother comes to visit for my birthday. As always, the hot wire tension zings between her and Gram. I'm relieved when they fight, because it means Gram isn't focused on me for a change. I feel guilty about experiencing relief at my mother's expense, but I can't help it.

On this occasion, I recognize a strange camaraderie between Mother and me. Gram half-raised both of us, so in a way we're more like sisters than mother and daughter, both of us at the mercy of the same powerful madwoman. Mother whispers things in passing, hinting at her true feelings, that she's always felt like a lost child, too.

"It's wonderful that Gram gives you the best things, your clothes and your lessons," she says. Then a warning tone creeps in. "But you need to be yourself. I don't want you to be like her." Sometimes Mother's comments are critical of Gram: "I can't understand why she hates your father so much; there's no good reason for it. He's a very nice man, and you should love and respect him." Or her tone is plaintive: "My mother is so mean to me."

Sorrow fills my chest on these occasions and I reassure her that it's all right, I'm not like Gram, I'll never be like that. I don't tell her much about the reality of my life. It's clear she doesn't want to know too much, and I'm sure the truth would worry her. I sense that she's genuinely grateful that Gram is taking care of me because she simply wouldn't know how. My life looks pretty good from a certain angle—my clothes, music, and grades—and Mother chooses to take that view.

A big birthday dinner at Aunt Helen's is planned for me. Over the last few months, she has cautiously returned to Gram's good graces. The depth of their friendship shows in their ability to be in the same room with no sniping. I credit this mostly to Aunt Helen's huge, happy Southern heart. Once she loves you, nothing short of murder can end it. I have never spoken of her betrayal of me, sensing that she has her own fragilities, though they are well hidden from the world. She's still my wonderful Aunt Helen, and I melt all over when she says, "God love ya darlin'."

Today even Gram is putting on a nice dress and some make-up. I can't remember the last time she left the house. As we wait for her, my mother's face and my own are reflected in the hall mirror. Mother leans up close to the mirror to touch up her mascara and eye shadow. She glances at me and touches the line of my jaw. "Hmmm, you could use a little make-up now. Here, stand still."

Carefully she applies a touch of eye shadow above my eyes. It tickles, and she tells me to stop wiggling. She sweeps blush on my cheeks with a huge fluffy brush, and gently applies mascara to my eyelashes.

"You're turning into an attractive young lady," she says, and my heart laps up her praise. "It's okay for you to wear just a little make-up, but not too much."

Gram comes out of her room and snorts.

"Now Mother, it's a special occasion for Linda. You should let her have make-up."

"This isn't Chicago, and she's only sixteen."

"She's a young lady." Then Mother turns her attention back to me. "Open your mouth, like this." She demonstrates, opening her mouth slightly and making a taut circle of her lips.

It thrills me for my mother to dip her lip pencil into the creamy rose color and carefully outline my lips. It tastes good, I'm careful not to smear it. We look into the mirror together, our faces side by side. My mother is much more beautiful than I, with her dark eyes and wavy hair, but we do look a lot alike now that I am growing up. Mother leans toward me and kisses my cheek. My chest aches, my heart opening to her sweet affection. If only she would be like this all the time.

Together, happy as mothers and daughters, we all go to Aunt Helen's for the celebration. "God love ya'" greets us with big, warm hugs. I have for the most part forgiven Aunt Helen for letting me down, though we have never talked about it. Tonight, I just want unblemished happiness. Uncle Maj clipped yellow daffodils for the vase on the table. I blow out all my candles.

You Can Wish Upon a Star

B<small>Y THE END</small> of our junior year, Jodie has auditioned at the Eastman School of Music and won her scholarship. I have a scholarship for the music school at the University of Oklahoma, but it isn't far enough away to suit me. Sometimes I feel a pang of guilt about wanting so badly to leave Gram, but then she goes into another one of her tirades and I remember that my only chance to live a normal life—whatever that might be—is to escape her.

The best result of Aunt Helen's intervention with Gram has been to give me a new perspective: I see now that my grandmother isn't perfect. Before last year, no matter what Gram did, I thought of her as an omniscient god, but she has fallen from her high perch. I don't know what's wrong with her, but I'm certain that her view of life—and of men, in particular—is twisted.

She has no friends. I think people are afraid of her oddities, even though they don't know the half of it. When Keith comes over to pick me up for symphony, she puts on a nice dress and acts aristocratic, so he has no idea that she's a screaming banshee the rest of the time, chasing me around the house, slapping and berating me.

I've learned to go underground, to hide from her who I really am and what I really think. As much as I can, despite her attempts at absolute control, I try to carve out a life of my own. At first I felt guilty about this—my Baptist voice yelled at me—but after a while, I realized it's natural to want a peaceful, positive life of my own.

The daily routine I have with Jodie gives me comfort: We are together in the morning, and we eat lunch together. Each day after school—in winter and summer—we walk the eight blocks to downtown. We go to the music store and listen to records, or stop at the drug store for malted milk or an ice cream sundae. When it's cold out, we huddle in the padded booths sipping hot chocolate, making faces at our reflections in the mirrors. I wait for the last bus from town, which gets me home after five in the afternoon.

From that point on, I have it all mapped out. When I first poke my head in the door, I size up Gram to get a sense of how bad an evening it might be. Then I fix dinner for us, do the dishes, and practice piano for two or three hours—this usually keeps her quiet. After that, I pore over five college prep subjects in the kitchen, writing papers and essays on a typewriter set up by the stove. Throughout all this, Gram hunches in her couch, watches TV, and smokes. Frequently, despite my best attempts to stay out of her way, she goes on a wild tear, and we have another loud and physical fight.

In the evenings, whenever Gram is out of the room, I peer through the window panels of the front door, sending my thoughts into the moon as it rises over the plains in the east, into the trees that blow in the wind. There, I find some beauty and peace.

To my great surprise, shortly after I turn sixteen Gram buys a gold Nash Rambler. She says she'll let me drive it, emphasizing that it's her car, not mine. She won't let me drive it to school, but on weekends I can take my time doing errands, and even meet Jodie on the fly. One afternoon in the spring, joyful with my newfound freedom, I drive the car out to the edge of town where the wheat is spread out under the sky. The stalks are green now, but soon they will become beautiful amber fields that undulate like a great sea in the wind.

I get out of the car and close my eyes—here, truly, God is in his heaven and everything is perfect. I run my fingers along the wheat stalks not yet come to a head, pondering creation. Birds fly by and cicadas start up their rhythmic chant. I vow to always immerse myself in nature, where the light and the natural forces of creation keep away Gram's darkness.

I've developed many strategies to help me survive, but I wonder if I'll ever be normal. Am I so damaged by what has happened in our family that I won't find anyone to really love me? Little do I know that at this very moment, my first love is not far away.

A few weeks later, Gram surprises me by arranging a visit to the Brauninger's in Kansas with Keith. Keith and I, together, on a car trip? I can't imagine anything more wonderful.

It's a warm July day when we set off, Gram acting unusually cheery. I wonder why she lives in the dark for so long, then perks up and becomes almost normal again for a short while. She's dressed up, wearing make-up; she even got her hair done for the occasion. She's like another person today, and I'm delighted. Maybe things will get better for good now.

Keith and I are sitting close enough for me to see the fine hairs on his arm and smell his aftershave. I'm soaring with happiness. For all these years he's been a constant in my life, the only boy to treat me with unwavering friendship and respect. He calls me Little Linda and always bows when he greets me, carries my cello, and teases me mercilessly. Jodie says that means he likes me, but I know he doesn't like me in that special way, just as a friend. For the last year, Keith has given me rides to Monday night symphony. Sometimes a group of us go out afterwards for ice cream at the Wagon Wheel or Goldspot's. Gram allows me these occasional forays into social life because she trusts Keith implicitly.

Today, the landscape is vast and golden, puffy clouds building into castles. Gram drives us up route 81, the old Chisholm Trail north into Kansas. When we arrive, Mr. Brauninger and Eva gather us into their arms. Mr. B. looks at me lovingly. "Our Little Linda sure has grown up." We have a joyous dinner, updating the Brauningers on the other musicians in Enid. Gram is charming and sophisticated, regaling everyone with tales of her trips to England. She has returned to being the Gram I love.

That evening, Keith and I sit next to each other at a symphony concert, watching Eva and Jim together on stage once again. I blink my eyes; it's almost as if no time has passed, yet I'm sitting next to Keith, and we are no longer children. I can see it in his eyes—Keith is looking at me in a new way. When his fingers brush mine and he gently clasps my hand, I am certain that things have changed. My heart is pounding hard by the end of the concert.

He asks Gram if we can take a walk around the campus while the adults go back to the house, and she agrees. The warm air caresses our faces as we stroll along, holding hands. I can hardly breathe, but I try to act calm, like Sandra Dee in the movies. This romantic moment with Keith seems unreal, yet I can feel the warmth of his fingers, hear his voice murmuring close to my ear.

I'm burning with confusion and unspoken questions as we walk toward a fountain in the center of campus. He talks about the moon and stars, physics and complex mathematics. I listen with only part of my mind; most of my attention is focused on how close he is to me, the heat of his body, the scent of his skin. We sit by the fountain, water splashing our hands. Keith is so close I can see the curve of his lips, his teeth. When he slips his arm around my shoulder, I fear my heart will burst. "See that star up there," he says softly, pointing. "Want to make a wish?"

I laugh and close my eyes. Sitting beside him, I feel so safe and happy. "Okay, I wish."

After a moment or two, Keith asks me, "What did you wish?"

I look directly into his face. "If I tell you, it won't come true."

His eyes grow large and serious. It's as if he's seeing me for the first time. "You're not Little Linda any longer," he says in a husky whisper.

I smile, wishing I could think of something clever to say, but instead I look back up at the star. If only, I think. If only he would love me, then everything would be all right. But it's not possible. Or is it? He is here, so close, only a few inches away. I can feel his warm breath on my face.

Suddenly childhood seems very far behind us. The future tastes sweet in my mouth as Keith leans close, brushing his lips against my cheek, my lips. Then his arms are around me and my thoughts fall silent. There is only the murmur of the water, the soft breeze, and Keith kissing me. I'm soaring as high as our star, my deepest wish coming true.

Wheat Fields on a June Evening

GRIT COATS MY fingers when I pry open the Venetian blinds of the living room window. Keith's two-tone green Chevrolet pulls into the driveway. I try to appear calm despite my pulse. I know I will be with Keith tonight in a way Gram would never approve. It is only three weeks after our first kiss, and I can't wait to see him again, to feel his arms around me.

"Don't be so easy. Get away from the window." Gram frowns.

Keith leaps from the car and quicksteps to the porch, slicking back his pomaded hair. I want to grab my purse and cello and rush off with him, but Gram is eager to use her old charms on a man, any man, even if he's her granddaughter's beau. Keith raps on the door.

"When is rehearsal over?" Gram blows a stream of smoke, shaking her head to direct me not to open the door yet. This means, "How soon will you be home, back in my clutches?"

I lie, telling her that we're going for ice-cream with the other kids, but Keith and I will park and explore the new landscape of kissing. We both know this with no words. I add for good measure, "We're rehearsing a new symphony. It might be later than usual tonight."

"Which one?" Gram asks. I throw a little truth in with the lies, stirring it all up in an acceptable brew. "Beethoven's Sixth."

Keith knocks again. I put my hand on the knob. He's so close, on the other side of the door, but I can't open it yet, not until Gram has had her fill of questions.

"Have you already translated your Virgil and written that paper on Charles Dickens?" She must enjoy torturing me like this, making me wait to let Keith in.

I say yes, knowing that in Latin class I can finish the translation as I go. Charles Dickens is easy. I can write the essay in study hall and still get an A.

Finally, she nods for me to open the door. Keith gives a quick bow of his head as he smiles at my grandmother, casting his eyes down lest they betray his feelings for me. We know it must be a secret for now. His mother sends her greetings, he tells her rather formally. Gram's face lights up with pleasure at being treated like a lady. I can see that he's nervous and eager to be gone. His kisses, by contrast, will be calm and slow.

"So you're going for ice cream afterward?" Gram asks, surprising me with her willingness to let me go.

Keith shoots a glance toward me, aware that he must deliver the correct answer. "With your permission."

Gram smiles, relaxing into his polite ways. "Don't be too late. Linda has lots of homework. She has to stay on the honor roll."

"Oh, yes, yes indeed, very important. I'd never do anything to . . ."

"Go on now. Play some Beethoven for me." Gram smiles and waves us away. Keith picks up my cello, careful not to touch me in front of her, and at last we go together into the night. He opens the door, stands back to guide me into his car. I am caught up in the love I feel, the scent of his car, the way the light glistens on his slicked back hair. His eyes so dark as he glances at me.

"Well, she seems to be in good spirits." His voice trembles as he shifts into first gear. I have mentioned to him that Gram has her bad moods, and that she mustn't get angry with us or else. He knows that she won't make it easy on any boy who wants to get close to me. Gram does not want me to have a boyfriend because she wants me all to herself, which makes me want to get away all the more. The few times she has allowed me to go out with boys, she knew I didn't like them all that much. She never gave her permission If It was a boy I liked. Because Keith is our old friend, it should be okay. Still, I don't quite trust Gram not to mess it up.

I haven't told Keith about the yardstick or the other awful things that go on in the house on Park Street. When he asked once about the blue welts on my hands, I told him I slammed a door on them. Another time I explained my bruises by saying I tripped and fell. I know the social rules—you never tattle on your family or air your dirty laundry. Everything is always fine; everyone is always doing great. You keep the secrets behind closed doors.

This is the first time since returning from the Brauninger's three weeks ago that Keith and I have been alone. I worry that he won't feel the same about me. Maybe he has forgotten how beautiful we are together; maybe I am too much trouble for him. I try to read the look in his eyes, but it's too dark in the car to quite see his eyes. I sit awkwardly against my side of the car. What does kissing mean to him? I don't want him to think I'm bad or loose because I enjoy it. Despite the Baptist in me, if it is wrong to kiss Keith, I don't care. It is the best feeling I've ever had—like flying.

At a stop sign, he looks over, his eyes full of warm affection. "Missed you," he says, reaching for my hand. I lift off the earth. The smoke-filled house and Gram's darkness is far away now.

When we get to rehearsal, Jodie reacts to us with wiggling eyebrows and sly looks. Dr. Wehner, the conductor of this adult symphony, whom we've all admired since we were young, steps up to the podium; the concert master sounds the A for us to tune up.

Beethoven sweeps me up in the swell and rise of sound, each instrument a voice in the conversation of intricate melodies and colorful chords. I see the green forests of Germany, castles, and majestic landscapes. The images and sounds soothe the hurt places inside me—fear of Gram and the future, the shakiness I feel that no one knows about. Beethoven is large enough to contain everything and transform it into hope.

Jodie looks at me knowingly, as only a best friend can. She understands that Keith is a wonderful oasis in the desert of my life with Gram, but even Jodie doesn't know the truth about what goes on. It's up to me to hold myself together until I'm old enough to escape. My survival is up to me and no one else, but it helps to have Jodie, Keith, and music to relieve my high-wire anxiety.

After rehearsal, Keith drives to a dirt road at the edge of town. He pulls over on the shoulder and turns off the motor. I can hardly breathe, anxious to be close with him again. The wheat fields are plowed under, the tops of the furrows catching flakes of moonlight. In spring these fields will be golden undulating waves. Now, in September, you can still feel some heat in the breeze, yet a hint of winter too.

He gestures toward the land—"Beautiful, isn't it?"—then gathers me close to him. His beard scrapes my face. Here is the learning I've longed for about the male species, through Keith's body, his scent, and how his mind works.

"Yes," I whisper, gazing out on the landscape I know so well.

"I don't want you to be late and get in trouble," Keith says with a tremble in his voice.

"It's not too late yet," I say softly.

What he means is, "I don't know if I should kiss you right now, but I want to." What I mean is, "It's all right, you can go ahead."

His kisses are so smooth and soft, like satin. The moonlight etches a silver outline along his cheek. I wonder what he's feeling. The car is thick with unspoken words. Then he says, "I think I love you." He pauses, looks away, then back into my eyes, and corrects himself. "I do love you."

Keith lifts my chin, a question in his eyes. Do I love him too? I'm afraid to declare myself. Love is dangerous. What might these words bring upon me, upon us? I have practiced words of love for Keith since I was eleven years old, not ever believing that my dreams would come true. We lean toward each other, our lips barely touching before we meld into each other. My mind fills with colors: purple, iridescent yellow, and red—the colors I see when I play music. The colors interweave with a feeling in my body of complete happiness and peace. I didn't know that such joy was possible. When Keith and I are together, I get to taste the life I want to be living, practicing mutual love, respect, and thoughtfulness.

<hr/>

Our state of grace lasts three weeks. One Sunday afternoon while Gram and I are talking and she's in a good mood, I blurt out that Keith has kissed me. Sometimes, when she is fun, when she is the Gram I knew when I was very young, I imagine that we can be friends like other mothers and daughters. But the look in her eyes after I tell her about the kiss, tells me that I've made a grave mistake, that I've spoiled the best thing in my life. Finally I am being loved, for myself, being appreciated and cherished in a way completely new to me. I want to curse myself for trusting her.

"What do you mean— how dare that boy take advantage of me like that!"

"That's ridiculous! He didn't do anything to you, he lov . . . likes me. He's not like those other . . ."

"He's a man, and men are all alike!" Gram shouts, her face dark with rage.

"I bet his mother would like to know what he's up to." She moves toward the phone. "You are going to college, I have plans for your life. Why are you messing about with some boy? How dare you disgrace me like this!"

"Keith's an old friend of our family. You have always liked him. This has nothing to do with you!"

"Of course it has. You are my granddaughter. You live in my house."

I block the phone with my body, but she pushes me away and picks up the receiver. I stare at her contorted face, fighting back tears and the urge to tear her to pieces.

She screams, "You slut, what do you know about love? You're like your mother. I won't let you ruin your life like she did."

Slut. There she goes, using that terrible word again. Kissing and being in love are that bad?

"I knew I couldn't trust you." Before I can duck, her ring stings my cheek. I back up and grit my teeth. I don't want to give her the satisfaction of my tears. The receiver is back on the hook, maybe I can stop her. I begin talking my way out.

"What do you mean about my Mother, what did she do?"

"She ran off and got married to some wet-behind-the-ears kid. I forced them to promise they'd never see each other again, and the marriage was annulled."

I'm shocked by this bit of news, but mostly concerned with my own survival right now. "But we aren't getting married," I yell. "We just love each other."

I can't let her ruin this the way she ruined things with my father. I make a promise to myself never to trust her again with anything that is important to me.

"Love." She spits the word. "A goddamned lot you know about love. You don't know what men can do to you." She plops angrily on the couch and lights a cigarette. She's determined to snatch away the little time Keith and I will ever have together. After this school year, he'll go away to graduate school and I'm going to college, which is part of my own plan to make my life better, not just Gram's.

"Men are all alike, I tell you. I'll not have you getting distracted from practicing and getting ready for college."

"Most girls go to college and kiss boys, too."

She leaps up from the couch and flails at me again, but misses. I hit at her, missing, too. More enraged than ever, she rushes by me to the phone and begins to dial.

<hr />

The next school day, Keith waits for me in his green Chevrolet. He kisses me and holds me, telling me that we will not let them break us up. Over the next few weeks, I develop the investigative skills of Nancy Drew. I call him at a pay phone and wait to see who answers. If it's his mother, I hang up. When Keith answers, we arrange a clandestine meeting. I drive around the block and wait for him to come running down the street. We send each other notes through his brother and develop a code: 451—the ignition point of fire—means "I love you."

Even during the winter, we brave a few moments together in the icy car. Ecstasy, the touch of his fingers on my face, the kindness in his dark eyes. Our stolen moments see me through Gram's ranting every night.

I worry that her foul moods are contagious. I worry that I will become like her. Each night before I go to sleep, I cry silently into my pillow, telling myself that everyone cries at night. This gives me a strange kind of comfort.

⌖

Gram screams at Mother on the telephone, refusing to give her money and blaming her for not being thrifty or for wasting her life on men or for being selfish. There is no hint of caring in her tirade, but after she puts down the receiver, she buries her head in her arms and cries, "Oh, my brown-eyed baby."

After a few days of raving, crying, and drinking endless cups of coffee, Gram shuffles to the telephone and wires money to Mother. Afterwards she paces back and forth muttering, berating herself, Mother, Daddy, and finally me, for the way things are.

Aunt Helen has information about Gram's secret past. Each week she picks me up to do the laundry at the laundromat. "Your grandmother sends your poor nitwit mother guilt money because she left her when she was a baby. You know that, don't you?" Aunt Helen folds the towels into thirds.

"She gets so mad at Mother on the phone, she screams and cries for hours."

"Well, honey, it goes a long way back. Besides, there's a lot you don't know about your gram, God love her."

I wait for Aunt Helen to go on while we each hold an end of a sheet to fold. "She used to come down to San Antone in the winter. That's where we met the Duchess, bless her heart. She was married to Bert, her second husband, and we heard that he was about to divorce her just before he died. She'd met a married man down there, and once she tried to kill herself over him. Silly girl. I told her he'd never leave his wife to marry her, but she got her hopes up. It was around that time you were born. She threw down the telegram and said, 'The little brat is born.' I declare, what a way to act about a little baby girl. And I told her so, too."

"Why didn't she want me?" I keep a brave face, but my chest squeezes in pain.

"She didn't want to be a grandmother, she didn't want to be old, just like your dad-blasted mother. They should be happy a little girl came into the world. Of course your gram did want you after all, but . . ."

Her voice trails off as we watch a freight train rumble by on the tracks. "And your mother, they're two peas in a pod, too much alike. They always fought over money. After that they started arguing over your father, and now it's about you. I think the Duchess is payin' for leavin' that little girl when she was young. This is what's happened because of it. You can't never get away with things if they're wrong. You have to pay for them someday."

⸎

Gram allows me to go on some field trips to the university—journalism trips, orchestra events. But even after she's agreed that I can go, she threatens me with juvenile hall or with dying before I get back. I think maybe I should stay to keep her alive, but deep down I see through her tricks. She wants to possess my soul.

One afternoon in late April, Gram greets me wearing one of her good dresses, her hair combed and a smile on her face. She's cleaned up the house and is wearing lipstick. I wonder what the heck is going on now. She orders me to sit down, and my stomach clenches. What kind of trouble am I in now?

"I've been thinking. It's almost the end of the school year, and there are those dances you wanted to go to. Keith's mother and I decided to let you two go, provided you come home when we tell you."

I stare at her. What's the trick? "Why did you change your mind?"

"Well, it's spring, and summer will be here soon and . . ." Her voice trails off as she lights a cigarette.

What she means is: "Keith is leaving for the summer and you are going to college, so you can't get in too much trouble. Besides, we mothers and the whole town are keeping an eye on you, so enjoy it while it lasts. You've got five weeks."

⸎

The warm spring afternoon smells of honeysuckles and roses. Fathers up and down the block have begun to mow their lawns on Saturdays, and Uncle Maj's roses blossom. Keith is my date for the senior prom—a dream come true. I wear a strapless dress with scalloped lace over powder blue satin. I inspect my face in the mirror, trying not to think about endings. Keith is slipping away, and Enid will soon be just a place to visit. My childhood is coming to an end. Jodie will be leaving soon, a fact we try not to talk about too much.

"You look very beautiful tonight," Keith tells me when he comes to pick me up. As he drives us to the dance, pink and orange clouds streak the sky, creating a beautiful sunset. I love the smell of his car and watching his hands as he shifts gears. His black hair is swept back; he wears his best black pants and a white jacket. We hold hands as "Where Have All the Flowers Gone" plays on the radio. A warm breeze blows against my bare shoulders. The moment is splendid, but my happiness is bittersweet.

The prom is at the country club, a place where neither of us is usually welcome since our parents aren't members. A full moon hangs in the sky, painting the trees and shrubs, the pathways and tables, with silver. The dance floor glimmers with mirrored lights. Couples cling to each other as they glide across the dance floor, everyone dressed up like adults in fine evening dresses and tuxes. Keith and I dance to the tune of "Moon River," close and warm, in ecstasy after the terrible, lonely winter when we had to sneak, or didn't see each other at all. We do not talk about how brief this period of happiness will be. We are content to dance and later to kiss for hours in his car, where we watch the moon make an arc in the plains sky and I make silent wishes on stars.

⟡

Finally, it is graduation night. Jodie and I grab each others' hands as we wait for the procession music. The wind blows her dark hair back from her face, and the setting sun brings out the burnished brown of her eyes. I get a lump in my throat—how can I go on without her? She cracks a joke, her light-heartedness making me laugh instead of cry. This is her particular talent when it comes to me and my tendency toward grief.

Jodie waves brightly at her mother. I feel keenly aware that my mother, Daddy, and Gram are all absent as I walk down the aisle. My representatives are Aunt Edith and Uncle Willard, Aunt Helen and Uncle Maj—the people who have always been there for me. I glance at Jodie, wondering what will become of us. Will we ever see each other again after this ceremony? I know that Gram will barely let me venture out of the house now, keeping control of the car keys and my time as much as she can. After we receive our diplomas, I think of the years ahead with an ache in my heart, uncertain of everything.

⟡

In the middle of June, Keith is ready to leave Enid for a summer internship, which means I won't see him again before I go to college. Our time together is over. I think of all the time we spent together since we were young children, and feel immensely grateful that he is my first love. I want to think that we'll go on, get married and all the rest, but I know it won't ever happen.

He drives us to the wheat fields at dusk to say good-bye, but we don't speak words of farewell. He remains cheerful and affectionate as he tells me matter-of-factly about his plans for the summer and the future and asks about my plans. These are the last moments of our saga, the final chapter of our lives together in Enid.

The sweet air is laced with the aroma of ripe grain and a faint smell of rain at the edge of the breeze. I look around at the landscape I love, the wheat stretching to the far horizon, an ocean of rippling, burnished gold. Keith and I stand together holding hands, awestruck by the beauty of the undulating stalks that rustle in their fullness. We wander into the middle of the field, entering the beauty. The sun has set and tendrils of pink are sketched on the sky. The old, familiar plains wind sweeps across the field, whispering its secrets. Gusts wrap my hair around my face and press my skirt against my body.

Keith and I cling to each other as the edge of the moon peeps over the eastern horizon. This moment sings of the past, the future, all that we are and ever will be. For a few minutes we are caught in a fold of time, suspended between worlds, embracing as the wind blows around us. It weaves us into this suspended moment, always in the landscape we love, always in love.

When we say good-bye that evening it is with gentleness, and for me at least, a terrible ache. Someone who has truly loved me is leaving. Keith and I will be close now only in my memory.

Who Am I?

DURING THE FIRST few weeks at college, "choose" becomes the most important word in my life. For the first time, I am able to choose what I wear, what I eat, and what I do with my time. Sometimes this means practicing less than I should, as I spend hours sitting on the beautiful campus, daydreaming or watching the bees and butterflies. I revel in the luxury of time to myself without Gram constantly asking me what I'm doing. I miss Keith, but understand that our separation and going in different directions was inevitable. Still, I feel sad and wonder if anyone else will ever love me.

I enroll in the required music classes, my mind stretched by the realization of how much I don't know. I arrive at my 8:00 a.m. class on music history half asleep, but Monteverdi, Palestrina, and Gregorian chants take me to new dimensions as we traverse time and space.

In this new grown-up world, stage fright—my childhood nemesis—returns with ferocious intensity. I tremble during piano and cello exams, stern-faced professors staring at me. We are to perfect scales and arpeggios and a performance piece, and every mistake counts. One day my fears will chase me out of music altogether. For now—as I did when I was more frightened of Gram than performing—I suffer through the night sweats, terror, and dread. But music soon takes a back seat to other college attractions.

At the first school dance, I meet Brad, a pre-med major from Tulsa. His brown eyes leap with good humor and his deep voice murmurs of possibilities—as do his kisses. Good girls are not supposed to kiss on the first date, but these boys are not the polite boys I knew at home. They are assertive and aggressive. If you don't respond, you're out. I like Brad, his offbeat sense of humor, the strength of his arms around me. He is nice, but very sexual. I'm nervous about what will come next but feel happy to be chosen by him.

After a few weeks we are going steady, with me proudly wearing his ring. In my dorm room I finger the little blue stone, amazed that a boy actually wants to date only me. Sharing a dorm populated by fifty girls teaches me how life is lived outside of Gram's prison. Over pizza and cokes, my dorm-mates talk about their lives at home—being cheerleaders, class secretaries, or homecoming queens. They know the subtleties of boys and dating, the facts of sexuality, and the ins and outs of the social scene, all of which leave me astounded. More than ever, I feel like an ignorant, small-town girl. I see how small my social world has been and realize that Gram hates people in general, not just my father, and that none of it is normal at all.

During the first few weeks of the fall semester, I read D. H. Lawrence's *Lady Chatterly's Lover* aloud to Brad as we sprawl on a blanket, allowing him to touch my breasts and French kiss. At dorm pizza parties, I discover that other girls like to be touched and are willing to talk about sex and feelings. I discover that intimacy with boys is not disgusting, as Gram would have me believe. The Baptist voice is in my head though, so it's hard to completely relax and enjoy my adventures with Brad. That voice warns me against the delight I feel and makes me wary of the strange new feelings surging within me.

On a Saturday night in late September, Brad and I stand in front of the Dairy Queen two blocks from the famous OU football stadium. Tonight he wants me to try alcohol. The Baptist voice says he is evil, tempting me on a path to perdition. "Drink will send you down the corridors to hell. Don't let him tempt you. Walk away and never talk to him again."

Brad says, "Come on, it won't hurt you. You'll see." His voice is soothing and his brown eyes beckon.

He orders two cokes from the blonde girl at the counter. I wonder if she can tell that I am about to grievously sin. He pours rum from a flask into the cups. Time slows down and the voice in my head gets louder: "You aren't lost yet. Walk away, don't let sin into your soul."

Trembling, I bring the cup to my lips, waiting for the awful punishment that will thunder down from on high. The concoction tastes good. Cars whiz by. The fall breeze brushes my face. A pleasant warmth flows through me and relaxes my muscles. I stop in the middle of the sidewalk, wide eyed, still waiting for some punishment but laughing, too. Brad smiles. "See, I told you nothing would happen."

He leads me to the lake where other couples lie entwined on the grass. We watch the stars shift across the sky and a sliver of moon grow orange as it slips under the horizon. Our explorations continue. He shows me his "private parts" and has me touch him. Again, I wait for the fires of hell to punish me for this brash encounter with flesh, but it doesn't happen. The Baptists are wrong. Gram is wrong. Men are appealing creatures, dangerous but thrilling. Of course I would never "go all the way," and I don't let him touch me except through my clothes, but it's exciting to explore these new pleasures, and to discover that nothing terrible descends from the heavens. I am suddenly very confused about God and his rules.

〜⁓⁂⁓〜

Brown leaves hang from branches by a single thread, waiting for the gusts of winter to carry them away. My folkdance class is gathered around the radio, listening to a special news broadcast. The governor of Texas and President Kennedy have been shot. Everyone huddles in shock as terrible words tumble from the radio—rifle shots, blood, book depository, hospital. After a few minutes, a stunned Walter Cronkite announces the death of the president. A horrified silence envelopes us, punctured by sobs. We stare at each other vacantly, trying to make sense of it all. We don't understand this kind of violence. It is not part of our world, yet.

As if in response to the horrible news, the November wind now comes whirling around the building, stripping the trees. Everyone is running. Frantic for details of the event, we search for a TV. In the dorms, girls line up in rows to watch the swearing in of Lyndon B. Johnson. Jackie stands by with bleary eyes, blood on her skirt. The casket is loaded onto Air Force One.

Regular life is suspended for days. We gather in little knots, talking, wishing that recent events could be erased. Funereal music plays all day on the radio. Starved for information, we watch the constant coverage on television. For days, the dorm living room is full of girls munching chips, attempting to have a normal day while watching live coverage in Dallas. We watch Lee Harvey Oswald being led down a corridor. Suddenly there's scrambling, a big Texas hat, a loud noise. Oswald crumples. The bad guy is dead, too. The news is full of photos of Lee Harvey Oswald, press conferences, and grim-faced men in dark suits.

We line up again in the dorm living room to watch the J.F.K. funeral footage: the horse with the backward-facing boot, the stately walk down the wide streets of Washington. A long, black veil conceals Jackie's face. When John-John salutes, there is sobbing in the room.

Eventually, life returns to something like normal. During frosty winter evenings, Brad and I stay out late, kissing as the icy wind rushes through our coat sleeves, kissing as if it would make us immortal. We are, or he is, tempted to go beyond kissing, but I always bring us back from the brink. It is not only the Baptist voice that I fear. I am mortally afraid, afraid to cross a threshold I hold sacred. If you are not a virgin when you marry, you are a disgrace to your husband, no better than a whore. Some part of me still believes this.

One night Brad goes too far, pushing past the invisible, shaky fence I have set up. Because he wants more, much more, than I can give, we break up. My few months of physical transgressions with Brad, and my keen enjoyment of them, ultimately have convinced me that I am a sinner after all. The crazy jumble of recent events and emotions—my confusion, my guilt, my fear, and the death of the president—send me back to church.

This time, though, I am not alone. I am embraced in the fold of a family whose mother gathers me under her wing, the way I have always thought mothers should.

Alma

ALMA IS MY boss at the music library, where I work ten hours a
week. Every day, she sweeps in wearing fancy brocade coats and
elegant linen suits, looking nothing like the other plain-Jane librar-
ians. Who could know that one night when she invites me home for
dinner, we will begin a friendship that will last for life.

She lives in bare-bones student housing with her husband, a graduate student in philosophy, and their three children. The older two, a
boy of six and a girl of seven, are wispy, blonde, affectionate children
who share their school assignments, books, and drawings with me. The
youngest, just a year old, nurses before and after dinner. I am somewhat
shocked to see a mother openly nursing a child, embarrassed to see her
bare breast.

Next to Blanche, Alma is the most efficient person I have ever
known. She holds the baby while she fixes quesadillas, food that I've
never heard of before, all the while chatting about world events, politics, and philosophy with her husband and some of his friends. She
quiets the children, supervises their homework, puts them to bed, then
returns to clean up the dishes, seamlessly handling these mundane activities as she inquires about my life, my family, and how I am doing.
I notice that she listens not just to what I say but also to what I don't
say. She responds to me on a more sensitive level than I'm accustomed
to. Alma invites me to more dinners, then to brunches and breakfasts,
where I find myself caught up in a sophisticated world of politics, philosophy, religion, and new friends.

I discover that church, religion, and God need not be frightening,
that maybe my transgressions don't mean I'm doomed to a scary hell. I
attend Episcopal services and learn about the origins of this quite different church, with its colors and symbols, incense and holy days. I like
the fact that I can kneel to send my prayers to God or Jesus. I enjoy
being still with my thoughts and feelings rather than being talked at. I
enjoy the candles and the deep sense of connectedness and intelligence
in the prayers.

At church and at Alma's brunches, I meet several interesting young
men. I begin to date like a normal person, without restrictions, and
learn once more that Gram's dire predictions about men are not true.
When Alma becomes pregnant again, carrying her large belly proudly
in front of her, I see that a woman can manage this extraordinary event

without struggle and drama. My Baptist skin begins to loosen and slip off. Alma and her family become my family.

I still have to go home to Gram during the holidays. I steel myself to face her depressing form hunched on the couch. Gram's life hasn't changed—it has stayed bleak and black while mine has been transformed into something wonderful. Through my new experiences, and especially my involvement in Alma's life, I see Gram in a new light. I understand now that she has turned her back on real living, choosing to exist in darkness, living a half-life. She goes out of the house only a few times a year, the rest of the time wearing her nightgown all day at home.

I am pleased that I have learned to enjoy life, the simple pleasures of good food and intellectual conversation. These ordinary things are like miracles to me. The candles burning at church and at Alma's promise life and hope, and I yearn for all the light I can find. At Gram's I feel tired, exhausted, and angry at the darkness I was forced to live in for so many years. When I visit Gram, the shackles snap onto my wrists as she wields the same old guilt and shame with alarming skill.

"So, have you forgotten your old grandmother? I raised you and gave you everything you ever had, and all you can do is send me one card. Why don't you write more often? How can you come here and see how I am and just leave me like this? You don't care what happens to me. You are selfish just like everyone else. I could die like this. You would come home and take care of me if you were really a Christian."

I have told Gram about my conversion to the Episcopal Church, hoping for her approval. She'd always complained about the Baptists, telling me that the Catholics had a closer ear to God, yet she never committed to a spiritual life herself and never attends church. Gram hunkers down, spewing smoke and hurtful words. It's clear to me now that she will always criticize whatever I do, and this knowledge is a kind of shield.

I've learned more about how life is lived, and can be lived, in the last three months than I did in all my years in Enid. There is so much more to the world than Gram's little hole. Her dark side had hoped to control me forever, to keep me captive in her negative world, but I have broken free. Ironically, Gram's other side, the part that wanted me to experience music and art, that insisted I study and go to college, helped foil her plans.

I begin to question everything Gram taught me. If she is so cut off from life, so different from normal human beings, then everything I learned through her bears re-examination.

Gradually, almost against my will, I begin to open my mind to my father.

I Have Been Waiting and Hoping

Early on an autumn evening in my sophomore year at the university, I stand at the window of the practice room watching the rain pour down in sheets. My friend Carlos comes in. His black hair and eyes show his Spanish heritage. He's the first chair of the bass section, and he often teases me about being the smallest cellist in the ranks. He's inquired about my family, at first expecting the usual story—mother, father, brothers or sisters. He knows now about my divorced parents and my grandmother, and from time to time seems curious or perhaps confused about it all. Despite the fact that he's an ex-Catholic, Carlos believes in the power of spiritual teachings and is always putting things in a philosophical context.

He leans against the wall. "Do your parents ever come for the holidays?"

I look away, the familiar ache starting in my stomach.

"I've never seen my parents for holidays—well, once I spent Christmas with my mother. As for my father—I've given up on him."

"Oh?" Carlos moves closer to me, his dark eyes lighting up with interest. "How can you give up on your own father? Where did you get that idea?"

"It's been like that for a long time." I wave my hand dismissively.

Carlos doesn't let things go by. "What made you decide you can just write him out of your life? How old is he?"

"I suppose he's about sixty."

"What if he gets sick or dies without you speaking to him? How would you feel then?"

Suddenly, I can't quite hear Carlos; his voice fades as my mind plays images of Daddy's kissing lessons and Gram's angry face as she fumes about him. I can't remember the last time I wrote him—months ago. I start to feel shivery inside.

Carlos sees that the subject is hard for me and takes his leave. On his way out he says, "You need to rethink your relationship with your father. A father needs to be forgiven. No matter what has happened, he is still your father." The look on his face is sad, not judgmental.

I pick up my bow and play "Kol Nidre"—a Jewish prayer for the dead, a beautiful melody that burns into my heart. I've buried my secret feelings and longings about Daddy deep so that Gram couldn't see them. Any connection I might express, any hint that I was ready to forgive and forget, would have made her even more determined to destroy our bond.

This heartbreaking melody of longing and loss penetrates the dark, tar-filled place inside me. When I have finished playing it, I wrap my arms around my cello and weep.

❦

As autumn passes, I think about the daddy I dreamed of for so long. I always wanted to know him, to have a father like other girls, but for as long as I can remember, Gram has made sure I wouldn't have any chance to love him. Eventually she won her campaign of hate. I have become exactly like her, speaking ill of him, refusing any contact for months at a time.

The next week, over coffee, I confide in Carlos about the fights between Gram and Daddy, keeping the kissing part to myself.

"You think he should come to you?" Carlos asks, his voice neutral.

"He's the father," I say self-righteously.

"Perhaps if I were him, maybe I would. But he is different. Maybe he's waiting for you to reach out to him."

"But . . ." I hesitate, looking down, avoiding his eyes. I can't tell him I'm afraid that Daddy will leer at me or that he might put me on his lap to kiss me.

Carlos must glimpse my deeper feelings in my face. "So, there's more to this story, isn't there? But he's still your father. What if you talked to him in person? Maybe you'd see that things have changed. You're not a child now. You can make it turn out different."

I leave the café wondering how Carlos came by so much wisdom at such a young age. The fall wind turns sharp against my skin. I look up at bare trees etched against the light of the rising moon and think: Maybe, just maybe, he is right.

❦

In mid-October, I finally write to Daddy, pouring out my regrets, apologizing for not telling him before that I managed to get away from Gram's negativity and am attending OU. I watch the envelope slide down the mail slot with a special prayer in my heart, and hope for the best. Every day that passes with no answer tells me that it was a mistake, that he doesn't care about me. Finally, a thick envelope arrives bearing his loopy, cursive writing. I tear it open and read hungrily.

"I have been waiting and hoping such a long time," he says. "Your letter was the answer to my prayers. I knew that you would grow up and realize your grandmother was wrong. I always knew you didn't write those letters, that she made you do it. Of course I love you and want more than anything for us to be father and daughter. I am sorry for all the years that we have lost, but we can make up for it from now on. Let me know if you want me to visit and when, and I'll come right down on the train."

My heart surges with joy. I fold and unfold, read and reread the letter. My secret cache of hope flares into full flame. I have a father after all. The bad and confusing memories are not gone, but they hover beside happier images of my father—our roller skating together, his exuberant hugs at the train, his great excitement about life.

I imagine a perfect father and daughter duo—he'll come to my concerts and we'll spend holidays together. He'll tell me all about his life. We have many years ahead of us to make up for lost time. He is sixty; he could live to be eighty at least. I am determined to do whatever it takes to have my father and even my mother belong to me at last. I vow to reclaim them, leaving my bitter grandmother smoldering in her self-made hell.

I wait in Norman by the station, gazing at the tracks that meet at the horizon, at that infinite point where the future resides. I face north, toward Chicago, the magic city where we all came from. The trains of my childhood came hurtling from that city in the clouds. The old stomach ache is there again since I opened up to my secret longings.

The train men drive carts of luggage and people buzz around like bees, waiting for the silvery horizon to produce the magic light of the train and the whistle that announces other times and places. The train sound is deep in my blood, ancient as cell knowledge.

All at once I hear it, and a rush of wind sweeps my hair. Tears bubble up from buried wells. The train ritual has me in its grip now, with its language of arrival and departure, the language of my life. I am ten years old again, and Daddy is coming. My old childhood joy surges, along with my tears.

I've seen my father only twice in the past seven years. As I watch people clambering down from the train, my stomach in knots, I wonder if he will even recognize me. Finally my heart leaps, as if his blood is calling to mine, and then I see him. He runs toward me, his coat flapping, his shoes slapping the concrete, crowing my name. He sweeps me up in his arms and around we go in our whirling dance of old. His beard feels the same on my cheek, his Old Spice is as comforting as it has always been. After a moment, he stands back and looks at me. "My girl, my girl," he murmurs, and clutches me to him. A missing part of me slips back into place.

We take a cab to his hotel. I perch on the edge of the bed talking about my life, telling him all the wonderful things I am learning, hoping he won't touch me except for the proper kind of fatherly hug. Joy and fear play tug-a-war battle inside me.

What a miracle it is to be with my father in the flesh, watching him hang up his clothes, doing ordinary tasks that normal families share. How little I know him, this stranger whose blood I carry in my veins. He looks older, with a slight double chin, yet trim for a man his age. His head is shiny and bald, with a fringe of dark hair. His eyes sparkle with joy as he looks at me.

"I play golf every weekend," he tells me. "I love going out there on the green. Maybe that's my way of worshipping. Nothing like the early morning dew on the grass, clouds against the blue sky." Daddy's eyes glow as he talks. He is still so alive, so passionately, thrillingly alive. No wonder I wanted so desperately for him to come see me when I was younger, to give me a strong dose of life as it can and should be lived. I needed his vitality to combat Gram, who I knew was sinking into a kind of soul death and trying to drag me along with her.

Daddy rushes about, his voice running up and down the scale of emotions. He is a passionate man—in some bad ways, but in good ones, too. Maybe I can have less fear and more courage now that I'm a grown-up, be optimistic instead of worried. At dinner, he orders himself a beer and a coke for me. He leans toward me and rushes through the stories of his life, as if trying to fit in all he should have told me through the years. I understand his underlying message: he needs to have me in his life now.

"You could go to school at the University of Illinois. You'd still be an in-state resident, and not so far away from me. I could show you Chicago. It's so terrific, all the wonderful buildings and museums. The city is almost a college education in itself. It's exciting, with new developments and research going on all the time. Growing up on a farm an hour away from Louisville, I thought Louisville was the cat's pajamas. But Chicago—there's really nothing like it." He bangs his fist on the table to emphasize his point, grinning from ear to ear.

"Remember, it's your life. Make your own decisions. Decide what you want and go for it. That's how I got to be an executive at the L & N. I came from nothin', just a freight boy with his first pair of real boots. I decided I wanted to escape the farm, and I did. Not many people do that."

He fleshes out his story. When he was sixteen years old, my father started working in the freight yards of a small town in Kentucky, and later moved to Louisville. His father owned land, but lost everything late in his life. Daddy loved being free of the burdens of farming, and worked his way up the ladder at the L & N Railroad. In his twenties he married for the first time. His brothers and sisters, aunts and uncles—whose names I know, though I don't remember meeting them—all lived nearby. His parents died before I was born. Daddy always believed in hard work and the school of hard knocks, but he thinks college is good, even for a girl, because now education makes a difference. I wonder how much my mother knows of his story. I know that she still cares for him. This whole saga involves all of us.

Daddy's eyes dance with images of the future he wants us to have. "I'll help you. Maybe it's time for you to break away from your grandmother. She had her chance; now it's you and me. We can have a lot of fun!"

It's wonderful to learn that my father wants me in his life. I'm still confused about the kissing, but that man seems so different from this one, who has proper, fatherly feelings for me and wants to help me get on in life.

❧

Too soon it is time for him to go. I watch him pack, the old ache reasserting itself. I memorize him—the stubble darkening into a beard, the rumble in his throat, his quick movements on gazelle legs. I wonder how long he will live. Will we get another twenty years to make up for what we've lost?

At the station, I weep in spite of my resolve. We stand together, faces to the bitter wind, arms linked. The train whistle blows; train men bustle with suitcases. My father turns to me. The look on his face speaks of the power of machines and of the dreams we can make come true.

Memories float like ghosts inside my head as my chest turns to liquid. Daddy's going again. I am losing him.

His sparkling green eyes and big smile are to help me, I know. He doesn't want to leave me looking desolate. "I am proud of you for leaving Enid and being on your own," he says. "You're doing fine, but from now on I'm going to help you." His arms bury me into his thick, manly coat. He turns to board the train, then looks back for a moment. "You know I love you."

Parts of my lost self knit together. The sky is rose and lavender, the colors of hope, as the sun eases itself down past the western horizon.

Endings and Beginnings

It is December in Iowa. The Mississippi River is frozen and the day is gray with spitting snow. Arching above the river is the old bridge joining Iowa to Illinois. The heater in Willard's car blasts hot air onto our feet. He turns up the hill, leaving behind the river and railroad tracks.

"Mama used to talk about crossing that bridge in a horse and carriage," murmurs Edith. Gram has been crying all morning. Blanche is dead. Willard is driving us to the same funeral home where family members have been laid out generation after generation. I look at Gram, her mournful early morning cry still in my ears. "Mama, oh Mama," she wailed. "How will I ever live without you?"

Earlier she sat smoking at Edith's kitchen table, staring at the empty rocking chair by the window. I stared too, expecting Blanche to reappear and take out her embroidery. She would wear her gold-rimmed glasses; she would sew for half an hour, then haul herself out of the chair. She'd find something to do—hang the laundry on the line, peel peaches, or snap beans. She'd hoe the weeds and pick the rhubarb before breakfast. She used to say that if she ever stopped, she'd die. Now, at ninety-two, finally she is still.

The funeral home is crowded with Blanche's seven children and their spouses, her grandchildren and great-grandchildren. Men whose normal garb is plaid flannel shirts and work pants with thick boots look awkward in their shiny suits, starched shirts, and off-center ties. I don't remember ever seeing my great-uncles so dressed up. Everyone lines up to pass by the coffin.

I am afraid to look, afraid of death up close. Gram nudges me, but I hang back and stand in line beside Edith. Eventually, I move forward and look at Blanche: a lifeless, deflated body, all bones and sharp angles, her tiny head with coiffed white hair sinking into the pillow. I remember her singsong voice as she talked to the flour, the fire, the dumplings in her potato soup. I feel bereaved but so grateful as I say good-bye.

Uncle Hal, his thick shoulders lumpy under his Sunday coat, breaks down. I'm relieved to see his tears and the tears of the other men, men who never express emotion, men so even-keeled, so full of jokes that I never imagined them being so tender-hearted.

Gram wipes her eyes. "Why aren't you crying? Don't you care?"

I stare at her, fumbling for words. "I do care, I'll miss her a lot, but she lived a full life. She was ninety-two. Edith told me she was ready to die."

"How dare you talk like that? Shame, shame on you," she hisses. I move away from her, sick of her constant venom. It makes me feel old and heavy myself. I make a vow as I skulk away: I won't let her negativity affect me any more.

A young minister comes to the podium. He talks about everlasting life, reads some scripture. Blanche had a Bible, but I never saw her read it. She was a practical person who appreciated the eruption of life in her garden, the birth of grandchildren and great-grands, but I don't know if she believed in God. In the stories she told about her life, she never needed a supreme being; she always saved herself.

Loving Blanche wasn't always easy. I have chosen to forgive, or forget, her grouchy side, the side of her that complained, cried, sighed, and cheated at gin rummy. I remember, instead, what she taught me. Because of her, I know how to grow potatoes, strawberries, and tomatoes. I know how to make potato soup and egg noodles from scratch. If I had to, I could start a fire and bake a cake in her old cookstove. I have gleaned a lifetime of woman's wisdom from my hours with Blanche.

❖❖❖

Shortly after I return to campus from the funeral, Mother sends me a letter typed on yellow legal paper. I read the letter many times, tears running down my face, surprised by her openness with me. I begin to believe that there could be a new chance for us.

Dear Miss Pudding,

I have been thinking lately about my childhood. Blanche had a farm, and I used to visit. I remember home-baked bread, warm milk from the cows, and a group of ladies quilting in the parlor; having a lot of fun with Gram's half brothers and sisters, home-made ice cream being made in the yard on a Sunday afternoon; thunder and lighting at night, and being scared. Little chicks being hatched, and horses, and oh all sorts of things that are fun to remember.

And when I was little, I lived with my great-grandmother Josephine in town, and Blanche would visit. I used to be so happy when she came, as I think I was very lonely. She always had a silk dress on, but when she was on the farm she wore aprons and sunbonnets, and worked in the garden.

I am surprised to hear that Mother has the same fond memories of the farm and our Iowa relatives as I do.

I would look for my father, who used to come to Muscatine every Saturday night without fail. But sometimes he didn't see me. I used to walk along the street looking for him, and he was usually there somewhere.

Mother went looking for her father? My chest hurts as I imagine my mother as a little girl, with the same feelings that I had. I can picture her as an innocent child, instead of the wild woman I know. How lost she sounds.

My mother used to come from Chicago to see me. This was wonderful, like a dream. She was very beautiful and soft and lovely, and I had a hard time after she left, because I missed her. She didn't come very often. Later, when she married Burt, I came to live with them.

It was nice to have my mother, whom I didn't know very well. I think perhaps I was very difficult. I am not sure, but I think so. Or else my mother wasn't used to being around children. I didn't know a single playmate, and I was so bashful and didn't know what to do, and everyone was so strange. Ugh, I hate to think of it. I was very backward, and didn't know anything, and sometimes I think I still don't.

I am getting older. It is very hard for me to realize I have a grown daughter. I am sorry that I didn't remarry and have you to live with me like my mother did, but it just didn't happen. Now I am worried about my future. I have always been very dependent on others.

I am not at all efficient, and sort of bungle things up. I didn't seem to be able to get things straightened around, so I just live day to day and do the best I can. I hope you have a direction to go toward. I guess your grandmother has trained you far better than I could have done, and I guess you know the things that you should know.

I never did know much about life, always too protected and too un-knowing about everything. I don't know whether people realized this or not, and I don't think I have changed much. I always thought people were different from the way I found them.

Anyway, your Gram is a very smart woman, and I would have just dreamed the time away. I am an idealist and a dreamer, and I would have taught you nothing practical. I sort of go around in a mist or something. I think perhaps you will know how to live and face life. I never could have taught you this, and you will need it. I am sure you will be a success, which I have never been. I know a little bit about everything and not much about anything.

My mother reveals so many things I've never heard before—how much she missed her mother, that she often felt awkward and uncertain. Did she remember her own childhood when she used to visit me? She always seemed decisive and stubborn—certain of what she was doing, not listening to anyone else. I know about this mist she talks about—sometimes life is cast in a thick fog for me, too. Did mother know that she'd never come back when she left me with Gram, or was it an accident, everything that happened to us?

Somebody always did it for me. I think others have even lived my life for me—I just went along for the ride, hither and yon. Very good, but now not so good, because no one is living for me. I am living myself, but don't know what I am living for—something? Somebody? Where am I going and what am I doing? Rather confusing.

Mother seems so lost, my heart aches for her. She thought others lived her life for her? Gram made so many decisions for mother, and in a way ran her life.

I am very sorry that you didn't have a mother and father together in the same house, but I think your father tried very hard under the circumstances—I know he loves you very much, and you are his only child . . . I didn't live with my father, ever, either, but this in no way impaired my love for him, and so must it not with you.

I suppose you have heard a lot of wrangling among adults through your little life, but don't pay any attention to this—people just do this sometimes. The adults' anger wasn't your fault. Everybody just loved you a lot. Too bad people can't be calm, but they haven't this much consideration. I have, but most people haven't. Adults didn't mean to quarrel in front of you; nothing ever was your fault. Everyone loved you and was vying for your attention.

This I can't accept. They fought for their own reasons. In her own mind, those fights have been rescripted. I don't buy her explanation, but I know it's her way of telling me she's sorry.

Anyway, you were conceived and born in the most welcome way. You were very much looked forward to, with a great deal of impatience, both by your father and by me. You were the most wonderful miracle that ever happened. I have never been the same since.

I just couldn't make things work right afterward. I got married for the express purpose of having you. I was married very soon after meeting your father, six weeks to be exact, and I said the first thing I wanted to do was have a baby, and so my wish was granted and you came into being, and it was all very wonderful, and I was very happy. You were born very quickly, nearly too quickly, one cold March morning, about 5:10 to be exact. It all happened so fast that it seemed it didn't happen at all. Truly, it was years before I could believe it.

My mother wanted me! She says I was her miracle! Some long-parched desert inside me soaks up her words, even as I struggle to understand them. I write her a long letter in response, asking her questions and sharing some of my own old feelings. I keep reading her letter, holding it to my heart like a talisman. Maybe our having shared these things will make the future better. Maybe the past can be over now, and we won't have to keep revisiting it.

I look through pictures from her childhood that I've tucked away. There she is at two years old, her hands folded as she sits in front of her grandfather's house in Wapello, her eyes telegraphing sorrow. Where is her mother? In another photograph she holds a baby and perches in a rocking chair, her eyes glittering. My little mother is a sweet-looking child. She was like me: small, lost, and at the mercy of her family. How did that little girl become the kind of woman she is now? I want to know more so I can learn from her mistakes. I must not let it happen to me.

Leaving at Last

I AM IN the Norman train station with several suitcases, wearing a brown suit with a hot pink lining, hose, new pumps, and a hat. Decked out like this, I feel ready for sophisticated Chicago. I've kicked off all traces of the small-town girl.

Sometimes it seems I have spent half my life at train stations, waiting for my dreams to be fulfilled. Again and again, throughout my childhood, I would imagine a thrilling reunion with my beautiful parents, only to be disappointed by the tarnished reality of them.

Now I am a grown woman and understand that Mother and Daddy aren't perfect, no one is. In Chicago, I will get to know them as real people. Most significantly, my time with them won't be marred by my grandmother's influence. I can no longer endure her misery and the guilt she wants to bury me in. For the sake of my spirit's survival, I have put great distance between Gram and myself. Now, at last, there's space in my mind and heart for my parents.

I hold onto my hat as the train roars into the station. A gracious conductor helps me into the car and I find a seat just before the train lurches forward. Soon we are clicking along on the tracks. I gaze out the window, waiting for the special station, Perry, a place of so much childhood longing. When it appears, it's just the same. Clutches of people swarm the train; men climb off and sweep children into their arms; women cry and wipe their eyes. I watch a small girl with long hair who reminds me of myself as she stands back and waves, her face etched in sadness. How I understand that look.

The train pauses for only a moment, then resumes its journey, hurtling me toward my future in an unknown place. I whisper good-bye to my grandmother. I don't wish her ill, despite all the years of abuse. I sincerely want her to be happy, but it will have to be without me. She is part of the past I am eager to leave behind. Still, her "Sugar Pie" echoes in my heart. If only she could let me go with love.

The train passes empty fields that have just been planted with wheat. I will miss the golden sea of grain rippling in summer wind, the songs of whippoorwills on telephone poles, the red earth of this prairie. It is dark when we click-clack into Kansas, leaving Oklahoma and my childhood behind. In the morning I will gaze at the skyscrapers of Chicago, no longer just a city in my dreams. I will spend time with my father in his own home, a first for me, and with my mother in hers. They will take me to wonderful places in Chicago and I'll become a part of their lives. At the same time I'll make my own way at a whole new school where I'll meet new people and make new friends. I can't wait to get to know my parents away from Gram. Through knowing them better, I'll find out where I came from so I can know where I'm going.

Anticipation zips like a current through my brain. I sleep very little as the train rocks me back and forth in its wonderful way. As the night passes, I imagine all the great things that lie ahead: a loving mother and father, a husband and children of my own, music and art and literature, the further ripening of all my gifts.

Some of this will indeed come to pass, but life is never quite as we imagine it.

Don't Call Me Mother

THE SHARP BITE of wind off Lake Michigan initiates me to the city that deserves its nickname—the Windy City. All my life I have yearned to see Chicago, and here I am. I feel triumphant as I stride next to my mother, holding up my head, proud the way Joan of Arc might have felt leading her troops. The battle here is not religious, though it is spiritual: my search for the Holy Grail that is my mother is over. Finally, at the age of twenty, I am in her territory, in the city where I was born and where she's lived all the years we were apart.

Crowds of intense Chicagoans hustle along with serious faces, heels clicking on sidewalks, wind plastering their clothes to their bodies like epoxy. My mother and I brave the wind, hunching over as a sharp gust bursts between buildings. We make our way slowly down the avenues between tall buildings that rise like mountains in this blustering city with its brilliant edges.

I sense my baby self as I walk here, imagining a little girl and her young mother living together in a small apartment on Armitage Street, before the severing of our bond when I was four, the event that broke our future and defined our lives. I can't help but wonder what would have happened if we had stayed here, if mother had not left me with Gram. Perhaps Gram raised me to make up for abandoning my mother so many years before. I shake my head to banish these thoughts. There are too many what ifs. Here I am now, eager to taste and feel all that I have missed.

I love the electricity of the city, the palpable energy coursing along its streets. I love the marble floors in skyscraper office buildings, the bustling cafés. People wear suits and stylish dresses, with an air about them of the big city, brisk and no-nonsense, talking with that nasal Chicago accent. This is nothing like plain-Jane Oklahoma where I grew up. I lift my head, hoping I don't give off the scent of red dirt and buffalo, hoping I won't embarrass myself or my mother.

My stomach trembles from the onslaught of new culture as I try to keep up with mother's quick, brisk steps. The wind blows her dyed auburn hair awry. She clutches it against her head with one hand, an unlit cigarette held between gloved fingers of the other.

She leans toward me, lecturing. "Hold your shoulders up. Don't slouch. A girl should always have the best posture and decorum. You don't want men to think you're dumpy, do you? And when you go into a restaurant, don't smile all the time. Just look ahead and make them take you to the table. All that chit-chatting—it's silly."

"But Mama, that's just being friendly."

"This is a fine sophisticated city, not some dumb cow town. Don't tell everything to everyone. Keep your own counsel. You talk too much."

My irritation grows as I listen to her. She always hates it when I "argue"—which means saying anything back to her.

"I like being friendly. People are nice."

"~~Don't be silly. People are not always nice; you need to learn that.~~" Mother turns to face a brick building and ducks her head down to cup cigarette and match against the wind. She tries twice, frowns, then stands to take a deep drag when the tobacco finally catches. The wind sucks my breath away.

She blows out the smoke, her dark eyes fierce. "Besides, you have to listen to your mother. There's a lot I haven't had a chance to teach you."

"I know, but I have to be myself, too." Fearing I've spoken too boldly and will trigger her rage, I soften my tone. "I mean, I'm just a friendly person."

She slaps me on the arm. "Quit talking back to me. Here's the jewelry store."

Like flotsam tumbling down Michigan Avenue, we are swept by the wind into the vestibule of a small store. Mother grabs my shoulder. "You stay by the door while I talk to the owner. Don't talk to me or join me until I tell you to."

"But Mother . . ."

"Shh . . . not so loud. And don't call me that." She smacks my arm harder, her face tight, angry.

Mother hauls open the door and we enter a quiet, brightly lit jewelry shop, display cases arranged up and down both sides. A middle-aged man stands behind a counter, inspecting something with a magnifying glass.

Mother starts her routine. "Oh, John, so wonderful to see you again." Hips rolling a little, she turns on her high voice of tense attraction. The desire to be flirted with and admired exudes from her like heavy perfume.

I scrunch myself next to the door. Whips of wind driving through the gaps in the frame make me pull my coat close. I shrink into a ball of misery as the minutes pass and Mother ignores me completely. The man glances at me once, then quickly looks away. Why won't Mother introduce me?

Scared of her anger and trying to be a good girl, I follow Mother's instructions to the letter, standing there crumpled like an old leaf blown in by an unwelcome wind. The whole jewelry store becomes surreal like in some noir movie. My legs ache, and Mother's flaunting, flirty cadence scrapes my nerves raw. Twenty minutes into my invisibility, she finally looks over. I open my hands as if to say, "What?" trying to convey polite impatience. It's my usual dilemma—how can I be myself yet keep her from getting angry. Is it even possible?

Mother turns back to the jewelry man, juts her hip out, and says, "See that girl down there?"—I am the only other person in the shop—"She's my daughter."

The man laughs richly, deep in his belly. "That can't be, Josephine. You're much too young to have a daughter that age."

Mother wriggles with pleasure and fixes her seductive eyes on the man. "Oh, really, do you think so?"

Smiling, I move forward a couple of steps to be introduced, eager to claim my status as her daughter. After all, she's beautiful and desirable, unlike me, her ugly-duckling. After all, she is my mother. Mother turns her body away from me, huddling closer to the man, draping herself over the jewelry case, still swiveling her hips. I stand there, obediently, waiting for Mother to pick up the thread of conversation and return her attention to me. Thirty minutes pass, leaving me in a hell of isolation, feeling helpless and confused. Outraged. How dare she ignore me like this? My own mother is ashamed of me? I'm sick of watching her flirt with this greasy, cold man, his velvet voice calculated to make her buy more antique jewelry. I'm disgusted that she's sucked into his fawning admiration.

I retreat back into the frigid pocket by the door, shamed by her snubbing and sick to my stomach over her outrageous flirting. The double fires of shame and anger temporarily warm me, simmering while Mother completes her performance and makes a purchase. Finally she leads me outside.

My shaking voice is gulped down whole by the wind. "Why didn't you introduce me?"

Mother stops to light a cigarette, her body cupped against a brick wall. "Now, don't you be like that. You have to understand—no one knows that I've been married. I'm 'Miss Myers' here. People are so nosy. If they knew I'd been married, they'd gossip horribly about my life; they wouldn't respect me."

· "But I'm Miss Myers. That's my father's name." The shock of her refusal to introduce me and her self-serving defense of herself leave me nearly speechless.

Her face grows stony with anger. "Be reasonable and keep your voice down. You should treat your mother with respect. When we got divorced it was easier to keep his name. I just said I was Miss, and that's all there is to it." Her hands twirl casually in the air as she leads me onward down the hard slabs of sidewalk.

There is a mighty roiling and misery in my stomach as I tumble into the deep, dark pit I know too well. I want my mother to save me, but I know she won't. "You mean, no one in Chicago knows about me?" my small voice whispers from below.

Her voice is edgy with impatience. "I told you, they can't know I have a daughter. They think I'm too young; you heard what John said. No one has any idea that I'm fifty. Besides, I can't have a daughter if I've never been married, now can I? You've got to understand how it is for me. I have to live here, and I don't want things disturbed."

Her illogical logic burns all the way down, but I try to swallow it. For years when my mother came to see me in Oklahoma, I always sensed that she was eager to return to her city life as she boarded those trains in the middle of the Great Plains, but I never dreamed that in Chicago she'd erased me from her life.

Emotional shock waves send pinpricks all over my body. Here I am in Chicago with her, finally, after so many years of longing for my mother. I glance at her. Yes, the physically beautiful woman I yearned for, cried for, needed, imagined, rushed to hug and clung to despite her cool reception, stands beside me, but not the way I wanted her and imagined her all these years. Now that I'm in college three hours away, I could see her almost any time I want. I thought we'd do mother–daughter things together, to make up for those lonely childhood years. Didn't Mommy want it as much as I did?

My dreams are crumbling as Mother rushes me along the gray streets, gum and cigarette wrappers flying at us like bats, people scurrying with frowns on their faces. Suddenly Chicago seems like a city of hard edges. In the café the waitress doesn't care, splashes the coffee. Everyone is quick, curt, cold. My mother doesn't see my disintegration. Tears pour down the inside of my body but don't spill onto my cheeks. The fire of anger still burns in me, but I manage a fake smile.

The January day closes in as I try to comprehend how my mother can deny me, even when we're together. My excitement has been spoiled

Don't Call Me Mother

by Mommy's coldness. There is no way I can know now that her denial will follow me, haunt me through the coming decades, all the way up to her death—and beyond.

She sits across from me, flashing a quick smile. "Cheer up. No one wants to be with someone who has such a sour face. Don't you think my new ring is beautiful?"

She lays her graceful hand across the table. I pause, caught up in my anger, then touch her hand. I'm surprised to find that the mere touch of her skin soothes the place in me that burns. I hold her hand, grateful for this flicker of warmth from her, ashamed of needing it, of accepting her on her own terms. The waitress returns to pour the coffee. This time she glances at both of us, her face flickering with a slight smile. I know she thinks we look alike, mother and daughter sitting oh-so-normally at a table in a café in Chicago, our secrets buried in each of us. My heart beats fast as I look at her, swallowing the hot coffee, swallowing everything.

Becoming a Mother

FOUR YEARS LATER, I've finally entered an eagerly awaited stage of life—I'm pregnant with my first child. I focus on the doctor's shiny bald head framed between my legs as I lie on the examination table. He removes his gloves and tells me to sit up. "You're pregnant—about two months. The baby is growing nicely."

Feelings of excitement and disbelief flood me. I sit up, a tingling like icicles all over my body. I'm ecstatic and Dennis, my husband, will be, too. Me, a mother? I never thought it could happen, figuring that because of my past I was destined to remain outside normal human experience. Yet now I am pregnant—a normal, pregnant woman.

The first time I feel the baby move, my life swerves into a cotton-candy dream. "Can this be real? I'm growing life inside me?" I feel powerful and awestricken all at once. My mother will become a grandmother, my grandmother will become a great-grandmother. I hope they will be thrilled by my news, but I'm not really surprised that their responses are less than enthusiastic. "You're so young. Shouldn't you have waited? Do you have enough money, with Dennis just getting out of grad school?" The subtext: Why are you making me feel so old by having a baby?

I try not to feel too disappointed by their letters. Reluctantly I've adjusted to their cynicism about me and about happiness in general. At least my father is excited and congratulatory. He actually looks forward to being a grandfather! I imagine frequent visits with him in Arizona, where he has retired. Daddy and I will make up for my lost childhood by playing with the baby, going to the zoo, doing all the things we never did together.

The day I first feel the baby move, I'm standing in the living room of our apartment in Portland, wearing a maternity dress that I made myself, a red print with a white cotton collar. My fingers gently search for the little protrusion, a leg or an arm, tiny round bumps rolling across my belly. I grab at one of them to say hello. The baby tucks in to escape my probing, as if to say, "Hey, that's my leg! Be careful up there."

I look in the mirror to check out my voluptuous new figure. Before pregnancy I was flat-chested and knobby and weighed less than one hundred pounds. Now I'm curvy everywhere and getting rounder every day.

Dennis and I have moved to Oregon, where he is an assistant professor. Though we've been married nearly two years, I'm still adjusting to being married and happy, no longer at the mercy of Gram and Mother bossing me around. I look up to Dennis and count on him to be the typical 1950s husband, despite our '60s ideals. I kiss him good-bye when he goes to work each morning. For the first time in my life without work or school to concern myself with, I'm trying to fit myself into the identity of homemaker. It's fun to throw myself into cooking, making fancy desserts that take hours, pouring over gourmet cookbooks, learning from the rulebooks of the '50s how to win your man and keep him. I learn how to cook Italian cuisine from Mama Leone's cookbook, spending hours making ravioli from flour and eggs, filling and crimping. I make sauce from scratch only to see my eight hours of labor disappear down the throats of our guests. We play pinochle late into the night, or attend professorial dinner parties, to which I bring more exotic dishes, holding onto my New Identity. I am Normal, how are you? My crazy childhood is a bad dream. I'm fine, thank you, content as can be in my happy, wifely bubble with Dennis.

We'd known each other for only two months before getting engaged when I was twenty-one. My virginal state was easily dispatched, thanks to the pill, Black Russians, and Bob Dylan. As I lay next to Dennis afterward, I wondered: Why the hell was I taught to fear this? Why the big fuss that Gram and the Baptist Church created about sex?

Dennis and I were buddies, got along well, and genuinely liked each other. Why not get married? Being unmarried at twenty-one made you an old maid. We were wed during the worst snow and ice storm in Illinois history, in January 1967. My mother and father both missed the wedding because of the storm. Gram was too angry to come, still furious that I had left her to move to Illinois. She sent me clothes and a cool, short note. I tried not to care, knowing I couldn't make her happy. Still, it made me sad. As always during my childhood, Aunt Edith and Aunt Grace were there for me. After our wedding at a little Episcopal church in Champaign-Urbana, Illinois, I pinched myself to see if it was all real. I'm finally a Missus, I thought. I'm married now; I belong to someone who's nice to me, who wants me. He'll protect me from the raging insults of Gram and Mother, as a husband is supposed to do.

<hr />

After a pregnancy in which my body amazes me by growing to huge proportions, I'm finally in labor. Bright lights nearly blind me and unbearable pains take away my breath as I writhe on the bed at Kaiser Hospital. The nurse tells me to get a grip, it's gonna get worse. I'm by myself for this, because Dennis insisted on scheduling an interview in Oklahoma on the baby's due date. I'd taken him to the airport only a few hours before my water broke—he waved cheerily, saying that babies never come on their due date. The pain slices through me; screams bounce off the gray walls in a voice I realize is my own.

I'd done everything right, visited the Kaiser pediatrician every month, devoured books on the subject of childbirth and labor, but found few exact details. The focus of both the books and the doctor was on having a saddle block to help with labor. Nothing has prepared me for this relentless pain. An angry nurse rushes in after a screaming-hard contraction and shouts in my ear: "Look here—you have to learn to count through it. It will be at least nine hours more! Count with me—one, two, three, four . . ." I shout the numbers with her, apologizing and crying. When I get quieter, she tells me I can yell and count all I want, as loud as I want, it's all right with her. Apparently the famous saddle block is available only toward the end of labor. It's a long, long night for me, in pain, desperate for any kind of comfort. I feel betrayed, abandoned. Bitterly, I tell myself I'm destined to be without family for every important event in my life. The rest of the night passes in a haze of Demerol.

Finally the nurses wheel me into the delivery room where they give me the saddle block and tell me to push. They gang up to press on my abdomen with all their might, trying to move the baby down, discussing me and my baby as if I'm not in the room. Finally, the doctor uses forceps to pull out the baby—a boy, I hear the nurses say. There's no crying, and I wonder if he's alive. I lean on my elbows, trying to see across the room. Without my glasses, I see a pink blur that is the object of the nurses' attention; they make bets about his weight. "Nine pounds, two ounces," they announce.

"What is nine pounds? Is he okay?" I've got to be too skinny to give birth to a huge baby.

"He's doing great. Your baby weighs nine pounds! Congratulations!"

A nine-pound baby from me? Wow, I really am a mother. Welcome to the world, Andrew.

⁂

Six weeks later, in the quiet of the early morning, the only sound is Andrew's nursing. It should be a sweet moment, but sorrow rises up in my throat and I break into a sweat. This is motherhood? I'm bone tired after five weeks of no sleep. Why didn't anyone warn me? So many long days alone with a baby I can't comfort no matter what I try. His wails rise to the ceiling of the small apartment, grinding at my nerves. I seem to be helpless with this tiny, mewling creature, completely inadequate. At six weeks, after no REM sleep for that long, I'm desperate for rest, and give in to bottle feeding, though that doesn't solve everything. When a nipple of one of the bottles gets clogged, I smash it against the wall and collapse in tears. Unable to bear any more baby screams, I wonder why I can't comfort him the way mothers on the Johnson's Baby Powder ads do, all serene and humming to their beatific, sleeping child.

Eventually Andrew outgrows the colic and turns into a smiling, good-natured baby. He still doesn't sleep enough, but we manage to get by on a few hours of rest. I know that I'm destined not to be a good-enough mother. I've already failed miserably. This inadequacy must be inherited.

That summer Dennis, Andrew, and I meander through the western states in a camper, stopping to see my father, Dennis's folks, and my Iowa family. While we're staying with Edith and Willard in Muscatine, Mother arrives on the train. My childhood of railway stations and mother-longing isn't over—the same old feelings sweep over me as I wait on the platform—a bone sadness, an ache that only deepens when Mother steps off the train and changes from the mother of my imagination into her actual self.

"Here's your grandson." I proudly lift Andrew up to her. He's a cherubic baby who belongs in a Gerber ad. I should have expected it: Mother doesn't take her grandson; she barely even looks at him. Instead she pulls out a cigarette, saying in her haughtiest tone, "I told you, don't call me grandmother. I'm much too young for that."

Edith blinks in shock along with me, and protests as we walk to the car. "But you are a grandmother. You should be proud."

Mother's high-pitched squeal grates on all of us. "Don't use that word, I tell you. Can't you listen to what I say? What's the matter with you?" Mother glares at me and jumps into the car. I'm stunned at her behavior, but why should I be surprised? She doesn't want to claim my child any more than she wants to claim me.

I get in the car, smothering in her smoke all the way back to Edith's. Andrew bobs in my arms, warm against my chest, his sweet baby smell and soft skin melting my heart. He's the next generation in the only family I have. I have to keep trying, I tell myself; I'll get her to change. Maybe when she falls in love with Andrew, she'll claim us all, and the barrier will come down at last.

That evening, after the usual Iowa dinner of fried chicken with gravy and corn on the cob, we all sit under the trees in the dusky glow, as we have for the last twenty years. The Mississippi River suffuses the air with its history. Between puffs on her cigarette, Mother glances at Andrew, who gives her a big smile. "He is kind of cute," she says, before turning away to blow out her smoke. Edith grins behind her hand at this, and Willard winks at me.

Fireflies begin to twinkle in the velvety darkness. Edith holds the baby while I sit on the edge of Uncle Willard's lap. "I'm not too old, am I Uncle Willard?" Still raw from Mother's denial and coldness, I need his comfort.

"You're never too old to sit on my lap," he smiles. Just as we did together so long ago, we grab at lightning bugs.

"Aunt Edith, can we make lemon meringue pie tomorrow?"

She smiles and gives a quick nod. Mother's smoke mingles in the darkening air with the magic lights of fireflies.

Return of the Bad Dream

THE BABY IS four months old by the time we arrive in Oklahoma, where Dennis is scheduled to start his new job in Norman. Furniture and boxes had been sent ahead of time to Gram's house in Enid. We've come to pick them up, and to show Andrew to her for the first time. My childhood memories floating before my eyes, I open the screen door to a smoky house. Gram, like Mother, doesn't react normally when she sees us. Her cool but polite greeting to Dennis and her quick glance at Andrew tell me all I need to know. Gram doesn't approve of any of this—marriage or baby. It makes her a great-grand-mother, a status she doesn't want.

Being in the house on Park Street is like returning to a bad dream. Gram has managed to clean up a bit; the books and papers are still stacked all around, but the house is clean and the piles are neat. A bor-rowed crib stands in the living room, evidence that she has put some thought into our visit. I blink my eyes to adjust to the dingy gray air, unable to take in the fact that I spent so many years here. I'm still embarrassed at its darkness and mess. It hurts to see this house through Dennis's eyes—he's shocked, but polite to me about it.

Gram relegates us to separate bedrooms, the anti-marriage and anti-sex message understood by both of us. Later in our visit, she upsets me again by complaining that Dennis has to use her bathroom, the only one in the house. "Men are so nasty. Can you tell him to be sure to wipe off the toilet seat and floor?"

I tell her I won't embarrass him like that, that he's a very clean and well-behaved male person.

"Why don't you mind me," Gram says angrily, "as a guest in my house?"

Oh, that's right, the place where I grew up is not my home. The fa-miliar old ache from the past slices through my stomach, the old heavi-ness on my shoulders, reminding me of where I came from and why I so desperately wanted to get away.

One afternoon, the baby is asleep in my room and Dennis has gone to the store, giving Gram the opportunity to launch into her old ways, picking a fight about nothing. We've been at it only a few minutes, but already her face has contorted into a mask of rage. She attacks, I defend. She still wants to control me, to win at any cost. I become angry and she raises her hand as if to strike me. Her Medusa face is a shock to my system, accustomed as I am to living in a reasonable and peaceful world. I flee to the garage, where I busy myself with going through boxes, hoping she won't follow me. She's raving, framed by the kitchen door, her hateful daggers pointing at me from wild eyes. Opening boxes and touching familiar objects of my life with Dennis comforts me, but only a little. How did I survive this house and Gram for so many years as a defenseless girl?

I no longer have the steel inside me to bear her ugly cruelty—her frizzed hair in a gray cloud around her face, her lips foaming with venomous words. Through a hazy film I watch her shouting, raising her fist, threatening me. I am frozen in place, motionless until the pressure inside me builds into a scream. "Shut up shut up shut up!"

In my imagination and against my will, I see myself stabbing her with a knife until she collapses into a blessed silence. When I snap back into reality, she's still yelling, and I'm awash with horror and shame. How could I imagine such a thing? Then despair comes flooding in—this is my heritage? I can't bear it.

The sound of Dennis's car pulling in the driveway on the other side of the garage door breaks into the living nightmare. I want to cry, but don't want Gram to know how miserable I am. She turns toward the living room, where she presents a slightly wild-eyed but otherwise sane figure to Dennis as he lugs in bags of groceries. I run to him, undone by a scene he knows nothing about, and wrap my arms around his neck. He pats me, unaware of my tripping heart, and goes on to the kitchen.

I escape to my room where Andrew is sleeping peacefully, his little legs curled up under his belly. I don't want to wake him, but I'm drowning with despair and I need to comfort myself by caressing his velvety skin, looking at the rosebud of his mouth, in love with his sweet, baby body. He twitches and smiles in his sleep. My tears finally come, and a silent prayer: "Please let us love each other always, let us never scream or fight. Please God, make this old nightmare go away forever."

Legacies

I T IS JANUARY 1971. I watch my breath puff in the air on the small side porch of the house Dennis and I are renting in Norman. I'm shivering from cold, or is it intuition, the wind of fore-knowledge in my veins? Daddy was scheduled to have exploratory surgery today, the doctors trying to find out more about the pains in his back and shoulder. It doesn't worry me too much, though surgery is always a serious matter. Daddy always had ulcers; perhaps they're acting up. The phone rings, and it's Hazel, my stepmother, her voice trembling. "He has pancreatic cancer, and it's in the liver. They give him three to six months to live."

The words hang in the air, destroying my fantasies of Daddy and me together, a happy future with Andrew, making up for our lost years. Kaleidoscopic memories of Daddy flash through my mind—waiting for him by the tracks, my delight as he swings me around on the platform, the scent of Old Spice, his rough beard against my face. My stomach writhes in pain as I think of our recent reconciliations: my first holiday with him—Thanksgiving at his house, fancy dinners at the Playboy club. Most of all I think of Daddy's boundless joie de vivre.

He's loved his status as an executive at the L & N, his social and professional clubs, his Cadillac. He retired at sixty-two to Arizona, where he enjoys golfing every day in the mild weather of Scottsdale. We visited him there last year, Daddy tanned and healthy-looking in his yellow golf shirt, his green eyes laughing as he watched Andrew toddle across the living room.

Now my mind surveys the future we might have had together: he would tell my children stories, run behind Andrew's bicycle, play catch with him. Older and distinguished, he would attend graduations and weddings. Through watching them do ordinary things together, the little boy and the grandfather, my own childhood would be healed.

"No," I hear myself saying to Hazel. "It can't be. There must be something the doctors can do."

<hr />

My palms sweat and tears sting my eyes as Hazel leads me down hospital corridors smelling of plastic, antiseptic, and sickness. Into the labyrinth we go, knowing that the monster at the center is death. We find Daddy curled up like a child in his hospital bed, tubes connected to his thin arms, his mouth gaping in sleep. He looks like an old, sick man. Where's my strong Daddy? He wakes as soon as we enter and sits up, a surge of vitality coming over him, but he's weak and can't cover it up. His arms shake as he lifts them to me, and I feel the bones of his ribs under my hands when I hug him. There is no scent of Old Spice, instead the bitter hospital antiseptic and urine. My voice catches in my throat, but I take a deep breath and paste on a smile. After all, it's my job in the family to be cheerful and encouraging.

"I'll beat this thing, you'll see. Nothing ever got me down in my life. I'm a fighter," Daddy says before collapsing back against the pillow. I find out later that they never told him the complete truth about his condition. I know it's important to never lose hope, but each upbeat remark he makes me have to lie and pretend even more. The prognosis is poor, but I'm supposed to go along with Hazel and Daddy that he will get better one day.

Two days pass, and we're alone in his room, talking about our past, and my mother and Gram. Daddy gazes at me with a look on his face I've always longed for—pride, affection, a sweetness I've never seen before. "You know, your mother was very, very beautiful. It was physical between us, I'm afraid. Married six weeks after we met. Of course, I didn't know her very well. It wasn't long before I found out how flirtatious and nutty she was. Always embarrassing me in front of people. I don't want you to be like her. I want you to have a good head on your shoulders, and I know you do. Your grandmother gave you lots of practical advice, and you'll need it."

At least he's not furious at Gram right now. I couldn't bear that. I tell him my plans to teach, to make a future for myself. He knows that Dennis and I aren't in good shape. The relationship seems to have died somewhere along the way, but we still hope to make it work. Daddy encourages me to stay married. He's worried about me, and I love him for it.

Sitting across from him, I bask in his full attention, soaking up his stories. The clock on the wall ticks out each hour as we try to make up for all those years, each hour and week and month that we lost. Our past is a huge mess, each fight and hate letter added to the heap until a high wall came between us, making it hard for us to know each other. So we try now to get acquainted, death nipping at our heels. I hate Gram at this moment for what she did to us. He tells me how many times he wanted to see me, how he tried to get Gram to send me to Chicago, but she never would let me go with him. Our history is littered with terrible mistakes. Everything I'd hoped for is too late. Those years can't be made up for the way I'd counted on doing for the next ten or twenty years after we made up. Inside I'm crying but outside I'm brave, chatting away.

Daddy gives me another adoring look, and says, "You're a Myers after all."

His putting our blood connection into words warms me, but there's a chilly note in those last words: "after all." What does he mean—was there ever any doubt about me being a Myers? The opportunity to ask him is lost when nurses and doctors with clipboards wander into the room. His cryptic comment will haunt me for years, until I finally find out what he must have meant.

• • •

Later in the day, Daddy regales me with stories from his early life, his childhood on the farm near Louisville. L & N freight yards bustled with activity in the small town nearby, and a love of trains grabbed him by the heart. He started working for the railroad when he was eighteen years old and ended up with an executive office in Chicago.

"You've got an education," he tells me, "but I came from the school of hard knocks." I smile at the phrase that always infuriated my grandmother. I can't help but admire the pride he's always had in working hard and making money, proving that he could rise up from the Kentucky farm and "be someone."

That afternoon Daddy tries to pack in a lifetime of lessons while I perch on a chair beside his bed, aware of the minutes slipping away as the Arizona sun slants against the beige walls. He talks of his own mother and father who died before my birth, of his regrets and his dreams of the future. It's early evening and his untouched dinner tray rests on the bed. Perhaps he was moved by reviewing his life, or maybe he sees the inevitability of his death. He begins to sob uncontrollably. "I don't want to die, Linda Joy. I'm too young, I'm so scared." I've never seen him like this before. I gather him to me, stroking his head as his tears fall. Sorrow for my own loss fills me to bursting, but I don't want him to see me cry. I whisper words of comfort to him, my own desperate entreaties unspoken: Please don't die, Daddy. Please don't die.

The day after his release from the hospital, we receive a call from Aunt Helen, asking me to come home immediately because Gram is sick and staying in a convalescent home. Aunt Helen says her condition is deteriorating, though it's not certain why.

In a surreal fog, I spend my last night with my father trying to say good-bye, trying to complete more of our unfinished lives, but he can no longer focus. He keeps repeating, "I'm going to be fine," smacking a weak fist into his palm. I prepare for bed, knowing that these are our last hours together in this life. I go to Daddy's room and put my arms around him, holding on, wanting to put our lives in perspective, but he can't bear to say good-bye. He says he's going to get better, and that's the way it is.

Daddy comes with us to the airport, so weak he has to lie down in the back seat of the Cadillac. I gaze at him an extra minute, searing his face into my memory. He falls back exhausted against the seat. I start to walk away, but turn for one more look. His long fingers make small circles in the air as he waves.

Gram

SPRING WHEAT SWAYS in the biting February wind. Despite winter storms—slashing rain and sleet and snow—the wheat keeps growing. In May the fields will be golden under azure skies, though that's hard to imagine now. I can never get enough of the wheat fields, these seas of graceful sage-green waves undulating under a pale late-winter sky. The Oklahoma landscape comforts me as I think of my father's impending death and Gram's hatred of him through the years. Dennis is at the wheel, driving up highway 81 to Enid so I can visit Gram at the convalescent hospital. Andrew is asleep in his car seat, his white-blond hair falling over his eyes, his baby cheeks flushed. I declare my new policy to Dennis: "If Gram says one nasty thing about Daddy, I'm going to walk out and never see her again."

Dennis nods, aware of how their fighting has defined my life. I feel sorry for him sometimes, putting up with me and my crazy family. Despite our difficulties as a couple, we are kind to each other, hoping it will work out. I wonder if it is all my fault that we are having such trouble with our marriage. After all, look at who my models are.

At the convalescent home, a nurse wearing a pink uniform and a big smile tells me Gram's room number is 203. Dennis wishes me luck. He's off with Andrew to the park so I can be alone with Gram. Sweat breaks out on my brow; my shoes squeak on the polished linoleum floor. What if she attacks Daddy again? Or me for spending time with him?

In the designated room I find an unmade, empty bed, a dresser, a chair. There is no familiar thing here to tell me I'm in Gram's room; everything seems too light and cheery. I check the room number again, then call her name. A lilting voice answers from the bathroom. "I'll be right out!"

I stay in the doorway when she emerges, unsure of my standing. Gram's dark eyes are like bright beads, impossible to read. The tense moment ends when she opens her arms to me, singing out "Sugar Pie!" Embracing her, I feel her delicate bones under my fingers.

Who is this jolly person inhabiting my grandmother's body? She looks like the Gram of my childhood, but something has happened to her. Before I can ask about it, she touches my arm. "Sit down by me. I have something very important to tell you." She pats the bed.

"You know that I was hospitalized at St. Mary's. A priest named Michael started coming around. He saw that I was crying a lot . . ." She pauses, assessing my reaction. "Each day I looked forward to his visit and we began to talk—about religion, but about other things, too." She looks like a different person. I keep staring at her—is this Gram?

She throws back her shoulders. "The most wonderful thing happened, Linda." Her fingers grip my arm with surprising strength. "Father Michael gave me the Last Rites of the church, washing away all my sins!" Gram's face is radiant with joy. I am shocked to hear that she was given the Last Rites, knowing that it's performed just before death.

"I could feel all my sins being lifted from my shoulders. I feel so light now. Maybe I'll even live a few more years!"

I'm too overwhelmed to speak. Does this mean she's going to die?

Gram leans close to me, grabbing my arm even harder. "I need to ask you something." She pauses, tears pooling in her eyes. "Please, please, can you forgive me for all those years I hated your father?"

My ears ring and everything is jolted out of focus. There are so many layers of that past I haven't dared probe. How can it be cleared away by a few words? In the beats of time between my racing thoughts, I search for a place in my heart where I can stretch myself to find forgiveness. I remember the Gram who cuddled me, the one who called me Sugar Pie. She was the only real mother I had, the only person willing to take me in and raise me when my own parents wouldn't. Despite all the pain, I remember our good times, too.

My heart pounds hard. I take her hand and look at her, barely controlling my tears. "Gram, I forgive you." She squeezes my hand.

"Sugar Pie, I'm so sorry your father is sick. Aunt Helen told me. I hope that you can see him and bring him some comfort." Her face is sweet, her dark eyes bright with life for the first time in years.

I feel as if I've been dropped into someone else's life. This isn't my Gram. I'm used to steeling myself against her, turning away from her cruelty. This old woman with a cheery attitude speaks to me with kindness. She seems real, but it's so strange. Her thin body makes hardly a lump under the blankets. Tenderness washes over me. I bend down to kiss her papery skin. Surely I didn't imagine her terrible power over me. I remind myself that however harmless she seems to me now, her awful rages and my struggles all those years really did happen. Now, suddenly, through some kind of miracle, Gram has been transformed from a monster into a sweet old lady in a convalescent home.

I perch close to her on the bed and we lace our fingers together, reminiscing about our summer travels to Iowa in the Nash Rambler, thunderstorms, the fun we had with Blanche and her brothers and sisters.

Rhubarb pie. The stars at night. She laughs, her voice soft, her dark eyes dancing. Hope fills my heart—maybe she will live. For the first time in years she wants to live. Good times are still ahead: She'll learn to like Dennis, and come to delight in Andrew's antics. Everything will be different if she doesn't die, I think. Then I remember the priest. The fact that he performed the last rites over her suggests he might know something I don't.

Late in the evening, I kiss Gram good-bye, my heart aching from being stretched wider than I could have imagined. My step is light as I walk down the hall toward Andrew and Dennis. If I hadn't seen it with my own eyes, I wouldn't have believed such a transformation was possible.

<hr>

The following days are spent monitoring Daddy, who's in Mexico receiving Laetrile treatments. I write him a letter, eager to share with him Gram's transformation and that she wanted to be forgiven. My heart pounds as I try to link these two enemies, whose connection to each other has been through me, and through their own wrangling and fighting. I hope they can each forgive now, and enjoy a peaceful end to their lives. It feels unreal—both of them dying at once. Will Daddy be able to read my letter? What will he say to this miracle?

Two weeks later Aunt Helen calls to tell me Gram has taken a turn for the worse, though no one knows exactly what's wrong with her. Mother is on her way by bus. Uh-oh, I think. There'll be trouble now.

That day I spend the afternoon with Gram at the hospital. She half-sleeps and dreams, calling out the names of people she once knew, murmuring about the past. I wonder if she's reviewing her life in preparation for death. I think about the spiritual teachings I've read about the dying—reviewing their lives, meeting departed loved ones. Is Blanche waiting for her?

All afternoon, Gram has slipped in and out of reality, but when Aunt Helen and Uncle Maj arrive she sits up, alert. While Aunt Helen is feeding her dinner, a nurse announces that a "Miss Myers" is downstairs. Aunt Helen and I respond with a moan. The nurse says, "I don't want anyone disturbing our patient."

We explain that Mother is "different," that she and Gram don't get along. I tell them I'll calm Mother down and check out her mental state before bringing her up to see Gram.

When I lean down to Gram to tell her that Mother has arrived, she stops eating, and her eyes fill with tears. "Oh, my brown-eyed baby," she says, invoking the phrase she always used when she felt tender toward Mother. I try not to cry as I walk down to fetch her. What were things like when Mother was a little girl? When exactly did Gram leave her? I don't really know what happened back then, only that it has left a tragic history never to be fully revealed now that Gram seems to be dying. Will Gram and Mother say words of forgiveness the way Gram and I did? I do know this—they have not laid eyes on each other for eight years. Aunt Helen told me that Gram "paid her off" with several thousand dollars to leave her alone and never come back. It's a shocking story—and it just might be true.

***

Mother paces impatiently in the lobby, well fitted-out with perfect make-up and hair, despite her two-day bus trip from Chicago. She peppers me with questions, obviously worried about Gram. I tell her that the nurse asked us to wait a few minutes before coming up. We chat about Mother's trip and the weather, unusually hot for this time of year, until she seems calm.

When we go up, she marches boldly into Gram's room and I follow. I'm surprised to find Gram lying down, the covers pulled up to her chin, her eyes tightly closed. The last time I saw her, she was eating dinner. How could she go to sleep so quickly during the few minutes I was downstairs? Gram doesn't move for several hours. Finally I realize that something must be wrong, and get the doctors and nurses involved. They examine her and declare that she's in a coma. It's uncertain why, and they can't say when, or if, she'll come out of it. I wonder if Gram managed to disappear so she wouldn't have to face her daughter.

Mother becomes more and more distraught, wild-eyed and wired as the hours pass. She paces and smokes all night while I try to get some sleep curled up on an orange plastic couch. She wakes me up to grill me about Gram's money—how much is there, when will she get it—subjects that I know nothing about. Finally I shout at her to let me sleep, but she won't. She even harasses the nurses and upsets everyone on the hospital floor. Constantly embarrassed, I keep apologizing to them for her insensitivity and rudeness.

I keep vigil at Gram's bedside, trying to prevent Mother from screaming her questions at me, but I can't stop her from ranting for hours about money and men, her usual subjects. After three exhausting days, I tell Mother that I have to leave. The plains weather has plunged from the seventies to the forties. Wearing the same flimsy spring skirt and blouse I arrived in three days ago, I'm freezing and just plain frazzled. I plan to go home, then come back with warmer clothes to take up the vigil again. Mother tries to stop me from leaving, threatening to slap me if I don't "mind." Despite all my years of independence, Mother scares me, but I stand my ground until she agrees that I should go.

I whisper my good-byes to Gram, telling her that I hope she will be all right wherever she is going. I tell her that I'm sorry for all the things that didn't work between us, and thank her for forgiving my father and me.

Her death will free me, but I can't imagine life without her.

<hr/>

Two days later, on my twenty-sixth birthday, the phone rings at three in the morning. The nurse on the other end of the line tells me that Gram is gone. The nurse says that Mother is sitting right there, but she doesn't want to speak to me. After I hang up, I try to imagine where Gram might be. Is she hovering nearby? Can she see me lying here beside Dennis, thinking of her? There are no tears that night, but they will come. Later, grief will run like a river. I will find out that death does not end a relationship; it is a beginning.

The next day, there are many small tasks to distract me: I play with Andrew, wash the dishes, and vacuum the house. Everything passes in a fog—it doesn't seem possible that it's both my birthday and the day of Gram's death. In the afternoon, the funeral home calls to ask me a startling question: "What are we supposed to do with the body?"

"You mean my grandmother?"

"Yes. We don't have any instructions."

"My mother said she would handle everything."

"I'm sorry, miss, but she's left."

"Left what?"

"She left town."

Typical. Mother had chased me up and down the halls of the convalescent home, screaming that we'd have a funeral in Enid, but I knew Gram wanted to be buried beside Blanche; she wanted a funeral with her Iowa family. None of that suited Mother. She would handle everything, she said in a huff, yelling at me to shut up and leave it all to her.

Now, it seems Mother has gotten on a bus and vanished.

The day after my birthday, I awaken in Aunt Helen's bed. Lying between sweet-smelling sheets, I stroke the empty side of the bed, remembering how Gram slept next to me on those carefree weekends of my young childhood. We'd cuddle together spoon fashion, her breath on my neck, the warmth of her body against me.

Gram was always her best self at Aunt Helen's. Perhaps she felt the most loved and accepted there. Nothing Gram ever did permanently tore them apart. The year after their blowup about the letters to Daddy, Aunt Helen came over every Sunday with a homemade dinner. Gram would rant and rave as always, and even call her names and abuse her, but Aunt Helen would just nod, saying, "Uh-huh, you don't say." She'd grin, nod, and burp. After Gram finished the meal, Aunt Helen would gather her dishes and head toward the door. "Now you quit those cigarettes and get some sleep, Frances." The next week, Aunt Helen would return, bearing fried chicken and chocolate pudding, or whatever delicious item she might create in her kitchen, and it would happen all over again. I would watch this constant loyalty from Aunt Helen, thinking, "So this is loyalty. This is the kind of friend I want to be."

Aunt Helen thought of it this way: Gram wasn't well. It was a simple, natural thing for Aunt Helen to offer her friend the food from her table and her undivided attention for an hour a week. She wouldn't let Gram break her spirit or destroy their bond. Those were the rules of Christian friendship that Aunt Helen believed in and lived.

Once I wake up fully, I remember that Gram is dead. Reluctantly, I throw off the quilt. I could spend the rest of my life in Aunt Helen's cozy bed, safe from the troubles of the world. Only the smell of fresh coffee, the soft shuffle of Aunt Helen's padding feet, and Uncle Maj's morning harrumphs make it possible for me to leave the bed and face the hardest journey of my life.

Aunt Helen and Uncle Maj drive me to Perry where I will take the train with Gram's casket in the baggage car to Iowa for the funeral. A pale sun flits between clouds as we follow the shiny black hearse down familiar roads threading between greening wheat fields. As I have done so often before, I wait at the Perry station for my future to unfold. Gram's casket rests on one of the old wooden carts on the platform. The train whistles, everyone gathers close to the tracks, and the railroad men roll the casket to where the baggage car will pull up. After the train arrives, the three of us watch Gram's casket being lifted into the train for her last ride.

The ironies of all this are with me as I board the train and wave at Aunt Helen and Uncle Maj until they grow small in the distance. As we cross Kansas, I sit alone, gazing at a perfect pink sunset. In the dining car, coffee is served in paper cups, and the sandwiches are served on plastic plates. I remember Gram and me in the compartment with our silver coffee service, the fancy white tablecloth and china, during one of our trips to Iowa. I lift my paper cup for a toast. "For you, Gram. For you." Tears wash inside me, but I am too tired to cry.

The train splits the darkness of the plains, whistling its lonely call all through the long dark night.

⚬⚬⚬

The Iowa family and I gather together at the funeral home high on a bluff overlooking the Mississippi River. Gram rests in a casket I chose for her on my birthday, wearing the clothes I selected for her on my birthday. She lies with her hands folded, looking peaceful the way Blanche did at her funeral. Mother sits quietly in the front row and barely nods at me when I come in. She appeared in Muscatine just before the funeral, telling a strange tale of being disoriented, blown into a building in Kansas City. No one knew if her story was true. To the farm people of Iowa, with their down-home logic and common sense, she wasn't entirely credible. Something must have happened to mother's mind, but she was irritating just the same, full of her usual bossiness and hysteria.

The minister speaks of eternal life, telling the basic facts of my grandmother's life: She was born in 1894 to Blanche and Louis. Married to Jasper Blaine. Had a son named Harrison who died at birth, a daughter named Josephine, and a granddaughter named Linda. Traveled to Europe. Lived in Enid. Died. What a sketchy outline of a complex person, whom in some ways, I feel I never quite got to know.

After the funeral, there's the usual party for the living. All the neighbors and Blanche's children, grandchildren, and great-grandchildren gather at Edith's. Everyone contributes to the usual Midwestern assortment of food: fried chicken, gravy and mashed potatoes; potato salad, ambrosia, Jell-O with grated carrots; chocolate cake and fruit pies. This delicious down-home food was made by these ladies in cotton dresses, whose worn, spotted hands are smoothing white tablecloths in the dining room, ordinary women who love their children and grandchildren.

Their conversations weave memories of the Iowa world for me: ripe tomatoes in August, Blanche embroidering by the window, a rhubarb pie on a summer afternoon. This is the place where my roots are, but I realize now that it will all disappear one day. Gram is dead and Daddy is dying. Edith, Grace, and the others will go someday, and I'll be alone with my mother, who seems to care about nothing but herself. Of course, one day she too will die, but the prospect doesn't sadden me as it should.

Suddenly, Mother's shrill voice punctuates the droning murmur. She's chatting with the minister, waving her cocked cigarette holder as she tells a largely fictional story of Gram's life, in which she, Josephine, is the star, she is the one who is put upon, wounded, and lost. I don't argue with her, realizing in that moment that my mother, who in some way lost her mother long ago, is entitled to her own way of coping with all of this. Maybe being the star of the show—sashaying around the men with her curves, her big-city attitude, and her perfect face and hair—maybe that makes her feel better.

My equanimity isn't seamless, however. As I listen to her stories about Gram's life and death, her own life and mine, I want to shout, "Tell the truth for once, dammit!" Of course, I know it would do no good. I've given up trying to tame the whirlwind that is my mother.

I wonder, not for the first time, what is wrong with her. She is so very odd, so different from other human beings. Suddenly an unbidden wish forms in my mind, that she instead of Gram had died. Guilt immediately grips me and I gaze thoughtfully at this wild woman, her high-pitched chatter rising above the deep voices of my Iowa family. I wonder if she can ever change, if she'll treat me better now that her mother is gone, or if things will get even worse.

***

The next time I see Mother is at Gram's house on Park Street, where she arrived a couple of days before me. Already she's torn up the place—the Oriental rug is rolled up, the books and the huge mounds of papers are gone. As I look around, the house is familiar and strange all at once. The wallpaper is still French green and maroon, the ceiling still seems to hover just above my head. But without Gram's brooding energy and cigarette smoke filling the place, it seems smaller and infinitely empty. My room has been stripped so I can't find my keepsakes— Storybook dolls and favorite childhood books in which I took refuge from Gram's rage and insanity. I find sealed black garbage bags full of my things heaped in the garage. Mother insists that I not open them, just take them away. I open the bags anyway to find a jumble of photos, clothes, and books, but so much is not there. I beg her to let me look for the Teddy bear Grandpa gave me, my school yearbooks, and other things I wanted to always keep, but she screams at me that everything is gone and tries to slap me to shut me up.

I'm raw to the core by the time Dennis and I drive away with the furniture that Gram has left me. I always hated it, but mother insisted I had to take it because she's closing up the house. We drive down the old highway that borders Enid, where the wheat sang to Keith and me as the moon rose. I'm so ragged with grief and stress, longing for a loving parent to soothe me. I send a prayer to my father: Please don't die, Daddy. Don't leave me yet. I'm not ready.

We drive through the empty, lonely plains under a moonless sky. No answer comes from the heavens. Only silence.

⚜

The next morning Andrew balances on my knees while I practice yoga in the living room. He giggles, his big blue eyes full of happiness to have me back with him. I touch his fine blonde hair, keenly aware of the preciousness of this simple moment with my son. He falls into my arms and we roll, laughing, over the floor.

The phone rings and I answer in a happy, playful mood.

The hiss on the other end tells me it's long distance, and suddenly my heart clenches. Hazel's voice: "I'm sorry, Linda, but your father died last night."

A chill comes over me and I start shaking. "No, he couldn't have died. My grandmother just died."

On the other end, a breath, then, "Honey, I'm so sorry, but he did die last night."

"No. No. He didn't die last night. He couldn't have died. Gram is the one who died."

More silence, a beat. A breath. "Honey . . ."

The room spins. Andrew grabs my legs and I collapse to the floor. Tears wash down my face as I hold Andrew, sobbing into his hair. His little hand pats me.

On the airplane, Bach's Brandenburg Concerto No. Five plays on my headset, but its uplifting strains can't save me today. Tears stream silently within while I struggle to keep my composure.

Once I get there, we stop briefly at the house, where I feel the emptiness of a world without my father. Hazel tells what happened with Daddy—they'd had to rush out of Mexico so he could die in the United States. On the last day of his life, she read him the letter I sent about Gram asking for forgiveness. She said he understood and everything was okay. I try to imagine what he thought, how he felt. What he looked like at that moment.

Soon, it is time to go to the viewing. Hazel and I march like wind-up dolls toward the limousine that takes us to the funeral home. Both of us are drained of tears, speaking matter-of-factly about what will happen in the next few days. Some part of me works desperately to suppress my true feelings, which are too painful to bear. A pill gives me distance from the pain, as if it's in a room separate from my real life. Everything becomes dreamlike—riding in the limousine, the funeral home, viewing my father in his casket. Hazel greets their friends one by one, introducing me as his daughter, the estranged child.

Being surrounded now by all these strangers reinforces my sense of not knowing my father. I stand a few feet away from his casket, unable to bear looking directly at his face, but close enough to see that the man in the casket doesn't resemble the father I knew. This man is emaciated, skin tight to bone, reduced to nothing. Then I recognize my father's hands. I rush to the bathroom, where it seems the tears won't stop. I'm losing control. I don't know how I can go back and face the strangers, how I will navigate the airport tomorrow.

The next day we walk like zombies through the corridors of the Arizona airport where we see Daddy's casket being loaded into the plane. We stand and watch the surreal scene while life bustles all around us. In Louisville dozens of relatives from my father's family come to the funeral home. One sister throws herself onto the casket in a fit of hysteria. I don't know these people, either, though I'm related to them by blood. The enormous sense of loss, a lifetime of brokenness with no way to repair it, overwhelms me utterly.

Daddy is placed in a marble crypt labeled with gold letters. I have seen him in his casket, there has been a funeral, but I still can't accept that he's gone. Someday, surely, we'll make up for all those lost years.

<hr/>

A month after all this, I leave Dennis, sharing custody of Andrew with him, and move back to Illinois to be close to old friends. I have no idea how lost I am. For a long time in my dreams, Daddy is not dead. He comes to me, at first once a month, then more often. He appears to me alive, shiny, energetic. It seems quite normal that he's walking toward me, arms ready to embrace me. I say, "Daddy, I'm so glad to see you! I thought you were dead. I knew we'd be together again. I knew you'd come back." He smiles and hugs me tight. Then I suddenly remember he's dead, that this has to be a dream. He begins to dissolve and I cry, "Don't leave me!" I crumple into grief, sobbing uncontrollably, clutching at the mist that he's turned into. I wake up, unable to stop crying. These dreams tear at my waking life.

A few months after coming to Illinois, Andrew and I move again to join Steve, a man I'd been friends with several years earlier. I love his belly laugh, his joy of life. Most importantly, he is known to me, a familiar old friend who likes me, admires me, and wants me. He buys me a long winter coat and a muff like one that Mother once gave me. He exudes charm like my father. He's my rescuer. Andrew and I weave our lives into his. For a while, the bad dreams stop.

Beside the Road

THE DAY IS gray-brown, an icy wind sweeping down the plains from the north. My son is huddled in his car seat, eyes closed, innocent of how his life will change today. His cheeks are still pudgy from babyhood, though he's taller now. He expresses himself more each day. I love it when he calls a bridge a "jib-es," a train a "nigh."

The windshield wipers fly back and forth, blurring my vision—or is it tears. Too much has happened recently for me to sort it all out—Gram's death and then Daddy's, leaving Dennis, trading Andrew with him every three months or so, adjusting to being in a new relationship. My every nerve is raw, and there is little peace in my heart. I hope Dennis won't be late to the Howard Johnson's rest stop next to the freeway. It's terrible to think of handing off our son as if he were a bag of groceries, but we try to be rational about it. We're thoughtful people, clear about how we must do things as modern, separated parents, sharing everything, even Andrew, equally, with no guilt. It's the guilt part that I'm not able to handle very well.

My inner voice bugs me, telling me that because Andrew is so young he still needs to be with me more than with his father, but maybe I'm just being old-fashioned. I reassure myself that he loves his father and his father loves him. I'm determined not to repeat what happened to me. A father and child need to be together, too. Besides, as a boy, he needs his father even more than I needed mine—that's how he'll learn to become a man someday. He won't miss me very much.

The green freeway sign says "Rest Stop—4 miles." My palms begin to sweat, slick on the steering wheel despite the cold. Today I got up early, driving down from Champaign, where I work in the university library. My stomach hurts from the war going on inside me. I keep telling myself I'm not deserting Andrew, I'm just giving him to his father. Out of the corner of my eye I see the sign for the rest stop.

"Andrew," I call out. "Wake up. Daddy, we're going to see Daddy."

He begins to stir. "Daddy? See Daddy?" he says in his sing-song voice.

"Yes, we're seeing Daddy. You're going to be with him again; won't that be fun?" I say cheerily. Nothing to get upset about. As I park the car, I see Dennis's green Ford pickup across the parking lot. We bought it when I was pregnant, expecting to take wonderful family camping trips when Andrew got older, things we'll never do now. Dennis watches me drive up, the wind tearing through his curly blonde hair. I have to look away from the pain on his face. Andrew is the best part of our marriage, the best part of who we were together.

Andrew bounces in his seat and waves his arms. "Daddy, Daddy!"

"Hey, buster, how are you?" Dennis opens my car door and buries his face in Andrew's neck, inhaling the smell of animal crackers and apple juice.

The ache spreading from my stomach to my ribs tells me that I am in dangerous terrain. The need to be fair to Dennis, to give Andrew to him for a while, wars with the part of me that knows Andrew and I are bonded close—it tears him up when I leave him. The other times we exchanged Andrew, he was younger, but I can tell that this time it will be harder for him. It certainly is for me. But what about Dennis? He looks torn apart too, but he's trying to act cheery, holding Andrew's hand as they go into the store to get milk. I watch the wind blow against the car, feeling the heaviness of rain in the gray world that surrounds us, as if there will never be another spring.

As they leave the store, Andrew trustingly holds his father's hand. When he sees me, he lets go and rushes to me, a look of wild happiness on his face. He buries himself in my legs, giggling with pleasure. I brush his fine blonde hair with my fingers. His blue eyes are wide and big, the blue of the plains sky in summer. "Andrew, you're going to be with Daddy. Be a good boy and mind him. I'll see you later. I'll call you on the phone, okay?"

Andrew stares up, his smile dimming, his eyes registering his grow-ing awareness of the purpose of this gathering beside the road. Dennis picks him up, sensing his brewing upset.

"Don't talk to him now, just get in the car and go," he tells me. Dennis is practical, a scientist. His philosophy is simple: Take care of the goal and the rest will follow. He rushes a blubbering Andrew to-ward the pickup. Perhaps he's right, but I run alongside, trying to hug Andrew one more time. The last time we did this, Dennis told me, "Don't worry, he always stops crying right away." Maybe he usually does, but the turmoil this time is worse—he understands more about what we are doing, and it's tearing his heart in two. He's kicking and fighting and screaming for me. Oh God, I'm hurting him, I'm ruining his life, he'll feel lost as I did, as I still do.

He's strapped in his car seat, his small hands pressing against the window. I wave and smile, trying to comfort him. "I love you. Be a good boy. See you soon." Andrew strains toward me screaming, "Mommy." I can read his lips through the glass.

As Dennis whirls out of the parking place, Andrew's eyes are glued to my face, tears running down his baby cheeks. "Mommy," he cries over and over again, turning around in his car seat to see my face for as long as possible. His horrified look seems familiar, but I don't know why. I sit in the front seat of my car, shivering, my mind awhirl.

Suddenly I recognize that face—it's my face as a little girl. There in the rest-stop parking lot, the full weight of my history crashes down on me. A chaos of memories, thoughts, and fears overtake me. My son is gone. I've turned into my mother after all.

Rachel

IT IS THE fall of 1974. The scent of burning eucalyptus leaves filters through the crisp morning. The pottery teacher tells us, "After
shaping your pot, we'll bisque it and put it in the raku kiln. Raku
means 'happy accident.'" That phrase best describes our arrival in
dream-come-true California, my second husband and me, both of us
attending Stanford. I've given myself over to my love of art and have
promised myself I would develop my creativity, beginning with pottery. The child in my belly flips and swims on this fall morning as I
grip the clay. Suddenly I know this baby is a girl. I am so certain of
this body wisdom that after class I buy pink baby clothes and pink
accessories.

My husband and I intend to stick together, and planned this baby,
but deep down I know that we need her to be the glue that holds us
together. In our small apartment near campus tempers often flare, trust
is broken, dishes crash. Sometimes I feel as if I've never left my childhood; other times we are desperately in love and pledge to do better.
With no model of healthy love to follow, I let passion sweep me along.
I surrender myself to its power, glad to forget my terrible past—until it
comes roaring back again, but this isn't completely clear to me now.

Every time I press my fingers deep into the clay, I dream about my
baby girl—we'll be wonderful together, we won't make the same mistakes that my mother and grandmother did. She'll grow up having a
father who loves her. One night I dream that she rests quietly in a blue
room, a silent and spiritual place where my father watches over her
from the other side of the veil between life and death.

My grieving for Daddy hasn't stopped, those endless dreams of finding and losing him. I send desperate prayers to the heavens, wondering
if I deserve help—according to Mother, I'm not living a proper life.
At twenty-nine I'm already divorced and remarried. I'm even an art
student, not the most stable thing to be. Society says that I should have
a different life. Occasionally I wish I do too, but I have no idea where
I'm going or what I should be doing except that I hold on to the idea
that if this marriage can only work, when the baby comes, things will be
perfect. I whisper a wish into the silence: to no longer be tormented by
these dreams. All this grief can't be good for my unborn child.

In bed one morning, I wake up with the sense that someone's hands have just touched my shoulder. I'm sure my father has visited me in answer to my prayers, that his presence is still nearby. In a dream I receive a letter from him:

> "Dear Linda. Oh, how beautiful it is here, green fields for golfing. There is nothing to fear. I am with you, I will be with you. You don't have to grieve for me."

The feelings and images in the dream are effortlessly translated into words, as if from another language, which I write in my journal.

For a few minutes I sit quietly by myself in the living room, my heart lightened. I understand the message of the dream: it's time to make the transition from death to birth, from darkness to light. It's time to focus on the impending birth of my daughter. The dreams of my vanishing Daddy stop that morning.

Andrew is living with me again, and cuddles up close, patting my tummy, whispering sweet nothings to the baby. My husband is gone most of the time. Having disappeared emotionally, he's involved almost constantly in his work. It's just as well. When he's home, our struggles return me to my childhood. The darkness, hopelessness, and pain are so familiar. It hasn't yet occurred to me that not everyone lives on an emotional roller coaster, and that I don't have to, either.

The baby grows inside me. I'm still convinced that it will be a girl, though there are no sonograms in 1974 to settle the question. Determined to make this a better birth experience than I had with Andrew, my husband and I attend Lamaze classes, where I learn to relax my muscles and practice my breathing. I visualize the birth I want, reading Spiritual Midwifery and learning to think in terms of "rushes" instead of pain.

At four in the morning two days before my due date, my water breaks. We leave Andrew with friends and rush to the hospital, but my contractions lag. The nurses hook up Pitocin to speed up the labor. It's intense, but thanks to the breathing methods I learned in Lamaze, I feel discomfort rather than excruciating pain. We hum along steadily for several hours. Suddenly I feel the urge to push. Only ten minutes earlier they'd told me it would be a while yet. The urgency I feel, the catch in my throat that makes me bear down, engulfs me. I insist that my husband call the nurse. Laughing, he says it can't be time to push.

I tell him again, as calmly as I can. The third time I scream it out. The nurses rush in to find the baby's head coming out. In a flurry, they lift me onto a gurney.

Suddenly, my normal perceptions shift. I'm not simply a body, I'm a part of nature. I'm the ocean, the trees, the wind on the plains. In a flash, I understand the unity of all things, my small self dwarfed by the expanse of the world in its spiritual complexity. Then my consciousness blurs, as does my awareness of all the people bustling around me and the bumpy ride to the delivery room. A few pushes later, the doctor lifts a baby girl high into the air. With her first breath her chest expands and turns pink. Her arms make little circles in the air, her cry is lusty and strong. Rachel, my daughter, is born.

She wears a little bow taped to her head for the newborn baby photograph. "I will not leave you," I murmur to her as she lies in my arms. "I'll be a good mother, I promise."

At home, my baby girl lies on one side of me while Andrew cuddles on the other. She nurses contentedly and sleeps like a dream—so different from Andrew at this age. This time I know what I'm doing. I kiss Rachel's soft cheeks, marveling at her little girl-ness, her femininity, wondering what my mother felt about me right after I was born.

When Rachel is only five months old, we fly to Austin to visit Aunt Helen, who now lives with her sister-in-law, Dot. The two women share a home in old age after being friends all their lives. Uncle Maj died three years earlier, another death I still find it hard to accept. We reminisce about Uncle Maj, his roses, and of course Gram. Aunt Helen knows us all so well, acting as our family historian, much as Blanche used to.

"Land sakes, just look at this beautiful baby. She looks like you, God love her. I can see that you're a good mother, Linda, not like Jo at all. Your mama, she calls me and wants to charge the phone call. Can you imagine—I'm on a fixed income! Oh, she's nutty, but she still loves her Aunt Helen." I consider the possibility that Mother sees Aunt Helen the way I do—as the nurturing mother figure neither of us had.

During our visit we drive down to San Antonio to see the Alamo and the hotel where Gram and Aunt Helen met. She tells me the story again, and then she says, "Darlin', your Gram was not what you thought she was. She hailed from another era, born at the wrong time, if you ask me. She was just bound and determined to have you be the way she wanted you to be; she'd do anything to make it happen. No child should be put through that."

Aunt Helen and I weave threads of the past together with the new generation that Rachel represents. When I say good-bye, I have no way of knowing that I'll never see Aunt Helen again.

Etchings of the Past

I OPEN THE door to the art store as if entering a cathedral, filling my lungs with delicious scents—linseed oil, canvas, wood, ink, erasers. And paper: creamy smooth parchment, watercolor pads in four levels of tooth, Bristol board. I'm one of those people who open books to sniff the inside—getting some kind of high from the glue, paper, the printer's ink. At the art store, I go into sensual ecstasy, musing and dreaming over the delicate fingers of color in oil pastel boxes. Paint brushes are soft against my arms, each with a different texture: sable, Siberian mink, blue squirrel.

Voices war within me: "You are an artist." Then, "You don't deserve to follow your desires to paint and draw." I've never forgotten the rave reviews I'd received in fourth grade for my art talent. Visiting university professors loved a painting I did of the wheat mills in Enid, yellow grain sprinkled on the ground amid the speckled gravel, the soaring march of alabaster wheat mills against a dark sky. The painting showed my love of amber crayon and the adoration I'd always felt for golden wheat fields. My teachers told Gram I should become a visual artist, but she insisted I focus only on music.

My daydream of being an artist has never left me, so I decide to take my first painting class. Once a week, we gather with the nubby paper, sable brushes, and paints, learning about the color wheel, how colors bounce and leap. After that, I enroll in a drawing class. I can't draw anything very well, but as we complete our assignments—sketching bowls, flowers, and eventually human models—I do improve. In art as well as music, practice is the way to learn—developing a new way of seeing, training the hand and eye. I love the silky ooze of oil paints melting across a canvas, and I learn how to build canvases with hammer and wood and stretched linen. Soon, I feel like more than a has-been musician. A few years ago, I gave myself permission never to play music again—unless it was for me. Every time I played, I had terrible flashbacks of Gram's yardstick, her angry eyes. I'd start shaking and feel sick. It was a huge relief to put it all away for good, but I hungered for artistic expression.

Next, I take an etching class. The smell of chemicals, ink, and acid for three hours once a week sends me into a kind of dream, where I part the curtains of the past and step into memory. For three months I labor over my first etching, savoring the technical aspects of creating an image. A deeply etched line divides the metal plate into several dimensions. Here, a little girl raises her hands to her father who Is trying to get through a door made of prison bars. There, a grandmother, tears pouring from her angry eyes, refuses to let the father into the house. A mother figure watches everything in passive sorrow. In another dimension of the etching, the tree of life reaches to the sky, its bare branches stark and leafless, and a quarter moon shines down on a road that leads out of the picture.

Every time I work on the etching, I return home to write in my journal, tears running down my face. For the first time I'm telling the stories I wasn't supposed to tell, releasing my family secrets, revealing the prison of my childhood. Long-buried images pour out of me in drawings, monoprints, and etchings. Blanche appears in a large painting, with her severe eyes and tight mouth, behind her a clock with no hands. She holds the finger of my grandmother, a baby with large, dark eyes who wears a white dress. Exploring through my art the history of Gram's life before I was born helps me to understand her better. At Aunt Edith's we had discovered old photos of Gram in Edith's photo box. She was once just a small girl with long blonde hair like me. How did she end up being someone who created a prison for a child?

By the time Andrew is seven and Rachel is two, my shaky marriage has dissolved. Months go by during which I'm barely able to get up in the morning and go to work, with little energy to care for the children. I do my best, fixing meals, making sure they have clean clothes. I take them to the park, enjoying their laughter and play. Andrew is a wonderful big brother, playing with Rachel, taking baths with her, making sure she gets her bottle.

Rachel is demanding, energetic, and headstrong, often leaving me exhausted by my efforts to keep up with her. It worries me that I'm neglecting Andrew in the melee. Dennis wants Andrew to live with him now, and several times has asked if he can keep him longer than the agreed upon period. He knows I'm having a hard time. Somehow it all starts to makes sense, so I tell Dennis he can take Andrew now, reasoning that my son needs more than I can give. The debate within me about how to mother the children, or how not to, hasn't changed over the years. I can't see clearly enough through my own history to know what is best for me, or for Andrew.

The night before he's to leave, I tiptoe in to watch him sleep. His cheeks are still chubby, his blond hair splays across the pillow. He clutches tight to his chest a yellow and purple snake, his favorite stuffed animal. I can't bear to see him so innocent, yet so tangled up in my own pain, my own inadequacy. I cry for a while on my bed, returning to look at him again, and feeling torn with indecision. I know that I can't give him what he needs; I'm hardly able to take care of myself. I stare at him in the dim light, whispering that I'm sorry. I love him, and so does Dennis. It will be all right, I tell myself, crossing my fingers behind my back.

On the way to the airport, I glance at his face. His eyes stare blankly, as if he's trying not to feel what he feels. At the airport, I reassure him, telling him I love him, but I can see in his face that he's holding back what he wants to say. I hug his small body tightly, and he clings to me for several moments, letting me know that he doesn't want to go. His white-blonde hair bounces with each step as he walks away. He turns around once to wave, his eyes hangdog and sad. We wave until he disappears around the corner.

I am not my mother. This is different.

⬥

One summer evening, Vivaldi pours from the stereo. Rachel is finally in bed after a day of diarrhea and temper tantrums, and my glass of wine rests on the coffee table. Outside, mothers and fathers tumble on the grass with their children. Lying on the couch, I can hear the sound of laughter, and I know that if things were normal here in my house, we'd be out there playing too. Not being allowed to play when I was young, I find that watching young children frolic makes me sad instead of happy. A profound grief about many things having to do with children and childhood has surfaced since Rachel was born. Suddenly, the full awareness of my situation hits me like a punch in the stomach: My son is already gone, and I am barely able to take care of my daughter.

I don't know the name of what is wrong with me. Naming my condition—depression—will come later. All I know is that I'm sinking into an impenetrable darkness, fear and shame slithering around me like snakes. Gram's cruel voice attacks me as I lie there: "You'll never make anything of yourself; you're nothing, nothing." As I sip my wine, I pour over the images I created in the etching: the little girl reaching for her father, the crying grandmother, the passive mother. Nothing is the way it was supposed to be. Is it fate that has created the life I have, or am I truly a write-off, another example of failure like those who came before me—those other crazy, bad mothers.

The voice in my head starts up again: "You are just like your mother and grandmother. You've lost your son, and you're barely able to care properly for your daughter." There's Gram, sitting as I am sitting now, consumed by dark thoughts, sinking into the couch. Somehow the cheer I had maintained for so long, a kind of Pollyanna hope that my childhood hadn't scarred me, has vanished, leaving me in despair. The only thing that soothes me is creating art, painting and drawing the stories that have filled my dreams and nightmares, stories I've been too ashamed to tell in words.

A friend who is worried about me refers me to a therapist. If I need a shrink, I must be crazy, like my mother. It means there's something terribly wrong with me. I make the appointment despite these fears drumming constantly in my head.

The therapist is a soft-spoken man with large blue eyes full of compassion. I'm a nervous wreck. I answer his questions about my childhood, crying, shaking, afraid to look at him. To me it is a shameful story, a story I don't want to tell, but I know somehow that I need to get it out. Finally I am beginning to unravel the tangled threads.

Compassion flows from him into me, soothing, subtle, and beyond words. He accepts me without criticism and listens attentively for an entire hour. He tells me to write about falling apart when the despair threatens to engulf me, to give particulars to all my thoughts and experiences. Sometimes I have to call him on the phone for reassurance, when the waking nightmares trap me. There are times that I can't clearly discern what I feel and believe. Being told so often as a child that I was lying when I was actually telling the truth has made me distrustful of my own perceptions. In Gram's house, she alone possessed the "truth." I feel guilty because of all the lies I told to protect myself from her, to escape from her prison, to allow myself a little life outside her influence. What is real? I wonder now. Who am I? I explore these questions with my therapist and in my journal.

❦

I discover that my process of recovery involves learning to face my worst anxieties and fears. My therapist and I spend much time in Vera's basement, at train stations, in smoke-filled rooms. We revisit Mr. Braúninger, Aunt Helen, and all my Iowa relatives. Now that I have a compassionate witness, I can learn to unpeel the layers of my past, but it takes many years.

Fear is my most constant companion, fear of falling and tumbling into a dark abyss, which sometimes happens for apparently little reason. I'm confronted with my mood swings and my impatience, my dreams of making a whole family with two parents, and my disappointment at not being able to do it. Each week, no matter how much resistance I have to overcome, I meet with my therapist. He teaches me about the path to myself, a path that gets lost in the woods where I have to double back to find myself again. There are times I don't want to continue—it's too difficult to face the ghosts that haunt me—but I won't let myself give up. I know this is the only way to break free of the generations of patterns etched so deeply within me. After several years, I take a break, then return on my knees after a relationship breakup that sends me to the depths of the loss of my mother, tumbling me into whirlpools of grief I'd repressed when she left so long ago.

Many different paths of healing, including Buddhist psychology and meditation, are presented to me. The idea that you can be present here and now, not caught in a sleeve of time, not defined by the past with its terrible pain, is new to me. In meditation I learn about relaxing the mind and letting go. I learn about appropriate anger and managing my fears. I rebuild myself from the bottom up, brick by brick, tearing down the old structure that never worked, trying to find out what love really means. It means opening fully to my children, my pets, my friends, the plants I learn to grow. I have to learn how to be here with them with my whole heart.

It takes a long time to learn how to love. Gifts come to me frequently in good friends who understand, in my children whose love shines from their eyes. There is much to heal between us, but we at least talk about our issues with honesty, trying to resolve them. This is a huge improvement in the old family dynamics. I learn that it's okay to be imperfect, though I was punished for it as a child. I come to understand that life is a work of art, an ever-dynamic process that flows and moves, imbued by energies we don't always understand, gifts that are truly given without asking.

I'm grateful for all the healing that comes to me, but one thing doesn't heal completely: the broken relationship with my mother. I cannot accept her rejection of me, which has continued through the years. I have tried for decades to prove to her that I'm a worthwhile daughter, and there are brief moments, precious moments of tenderness between us, but then comes the usual fight, her grinding criticisms of me. Though we are destined to find our way to each other, it will not be an easy road. At the very end we will meet each other eye to eye, but only when there is no way for her to escape.

For the Grace of Dan

BATTLE-READY, RACHEL AND I stand nose to nose in the kitchen. At fourteen, her golden-brown hair is streaked with various shades of red and black, her eyes ringed like a raccoon's with black eye liner. In some subconscious way, she's modeling herself after me, even wearing my trademark black leggings and tunic shirt. I know she's at the love–hate stage all teenagers go through, but mothers' and daughters' love–hate relationships are terrifying for me. I'm afraid these yelling matches mean we're turning into a version of my mother and Gram. Rachel and I have fought and made up since she was eleven, but today there's a new edge to it.

During the argument, I tune out Dan, our aging golden retriever, who sits beside us with his tongue hanging out, waiting to be fed. My youngest son, ten-year-old Thomas, chugs his third glass of milk in front of morning cartoons instead of eating his breakfast. I reflect sadly that the dog and Thomas are used to scenes like this between Rachel and me. Today I have the flu, and all I want to do is go back to bed with a hot water bottle. My daughter is more adamant than usual, though, so I have to stand my ground.

"No, you absolutely can't go hang out somewhere today. There's a ton of homework waiting for you. That report on the Miwok Indians is due on Monday."

"But Mom, it's so important. They're my best friends, I have to go." This is her cajoling phase, but I know that soon she'll turn more angry and demanding.

We go on and on, our voices rising as we pace in endless circles around the kitchen, shrieking our way to an impasse. Finally, she rushes into her room and slams the door.

It's hopeless, I think. How could I ever believe it possible to break the mother–daughter pattern I witnessed so many times during my childhood? Apparently, it's in my genes. Can there ever be a resolution to decades—nearly a century, in fact—of this stuff? I'm not quite used to having big arguments and conflict with Rachel. For a long time in her childhood, though she was stubborn and we had struggles between us, she showered me with hugs, little drawings with hearts, love notes, and adoration. I soaked it all up, yet there was a small part of me I kept from her, as if afraid to allow my heart to open all the way.

Heavy in body and soul, I spoon a few reluctant bites into Thomas, feed the dog, and slink back to bed. Every few weeks it seems, I'm felled by another bug. Burrowing down under the quilt, I feel miserable. I'm a failure for getting sick all the time, for having a daughter who's barely interested in school. What would my therapy clients think? After all, isn't a therapist supposed to have it all together?

Over the last eight years, I've completed a master's program, earning a license to practice psychotherapy after putting in three thousand hours of internship and passing a state exam. I have a private practice and a twenty-hour-a-week job at a family agency, where I help people like Rachel and me resolve their problems. I should feel good about all this, and I do, but the dark times still come and go, as they always have, setting off moods I find hard to combat.

During the years of study and internship, I gave birth to Thomas, and shortly after that my most recent marriage ended—another good reason to feel bad about myself, though I know that staying would have been worse. It's a sign of good mental health not to stay married to men who remind me at times of my grandmother, but I have to wonder why I keep bringing people like that into my life. Don't I get it yet? How much therapy will it take?

I sink back under the quilts and finally fall asleep. In the dream world, I find myself wandering through shadowy labyrinths in Vera's basement. She is screaming at me, her vicious eyes gleaming with an eerie yellow light. She morphs into Gram, then Mother, then back to herself. She chases me through haunted, lonely landscapes. I'm afraid of every sound and every movement in a foggy world of leafless trees, an eternity of doom.

Dan soon snuffles at the door, waking me up. He finds a crack, pushes, and wanders in, waving his tail back and forth, a smile on his face. I'm glad to see him; he's such a cheerful antidote to my bad dreams. Generally, I'm a cat person, but I got Dan from a rescue agency because I thought a dog would be good for the kids. As it turns out, he has been good for me, too. He's taught me more about self-acceptance and unconditional love than any human I've ever known, except for Mr. Brauninger.

Thomas was with me when I went to pick up Dan. When we arrived at the rescuer's house, Dan rushed up to me, tail wagging, eager for a new home with us. Unaccustomed to this enthusiastic doggie reception, I wouldn't let him lick me. Once we got him home, I offered him newly purchased dog food and took him for a walk with our new leash. Later, I noticed that Dan kept following me from room to room, even into the bathroom. I knew he had eaten and I had just taken him for a walk. As I had with the children when they were babies, I ascertained that Dan had all his needs met. Still, he followed me from room to room.

Perplexed, I asked Thomas, "Why is he following me? What does he want?"

"Mom," said Thomas, big brown eyes peering at me over the rim of his glasses, "he just likes you, that's all."

I stood thinking for a moment. We'd just picked Dan up that day. He didn't even know me. "But I haven't done anything to deserve it."

"Oh Mom," Thomas explained patiently, as if he were the adult and I were the child, "you don't have to."

I was taken aback. What do you mean I don't have to do anything to deserve such devotion? I stared at Thomas, then at Dan, who sat in front of me, panting slightly, his pink tongue lolling out of his mouth. I realized that the look on his face was a dog smile, and patted his head. He made a move to lick me, then stopped, as if respecting my wish not to be licked. Moved almost to tears, I kneeled down in front of him and gazed into his eyes, trying to understand this radical notion of unconditional love, such generosity of spirit.

⁂

Now Dan is tending me in my illness the best he can, checking on me, making sure I don't lose faith. He is a spiritual being, emanating peacefulness and patience. He's certainly more spiritual than my mother, and much more accepting. She's never given up her position of denying me, and in recent years she's extended it to my children. Dan, just a dog, is an advanced teacher of love and acceptance, showing me that it is indeed possible. My mother, on the other hand, hasn't got a clue. Yet I keep trying to win her over, desperate to prove to her—and, I suppose, to myself—that we're a great family and I'm a good mother.

The California Zephyr

Through the years, I've returned to Iowa many times in summer to see my relatives, always staying at Aunt Edith's, where we've kept up our tradition of working in the garden together and making lemon meringue and rhubarb pies. This year, Rachel and Thomas have come with me on the train, the California Zephyr, all the way from San Francisco. It's important to me to introduce them to the hypnotic rhythms of the train as it chugs up the Sierras and across the rocky wilds of Utah. They get to see the Rockies, winding between canyons that follow the Colorado River, sleeping through the night as the train rolls through Nebraska. On the way they learn about the gold rush, the forty-niners, the Donner party, and other histories of America, encountering a world larger than themselves.

Once we get to Edith's house, I show the kids how to cultivate the squash and tomato plants on August evenings, imagining Blanche beside me, her voice murmuring in my ear: "Don't give up keeping the garden. You can trust the cycles of nature. You can count on the tomatoes, year after year." Back in this place that always feels like home, I surrender to life's simple pleasures. At night, after a dinner of pot roast and vegetables, fresh tomatoes, and pie, as always we sit out in the slow summer evening, watching the fireflies and telling family stories, initiating my children into the quiet rituals of country life.

At night, after Uncle Willard winds his seven chiming clocks, I tuck the kids into their sleeping bags and ascend the stairs. In my mind's eye, Blanche is clump, clump, clumping up the stairs ahead of me. I settle into the bed we used to share, all those years of my young life captured in a patch of silver moonlight on the ceiling. My heart aches as I settle in, yearning to sleep with Blanche one more time, listening to her in the dark.

She whispers, "Don't you give up, you hear me? I never did think your mama or Gram did right by you, but you have to go on."

In my mind, I answer her. "I've been in therapy all these years, but I can't seem to get over the past. When will Mother accept me? When will she just realize that I'm her daughter and it's all okay?"

"You got to be yourself, that's all you can do. Your mother has a few screws loose, but she's still my little Jo'tine."

"Blanche, I wish I could see you again. I miss making potato soup on your wood cookstove. You could teach me so much more now. I loved all your stories. Tell me one more time about baking bread, canning tomatoes . . ."

Silence. The reason death is so hard is that even when you tune in and listen, imagining what the dead would say, in the end you find only silence. Too much silence. I'm grateful, though, that Gram doesn't haunt me as she threatened to. It seems like a miracle, but most days I don't think of her at all. Perhaps that's the gift of forgiveness.

⁘

The next afternoon, a car pulls up to the house and a white-haired couple—great-uncle Earl and his wife Dorothy—come up the steps. Edith whispers to me, "That's Vera's sister."

At the mere mention of that name, my stomach tightens and my breath nearly stops. My children notice I've gone pale and ask if I'm all right. We all greet each other politely and the woman seems perfectly nice. As always when guests come, fresh coffee is brewed and pie is served a la mode. Everyone chats about the usual Iowa subjects—the weather, the price of hogs, the tomatoes. I stare at Dorothy, trying to breathe evenly, my memories of Vera as vivid as if I'd seen her yesterday.

Dorothy must notice my discomfort. She pats my arm and says, "I'm Vera's sister, but I'm nothing like her." I smile and swallow hard. Do I look that scared? I tell Dorothy I've thought of seeking Vera out and talking to her as part of my healing process.

Dorothy frowns. "You don't want to do that. She's still a very angry person." She pauses to sip her coffee. "I remember you, though, when you lived there." When she puts down the cup, her chin quivers. I don't remember her, but it seems pointless to say so.

As they prepare to leave, Dorothy pulls me aside. Her face is drawn and her cheeks are trembling. "Linda Joy, there's something I have to ask of you. Please, please forgive me." She begins to cry, leaning against me. I ask her why, what is it she's done to me?

She says, "I know what happened to you at Vera's. I saw it. I knew that she was mistreating you. You looked so frightened and unhappy. You were just a little bitty thing. I've felt bad all my life that I never told anyone about what she was doing. It was wrong, I know it. Can you forgive me? It must have been terrible for you. Vera was always different from the rest of us, so angry."

I murmur reassurances, my mind in shock. I never believed that I'd made up what happened, but I did wonder why it still had such power in my memory, why I still had nightmares that ended in that basement. Dorothy hugs me again, her blue eyes big and watery.

"I am so sorry, Linda Joy." She sobs into her handkerchief.

"It's all right. Don't give it another thought." I pat her back, trying to comfort her, but she seems inconsolable and is still crying when they drive away.

In a low voice, Edith tells me she heard that Betsy, Vera's daughter, had killed herself a few years ago. I sit down, trying to absorb the shock, wondering what might have happened to that other little girl.

Don't Call Me Grandmother

THE NEXT DAY, Thomas, Rachel, and I get into an old rented station wagon for the trek to Chicago to see Mother. She hasn't ever
met Thomas, and has met Rachel only once, when she was a babe
in arms. She's already given me strict instructions and a long lecture
over the phone. "Don't tell them you're related to me. I don't want
anyone to know my business."

I fought with her, angry that she could be so cold and self-absorbed.
In response, she shrieked so loudly I had to hold the phone away from
my ear.

"I told you already—they don't know I've been married, so I can't
have a child. God forbid, grandchildren. That makes me sound so old.
I'm the youngest person in my building, and I rather like being treated
like a youngster." Mother went on, unaware of my heavy breathing. I
was sweating with rage at her stubbornness, but I'm hardheaded too. I
can't seem to give up hoping that one day she'll claim me and my children, the pride shining in her eyes. It's probably a ridiculous dream, but
I still believe it will happen someday, if I just keep trying.

Of course, if the past is any indicator of the future, this dream isn't
likely to come true. The worst memory I have of Mother's overt rejection of me happened fifteen years earlier. On my way to Europe, I
stopped to see her overnight. I got off the elevator and my heart raced,
as always, when I saw her coming toward me down the hall. She was
smoking, of course, and kept her eyes cast down as she walked within
inches of me. I waited for her to say hello, certain that she knew it was
me, but she passed by without a word. Stunned, I called her name.

She turned, surprise registering on her face. "Oh, I didn't see you." I
stood there in shock, grief-stricken that my own mother didn't recognize me. After all, I was the only other person in the hallway. Had she
really become so oblivious to the rest of the world?

We went into her suite then, where I was grateful for a pleasant
hour of conversation. The first part of our visits was always calm; she
didn't get mean or strange for about three hours. After talking for a
while, we got dressed to go downstairs for dinner in the hotel. In the
elevator, she looked me up and down, examining me closely, survey-
ing my clothes, my face, my hair. Her eyes flickered and a slight smile
appeared on her face.

I began to smile, too, sensing that she was pleased with me. Then

she looked away and said, "I hope no one thinks you're my daughter."
She went on talking, but I didn't hear a word. Stabbed in the heart, I
gasped for breath, trying to suppress my tears. As the elevator made its
way down to the restaurant, my mood plummeted, too. I felt crushed
like an insect under the spike of mother's high-heeled shoe.

───※───

On the way to see Mother today, I coach the children, "Don't tell
anyone you're her grandchildren, and don't call her grandma."

"But why, Mom?" I can tell by Thomas's serious expression that he's
trying to understand something that makes no sense, and wants a reasonable answer. I fumble for words, but just end up repeating Mother's
instructions. Rachel leans over and kisses my cheek. "Why doesn't she
want you? She should be proud of you."

I stare straight ahead at the road that bisects oceans of corn, unable
to find an answer to my children's questions. I wipe a tear off my cheek
when Rachel isn't looking.

Mother's building is in a neighborhood of lively shops and tree-lined
streets. Children's voices echo across the avenue from the Lincoln Park
zoo. My kids are restless to get out of the car, but I circle round and
round in frustration—there's no place to park. I decide to drop them off
at the hotel with stern instructions not to tell anyone who they are.

As I drive away, it suddenly occurs to me that I'm doing just what
Mother has demanded—accepting her crazy logic and passing it on
to my kids. I keep feeling compelled to seek her out, though I'm still
deathly afraid of her temper. She's so unpredictable, fully capable of
a dangerous, irrational rage. I want to protect my children from her,
but I also want us to try to get along together. Everywhere I go, I see
"normal" families sharing vacations and holidays. That never happened
with us. When I was young, no one got along well enough to share a
holiday. The few times Mother did come for Christmas or Easter, the
day was memorable only for how terrible the fights were. Usually she'd
go storming off and return to Chicago early.

When I get to the hotel, Rachel runs to me excited, her cheeks
flushed. "Mom, everything is all right. The desk people asked us who
we were, so I told them we were there to see Miss Myers, that we're
her grandchildren, so they called her and told her we're here! Nothing
bad happened."

"You what? You told them? I told you not . . ." I hear Mother's words
spilling from my mouth. Shocked, I stop talking, but I'm worried about

the kids. If they displease Mother, what might she do? By the time we arrive at her door I'm breathless with anxiety, but she motions us in with no fuss, and the visit proceeds without any disasters. I observe the children watching my mother, their solemn eyes taking in everything. It is clear that they're uncomfortable when her sharp voice corrects them, telling Rachel she must have perfect posture at all times and telling Thomas not to bite his fingernails. They look at her as if to say: You're a complete stranger, so why are you telling us what to do?

After dinner, Mother ushers us through the back door of the hotel, and Thomas whispers to Rachel, "She doesn't want anyone to know we're hers."

My children are wise beyond their years, healthy enough to see through Mother's crazy logic, which is more than you can say about me. I'm stuck in my own kind of madness, still believing that if I just keep trying, someday she'll turn into a loving, welcoming grandmother.

It will be my youngest child who finally gets me to accept the ugly truth.

⚜

The next summer, I repeat the routine, going to see Mother once again, this time only Thomas at my side. Rachel is staying with her father. Thomas asks me if we can tell anyone who we are. I just shake my head, unwilling to mouth the same stupid instructions of the year before.

The three of us eat at a café close to her hotel. While I'm out of the room making motel reservations, Mother has Thomas all to herself. I don't know what she says to him, but when I come back, he's been alone for several minutes, and now he's acting strange. He's limp, and his head droops onto the table in some kind of stupor; it takes some effort to rouse him. Finally, he sits up and opens one lazy eye, staring at me with an empty, forlorn expression, as if a vampire had sucked away all his personality. I'm horrified. I'm so used to Mother, I don't notice how drained I feel when I'm with her, but my son is not used to her. That is a good thing.

Thomas stares at me flatly, finally opening the other eye. "Why do you bring us here when she doesn't want us?"

His words stun me into a whole new perspective, but right now I just want him to be okay. I get him to stand up and put on his jacket, desperately hoping he'll turn back into a little boy again and not this zombie-like person. My heart is pounding, everything is tumbling around in my mind.

He's right: Mother doesn't want us. She never has. All my life, I've tried to get this woman to do something she simply isn't capable of doing: to love.

I kneel down to look Thomas in the eye, a prickly, sick feeling spreading throughout my body. "You're right, Thomas. I'll tell you this, and I mean it, you'll never come here again, and neither will I."

I make a silent pact with myself never to come begging to Mother again. This is the last time my son ever sees his grandmother.

I find my mother, who acts as if everything is normal. She thanks us for coming and tells Thomas and me to write to her. I politely kiss her on the cheek, and we take our leave. Mentally, I say good-bye to the woman who gave birth to me, the decades of her betrayal burning through my body, my sense of who I am and what kind of mother I have have been stripped down to the basics.

How this afternoon has changed me will become more evident over the next few hours, and the next four years. I will find that leaving my mother behind, and abandoning the dreams I'd always had to win her, isn't so easy.

Lost

Aʟʟ ɪs ʙʀᴏᴋᴇɴ, *dark and ashen, with no hope in sight. The landscape I have fought against for so long is all around me now. Rumbling thunderclouds hover overhead, gray and empty of life. No one inhabits the world that I am lost in. I am alone, without comfort or nurture. There are no trees to reassure me, only scorched earth, powdered dust. I stumble and fall, my cries echoing across the emptiness.*

No, no! I cry out my protest, but to no avail. A voice tells me that this is the way it is, this has always been true, this darkness. All my life I have tried to make it not so, and at last I have failed. This darkness is the fundamental reality of my life. My mother doesn't want to be my mother. She never has.

Scenes march across the landscape from my past: my eager waiting for her at the train station, my excitement when she arrived at the door on a surprise visit. I feel again the grief that swallowed me every time she left, my pain at her obvious delight in leaving me in Enid with Gram to return to Chicago alone. I finally admit the truth to myself: That is where her heart always was, in that other place, where I was not.

No! I can't bear it. My mother doesn't love me. Vera was right; my mother doesn't love me . . .

Finally, I can't fight any longer. All right then—I admit it. I have no mother. You don't want me, Mother? I am not your daughter? So be it. I will stop resisting. You win.

We are not mother and daughter.

So now I belong to no one. No one will hold and comfort me. Okay, I can survive that. You never nurtured me anyway. It was just a fantasy I had.

I am alone? Fine. It's better than trailing after you like a lost puppy. All you do is criticize and abuse me anyway. Why the hell do I want you? What good are you to me? All you do is hurt and reject me. I won't let you do the same thing to my children.

Have it your way, Mother. I do not exist for you.

I promise to leave you alone.

I'm Not Your Daughter

THAT VERY NIGHT, after cutting short our visit with Mother, the threads of my previous history snapped.

My new story began ragged and raw. I screamed in the bathtub, a towel in my mouth so that Thomas, asleep in the motel bedroom, wouldn't hear me. A lifetime of grief and rage poured out of my body, wrenched from the depths of my being. Words of surrender and protest, sorrow and anger, repeated over and over again in my mind. Everything I'd held onto, everything that had given my life purpose, broke into pieces. For a time that night in a motel bathroom in the middle of the Illinois cornfields, I had no identity. The person I had called "me" ceased to exist.

Everything I'd tried to do to heal the past, to create a better future for my children and me, now seemed futile and pointless. Layers of shock eventually wore away, and in my new consciousness I could see so clearly what was true and what was not true. I began to accept this new reality. It was clear that I had defined my life around an illusion: that one day my mother would wake up and see me. She'd open her arms and take me in, sobbing her apologies. That one day she would be proud to call me her daughter.

I felt clear in my decision not to write her, call her, or try to manipulate her into being different. There was nothing I could do to make her love me or accept me. I had tried everything.

Whether from newfound clarity or the unmet need for a positive end to our story, I made another promise to myself that night: when Mother became ill and was dying, I would attend her despite everything. I believed in the possibility of transformation at the end of life such as what happened with Gram. I didn't want to miss that chance for Mother and me.

Four years would go by before our next contact. And when it came, all our history, all the generations of mothers, lost and found, would rise up like invisible ghosts.

Motherless Child

Sometimes I feel like a motherless child
Motherless children have a real hard time
Motherless children have such a real hard time,
So long, so long, so long.

FROM A NEGRO SPIRITUAL BY HARRY BURLEIGH

OVER THE NEXT four years, my healing journey continued. My spiritual quest, a search for peace, love, and forgiveness, kept me going during many periods of inner turmoil. Approaching fifty years of age was especially difficult. Memories of Gram lurching around the house like someone half dead and of Mother behaving outrageously made me terribly anxious that I might become like them as I grew older. I was constantly vigilant for signs in myself of their irrational qualities.

My search for understanding, along with my unresolved emotional pain and dark moods, had led me long ago to leave my Baptist and Episcopal roots and discover other forms of spirituality. I read the works of spiritual teachers, practiced mindful breathing, and developed a calm centeredness in meditation. Though I never attended meditation retreats, I learned that flashes of enlightenment can occur at any moment—while walking down the street or petting a cat. Nurturing plants, chopping vegetables, and interacting with a child can all provide a means of paying close attention, being present, and finding inner peace. Of course, my work as a therapist, listening with complete attention to each client, had always been a healing meditation.

During this time, I became even more dedicated to my old standby—journal writing. It was an extraordinarily liberating practice for me to capture in writing my agonies and insights. Little did I know that writing would someday play such a significant role in my work and my life.

On Easter Sunday in 1995, four years after my self-initiated break with Mother, I found myself reflecting on the theme of resurrection, viewing it as a symbol of ego death and renewal. I asked myself, "What needs to be attended to that I haven't had the courage to face? What aspect of my life needs renewal?" The answer came swiftly: my relationship with my mother.

I had begun to wonder if she was well after receiving various legal documents in the mail, including her will, in which I was named her only heir. I signed the papers as she requested, but included no personal note, in keeping with the promise I had made to myself. I wasn't ready to let her back into my emotional life.

Since my breakdown in the motel room, my general attitude and sense of self-worth had improved. After all, Mother was no longer tearing open my rejection wound several times a year. By refusing to contact her, I was breaking my see-saw pattern of thrilling hope followed by devastating defeat. I was no longer holding onto a fantasy about my mother that had only hurt me in the past. I knew it was essential in my growth and healing work to keep saying no to further abuse. However, I was concerned about her health.

Shaking with nerves, I dialed her number, stopped, put the receiver back down. What if she's nasty to me again? What if she attacks me? I took a deep breath. If she does, I'll just hang up. I tried again. Tingles went up and down my body when I heard Mother's voice on the other end of the phone, a voice I'd always loved. I was surprised to find her in a tranquil mood. Relieved, I made normal conversation, filling her in on my activities and those of my children. She said she was sorry she hadn't heard from me for so long, but there was no blame in her voice. The conversation led into reminiscences about our Iowa relatives, and eventually our past. I told her that I'd put it in perspective by now. She spoke the oft-repeated phrase—she had done the best she could when I was a child. Suddenly it became clear to me that this simple statement was true. She had done all she was capable of. Now it was up to me to accept it and find whatever peace and forgiveness I could.

A deep sense of compassion for my mother as an abused and abandoned child in her own right came over me, and I felt sorry for that little girl who had lost her mother too. Before hanging up, we said we loved each other. Words of love had so infrequently passed between us, it was like a beautiful dream to speak them and hear them that day. After I put down the phone, I sat without moving for a long time, absorbing our surprising conversation. My four years of serious psychological and spiritual work—letting go of the past and knitting together a new sense of self—had borne fruit. I wondered if Mother had sensed my acceptance of her, and if it had influenced her, in turn, to be more accepting of me.

⬥

Six weeks later, my intuition that Mother might be ill was proven true. I received a frantic call from her, which led to a conversation with her doctor about a spot on her lung. Even more terrifying, she had a brain tumor. On the phone later that same day, Mother demanded that I be on hand when she entered the hospital for further tests the next day. My heart pounding wildly with the shocking news, I chose not to challenge her imperious tone and simply agreed. I put everything else in my life on hold and took the red-eye to Chicago.

After the long flight from San Francisco, I felt I had entered a dream. Suddenly I was off the plane and in a cab riding through the bustling city, the Sears building looming before me. The city bore many memories for me of those years when I had gotten to know Daddy and Mother away from Gram's negative influence. I frequently came up on the train from college and imbibed of my parents' love for their city. From the time I was little, Chicago pulled at my heart. It had seemed to me then a magical and magnificent place, where my fairy-tale parents lived without me.

During the cab ride through a city filled with vibrant green trees and lawns—so unlike dry California—I thought about the cycles of nature and about the cycles in my own life. Now it looked as if Mother's life would end in this city where mine had begun.

Making my way to her place with the usual knot of anxiety in my stomach, memories swirled around me. She let me into her small apartment, kissing me hastily on the cheek. Her sweet scent enveloped me as I clung to her for a moment, still unable to believe that she wouldn't live forever.

I soon realized that she had developed some memory problems. She left cigarettes burning in ashtrays, and left stove burners blazing long after she was finished using them. When the time came, we made our way to the hospital by bus rather than cab, because she insisted on it. The fact that it was raining, and that I was fatigued from my trip and had two suitcases to carry, couldn't change her mind. Despite her illness and its attendant anxieties, she was as stubborn as ever.

At the admissions desk, Mother was given forms to sign. I was horrified to see "TERMINAL" written on them in big letters. I wanted to grab the papers out of her hands, to protect her from this awful pronouncement. Mother and I hadn't spoken about her diagnosis, but the doctor had told me she was likely to die within three months—by August.

She became frantic when she couldn't find something in her purse. "It's all lost, it's all lost," she wailed, sounding like a child, and I realized again that she was not quite herself. She must be feeling vulnerable and angry all at once, I thought—a dangerous combination. I held my breath, remembering how unpredictable her behavior could be, even when she was at her best. One thing I knew for certain: At some point, the denial of me as her daughter would come up. I was prepared, but my heart beat fast as I thought about confronting her, as I knew I must.

We followed a burly man down a warren of polished corridors until we reached the oncology unit. Mother's roommate, a kindly gray-haired lady, and her attendant greeted us politely. I immediately felt sorry for her, having my mother as a roommate. Poor thing, I thought, you have no idea what you're in for.

Don't Tell Them You're My Daughter

IMMEDIATELY, MOTHER BEGAN holding court, sitting on her bed in her street clothes, brandishing an unlit cigarette between her fingers. Various hospital personnel bustled in and out to check on her. After about an hour, a perky-looking woman carrying a clipboard arrived, saying she needed some more information for the records. When she noticed me standing on the other side of the room, she broke into a cheerful smile and looked back and forth between Mother and me, taking in our faces, no doubt observing our family resemblance. Squaring my shoulders, I took a deep breath. I knew what was coming.

"Are you two related?" she asked me, expecting the typical response. "You look so much alike."

Trying to keep my voice from wavering, I answered, "Yes. I'm her daughter."

The intensity of Mother's response took even me by surprise. She jerked to attention on the bed and screamed at the top of her lungs, "Don't tell them you're my daughter!"

The scene that ensued would have been hilarious if not for its tragic history. The cheery lady with the clipboard was speechless with astonishment, her mouth dropping nearly to her chest. The roommate gasped, and the attendant who sat beside me froze in mid-breath.

I spoke again, in placating tones. "Please, Mother. Don't be silly. You know I'm your daughter."

The woman with the clipboard regained her composure and managed to complete the interview. I could imagine her thoughts as she left the room in a hurry: "I've met my share of crazy people, but these two take the cake."

I knew Mother would deny me. I had meditated about it, worked on it in therapy, told my close friends and my children that I was sure I'd have to confront her rejection once again. Yet despite all my preparations, I felt the blood drain from my face, my emotions in turmoil. I felt cursed again by my own mother, under her old spell again.

I took deep breaths, trying to restrain my tears, but one escaped and meandered down my cheek. When a small moan slipped from my lips, the roommate's attendant looked up at me with kind, soft eyes and said, "There now, it's all right. It's all right, dear." She touched my arm. "Don't let it get to you, honey. Some people can't help themselves."

Her simple kindness brought on even more tears. I allowed myself to weep silently, comforted by this stranger who had witnessed my mother's denial of me. For the first time in my life, someone objective was validating my perception that Mother's behavior was wrong. This woman's sympathy and support convinced me at last that I wasn't the one who was crazy. In that moment, an old, old weight was lifted from my shoulders.

But Mother's abuse wasn't over. The next day she slapped me for not handing the phone to her on demand, and she let me know that I was still persona non grata with her friends. "Don't you try to talk to anyone about me. No one knows about you, and it's too late to start now."

I spent hours pacing up and down the hospital halls.

***

Mother's moods were mercurial, as always. The first evening at the hospital, she lay on the bed, curled up like a child. She looked small and helpless, her dark hair spread on the pillow. Poor little Mother, I thought. She seemed so lost. She smiled weakly at me and asked me to rub her back, returning us to one of the few tender things we had ever shared. She moaned under my touch, telling me how good it felt. I had been trained in recent years as a masseuse, and I suspect she noticed my expertise. Nothing more was said, but for many minutes we were connected as mother and daughter once more. When I tucked her in and fluffed her pillow, she looked up at me with such innocence. "Where did you learn to take care of people like this?" she asked with a kind of awe.

"I had children, Mother. I learned by taking care of them."

I don't know if she caught my deeper meaning, that children can teach us to be tender and loving, something she didn't allow herself to experience. She only smiled again and said, "You are very good and kind."

I walked away in a peaceful frame of mind, grateful for her acknowledgement. What would be next for us, I wondered, on this journey to her death?

***

The day of the biopsy, Mother was upset and irritable, as one would expect. She hated to have to wear a hospital gown, she hated having to do what others told her to do. She fought and complained all the way. When she returned from the procedure, she put her street clothes back on and told me stubbornly that she was going home. I knew better, but didn't argue. In fact, I had no idea what arrangements were being made for her.

As we had feared, the spot on her lung was cancer, but the doctor told me it was the brain tumor that would kill her. My breath caught in my throat at this news. Right now, Mother's will seemed so powerful. She was certain that she would live, and it was hard not to believe her.

The doctor went on to say that Mother had been disruptive the night before, sending nurses home in tears. He assumed the brain tumor was causing her erratic behavior.

"Oh, it's nothing new," I told him. "She's always been abusive and nasty, but usually she just focuses it on me." I gave him a few examples of her bizarre behavior patterns.

"Let's get a psychiatrist up here," the doctor suggested. "We'll see what he has to say."

For the most part, Mother treated me like an interloper. She ordered me not to get involved in her care, not to make any decisions. She said she had an attorney who was in charge of everything. I didn't challenge her, but I ran my own show behind her back. She was clearly not fully capable of making her own decisions. I had behind-the-scenes conversations with each of her doctors.

One afternoon, Mother let me know that I was not welcome in her room. "I'm expecting company," she announced. She smoothed her best dress and put the finishing touches on her blush and eyeliner. Obviously, the expected visitor was a male.

"Who's coming to see you?"

"None of your damned business."

I took a deep breath and asked, "Mother, don't you think it's time you introduced me to your friends? After all, I'm here to help take care of you."

"It's just too awkward," she snapped. "People like John from the restaurant don't know about you, and it's too late now."

"Let me see if I understand you, Mother." Here I was, fuming again despite my intention to stay calm and cool. "You've never told your friends that you have a daughter or grandchildren?"

"I've told you before!" she snarled. "It's too late. They've known me for fifteen years and they'll wonder why I never told them before. It's too complicated. Just go away for a few hours."

I slammed out of the room and took a cab to the Chicago Art

Institute, where I tried to soothe myself with art. I saw such beauty in the paintings of the Impressionists, my favorite artists, but I couldn't surrender to it. I ached with the knowledge that, even as she approached her death, Mother could casually toss me aside in order to keep up her pretense. I stormed through the museum, at times inspired by the light and color of the exhibit, but mostly weighed down with misery.

I was still steaming when I returned to the hospital. I stepped from the elevator and immediately saw Mother charging frantically up and down the hall, clutching an unlit cigarette. She started screaming at me on sight. "Where have you been? I've been waiting for you for hours!"

Full of my own frustration and fury, I shot back. "I got out of your way, Mother. Like an idiot I continue to do as you tell me, disappearing conveniently when you want me out of the way." I stood a couple of feet away, glaring at her. "I am your daughter, do you understand me? I left my work and my children and flew here to help you because you are my mother and you needed me. How can you pretend that I don't exist?"

Mother and I went on shouting as we paced the hallway. People looked at us aghast, but I didn't care. This was my last chance to say words I'd never spoken, and I wasn't about to stay silent.

"Mother, you've pretended you didn't have a daughter, you've refused to introduce me to your friends. Stop denying that I'm your daughter. I can't stand it any longer!"

By now we were standing in a waiting room, looking out at rain falling on the rooftops. Suddenly, she fell silent for a moment. Then, in a childlike voice, she asked, "I did those things? When?"

Instantly, the fight drained from me. I'd said what I needed to. I wanted Mother to say she was sorry, but I could see that she had no recollection right now of what she had done in the past—whether from the brain tumor or simple denial, I couldn't say. All I knew for sure was that she was dying. I put my arms around her and held her close.

"Mother, don't worry about it. Let's go have some lunch."

Her demeanor had completely changed. She seemed at that moment more like a little girl than a grown woman. Finally I had told my Mother the truth. I had stood up for myself.

Emptied of the feelings I'd always suppressed about her rejection of me, my heart felt peaceful as we walked to her room, my mother small and helpless beside me.

The Diagnosis: Manic Depression

THE PSYCHIATRIST WAS a soft-spoken man in his late forties. He was handsome, with dark hair and eyes and a gentle, well-bred demeanor. Mother had spent all morning preening, putting on her make-up and fixing her hair. When Dr. Hart greeted her, she minced a couple of steps toward him, chattering wildly. She carried her unlit cigarette aloft in a haughty gesture, acting every bit like Gram used to in her over-the-top way.

Mother flirted shamelessly with the doctor, sashaying across the room, acting so much like an out-of-control teenager that my face flushed. Didn't she realize that her every word was being noted and analyzed? Did she really think that he would be romantically interested in her? I watched in fascination, but soon she waved me away, desperate for his full attention. I motioned to him as I left, affirming a previously made arrangement to talk on the phone after his meeting with Mother. She shouted after me, "Now you stay away. Don't you talk to him behind my back!"

For the next hour I wandered the halls, circling around the nurse's station, going down the elevator and coming back up, curious about what the psychiatrist would say. To my knowledge, no mental health professional had ever assessed my mother. A few years earlier she had told me that a doctor suggested she see a psychiatrist. She'd laughed uproariously in her trademark cackle. "I don't need a psychiatrist. Why, they're all crazier than anyone, aren't they, Linda?" It was a typical dig, her asking me, a psychotherapist, to agree with her outrageous statement.

Eventually, I spotted Dr. Hart talking on the phone. He waved and told me to wait for him in the next wing. Ever vigilant, Mother yelled from down the hall, "Don't you dare talk to him. Go away. You're nosy and rude!"

I ran off to our secret rendezvous. It was farcical, Mother chasing the doctor around the halls, trying to keep him away from me; Dr. Hart and I surreptitiously making arrangements to talk. I hiked to the next wing, and he joined me a few minutes later. We sat in comfortable chairs that faced each other in a room dimly lit by sunlight filtering through Venetian blinds. He gave me a conspiratorial grin and said, "I don't think she'll find us here." He leaned on his elbows, his eyes the most striking thing about him as he asked me about our history.

I told him the whole story.

"My mother was abandoned as a baby when her mother left her to work in Des Moines, then Chicago. I don't know much about her early life, but I was told that she wandered from place to place, living with her great-grandmother Josephine, for whom she's named, and with an aunt on her father's side. When Mother was thirteen, my grandmother finally brought her to Chicago, where she felt unhappy and out of place. They had a violent, screaming relationship. Mother ran away to get married when she was seventeen, but her mother insisted the marriage be annulled." Dr. Hart listened silently, occasionally jotting something down in his notebook.

"I don't know anything about her young adult years, but she married my father when she was twenty-nine soon had me. They divorced when I was one. I was with her for only four years. For a brief period we lived with Gram in Wichita, but mother decided to go back to Chicago and we never lived together again. She would visit me occasionally when I was little, but once I got older and started coming to Chicago, she didn't want anyone to know she had a child or grandchildren. She won't let anyone she knows meet me even now. I don't know what we'll do when she leaves the hospital; she's told me nothing about her arrangements. There's some attorney she's having an imaginary love affair with who's supposed to take care of things."

The doctor watched me attentively, absorbing it all. I went on.

"Gram, her mother, who raised me from the time I was six, sat in a hole in the couch for years, crying, raging, and ranting. She hated my father and tried to live her life through me. Mother and Gram were a lot alike, negative and critical, staying up half the night, ranting and raving for hours when they got mad." As I talked I realized how much Gram and Mother approached the world, and me, in similar ways.

When I had finished pouring out the story, he was silent for a very long moment. "Your life must have been very difficult," he said, his eyes reflecting his compassion. Laying out my entire life in one sitting to a stranger had a profound affect on me. I felt like crying with joy and relief. He had seen with his own eyes how my mother acted; he understood how it had shaped my whole life. I bowed my head and thanked him. Then Dr. Hart delivered his assessment.

"My diagnosis is bipolar disorder, but manic-depression better describes the mood swings, the ups and downs. I'd say your mother is hypomanic." He went on to say that there was underlying depression, but that Mother was more obviously manic in her behaviors. I asked him about Gram, her moodiness, her bouts of crying, the hate letters. "She was more melancholic, more on the depressed part of the spectrum, but it all falls under the same diagnosis."

I stared at him in silence, all the puzzle pieces fitting into place. The monster that had haunted my family for generations finally had a name. I had given both Gram and Mother a dozen different diagnoses over the years, but this one suddenly made perfect sense. As I sat there absorbing Dr. Hart's words, it dawned on me that medication existed for this illness. I asked if treatment could have helped them.

"Medication could have helped, but the problem is making the diagnosis. These kinds of people stay away from psychiatrists. Most of them don't like to take their medication anyway, especially the manic ones—they like their highs. Nevertheless, I plan to recommend it for your mother."

I sat with him for a while longer, trying to comprehend the full meaning of what he'd told me. Naming Gram's and Mother's disease swept the scattered ashes of my childhood into orderly boxes. There could have been solutions, if anyone had named it before. There might have been a better outcome . . . "if only." I saw Gram and Mother through a new lens now—they were mentally ill, unable to control and come to terms with their own pain, urges, wishes, dreams, and ultimately their very lives. The sorrow of it all weighed heavily on me. I also saw my own struggles anew—my dark nights of the soul and the ups and downs of mood. While not as striking as theirs, they were still a significant influence on my life and my children's lives. This illness has lived in our chemistry, an unwelcome but real guest in our family. All this was so complex. I knew from my studies that the disease includes an alive, creative, and exciting element. What a paradox.

<hr/>

Mother no longer needed to be hospitalized, but the psychiatrist agreed she wasn't ready or able to live on her own. When I explained that she wouldn't let me make any arrangements for her, he said that he might be able to help.

It was a strange day when my mother officially became a psychiatric patient. An entourage of attendants and I led her from her room in oncology to the geriatric psychiatry ward. She had been told that she would be more comfortable there. She said she loved the "nice, kind, doctor." I suspected it was because on some level she knew she needed the kind of help he could provide. One person in the little parade was a jive-talking orderly who obviously enjoyed kidding around. He noticed the family resemblance and asked if the patient was my mother. I said she was, watching mother's reaction carefully, prepared for her scream of denial. This time she said nothing.

I settled her into her new room. The nurse's station was in the middle of the ward, with patients' rooms splayed out around it like the spokes of a wheel. I saw families gathered around some of the patients, and wondered about their histories. How had their lives been affected by mental illness?

Mother became disturbed when a nurse wanted to take her purse. She didn't understand why, and clutched it to her chest. The nurses, used to handling irrational patients, finally convinced her to let it go, but Mother was too nervous and disoriented to sit and talk with me as I prepared to say good-bye to her. I had been in Chicago for a week and needed to go home. I stood a few inches away from her, wondering what to say, aware that we had so little time left. Never one for emotional good-byes, Mother turned her back to me. I tried to hug her, but she just kept murmuring, "Why did they take my purse?"

I kissed her on the cheek and walked away, my mind reeling with the astonishing idea: "Mother is in a psychiatric unit. She really is mentally ill."

After so many years of not understanding her, I felt great relief with this new diagnosis. At last she was in a place where she might feel understood and accepted. It was easier now for me to feel compassion for her, to understand more deeply how difficult it must have been to be so alone with her demons. I didn't know my mother, not really. I had no inner knowledge of her as a person, and perhaps she didn't know herself either. She was lost, and always had been. Those were my thoughts as I walked away from the hospital, not knowing if I'd ever see my mother again in this world.

Mother was happy in the psychiatric unit and often told me on the phone how much she liked the "lovely" doctor, but after two weeks she was scheduled to be released. In the meantime, I'd had several conversations with the attorney she had recently hired. This new young and handsome attorney was shocked to find out that Josephine had a daughter or any living family. He had said during our first phone call that he would discuss nursing homes with her. I warned him of her bad temper and stubborn will, of her irrationality and furious demands. At first he wasn't concerned, but after a week he was calling me for advice nearly every day. When he suggested a well-appointed nursing home as the next step, Mother would have none of it. It almost amused me to watch another person go through the same kind of hell as I had with her. The lawyer was persistent, however, and finally—with the help of the nursing home director, an angel named Margie—Mother moved in.

Margie became a maternal figure. Mother would curl up on the couch in her office, talking nonstop. Margie had been a nurse for many years and understood old people, the mentally ill, the dying. Mother seemed to sense this woman's compassion and deep soul acceptance of her. Perhaps she had never felt such an unconditional presence before in her life.

At the nursing home, Mother's queenly demeanor was indulged. She was allowed extra favors and given sterling attention. When she acted out by running off to have dinner at her favorite restaurant across town, she was brought back with gentleness. Mother loved it when Margie hugged her and tucked her into bed like a little child. During this period, Margie tried to help Mother face her impending death, but Mother always laughed her off.

As for our relationship, Mother still treated me like cast off rags. Once, I recorded a phone conversation with her, just to preserve the sound of her voice. At times it was her usual throaty monologue, but when I said something she didn't like, she responded with a scathing attack in a high-pitched rant. To this day, I can't bring myself to listen to that tape.

During that summer I kept a journal entitled "Requiem for a Ghost Mother," chronicling events from the day she was moved to the hospital's psychiatric unit.

A deep purple sorrow rides within me. I ride it, like the horse of death. I am chained to it as we careen through this dark time, galloping as if the devil is chasing us. Sometimes it feels that through my mother—and before that, my grandmother—the devil has been chasing me. Some people romanticize mental illness. For me, there is nothing interesting or fascinating about it. It is pure pain, the kind of thin, trilling pain you feel when the dentist drills with no Novocain. The pure pain when you slice your finger or have one of those late labor contractions. It doesn't go away. It doesn't get pretty and light. It is what it is. Pain is.

Who am I? Who are we? What is it about, this trip though the vale of earth shot through with flashes of light? I have tried to understand it all by becoming a therapist. I thought there was a way out. This kind of ending with my mother makes me feel as if I'm strapped in a jet plane. There is great, frightening turbulence, and I can't get off. I have to stay here until the turbulence stops or we land. No escape.

She is lost, the woman inside the illness. She is lost, the mother I always looked for when she came to visit. I'd wait and watch for the human to come out of the demanding, whiny child in a woman's body. I'd wait for her, holding my breath. She always showed up, for a few minutes—when she played Liebestraum on the piano. When she asked me to scratch her back.

I hadn't predicted that I would experience such pain about my mother's death. I thought I would escape.

Mother kept up her old ways, trying to control my access to the lawyer and to Margie, but behind the scenes we all worked together. I told Margie I might want to be with Mother at her deathbed, and she agreed to let me know when that time came. I was torn. I wanted to keep my promise to myself that I would be with Mother when she died, but there were still occasional torrents of abuse. My stamina was wearing thin. Despite feeling more sorry for her, I couldn't take any more of her attacks. I was afraid I'd lose control if she tore me down one more time. Fifty years was enough.

As it turned out, the effects of the brain tumor made it possible for me to honor my vow. During the first week of August, Mother lost her ability to speak. Margie told me Mother was failing fast and that now was the time to come. All summer, Mother had told Margie that she didn't want to see me. The week she lost her speech, Margie said, she became very docile and weak, sweetly smiling at everyone. The last day Mother could speak, she said yes when Margie asked if she wanted me to come.

I got on the red-eye at once and flew to Chicago.

Requiem for a Ghost Mother

I ARRIVED IN hot, muggy Chicago as a reluctant visitor to the valley of death. I wondered how I could spend time with my dying mother without succumbing to her anger. I followed the orderly down the carpeted halls of the nursing home. On each side of the hallway were people in various stages of illness, people who had once been young and vibrant. They had all been sent to this place to die. The nursing home was well appointed, clean, even luxurious, with its stylish furniture and modern paintings, but a heavy sadness filled my chest.

The orderly gestured toward a room and left me. Confused, I lingered in the doorway, noticing a woman lying in the far bed. She had long gray hair and a sharp face, and she stared at me with suspicion. In the other bed was another old woman I didn't recognize. She was bald. IV tubes hung from arms that repetitiously lifted and fell back to the bed. This couldn't be my mother, I thought, yet there was something familiar about her. I looked more closely and a moment later noticed a white birthmark on her left eye. I caught my breath. This must be my mother, but where were her lovely dark hair, her beautiful face?

I was still hesitating at the threshold of the room, trying to grasp this horrifying reality, when Mother caught sight of me. She cried out, an animal-like keening that cut through me, her trembling arms held out to me, begging me to come to her. I crossed the room quickly and gathered her up. "Mommy, oh, I'm so sorry," I whispered, draping myself gently across her chest while she clutched me like a terrified child.

In that moment, our past melted away. My mother had always been a lost soul, she'd never felt truly loved, and now she was helpless and dying. She sobbed and wept uncontrollably, clinging to me. Out of her desperate need, she seemed to realize that I, and only I, could help her. We clung together for a long time, weeping. My heart was broken by her pitiful condition, the depth of her wounds and fear. I broke away to wipe her face, but with surprising strength she pulled me back to her chest, where she held me so tightly I could barely breathe, sobbing, crying, for everything in her life it seemed. The nurses stood by, silenced by the pathos that was unfolding in front of them. They and the old woman in the other bed stared at us; bells and footsteps continued in the hall, but mother and I existed in a separate world of our own.

Finally, after an immeasurable time, I stood back to look at her. She had the look of a trapped animal, her eyes constricted in abject terror.

She was dying, and she could no longer deny it. She clutched at me again, her fingers digging into my skin. Never before had I felt such tenderness toward her. After a while, she allowed me to sit in a chair beside her but she wouldn't let me release her hand for hours. From time to time, she gathered me to her chest, wailing. For hours, my mother's grief, and my own, swelled to the surface in waves.

All I could do was take care of her basic needs, wiping her mouth, caressing her forehead. For the first time in my life, performing these age-old human tasks, I felt whole. When Mother drifted off to sleep, I walked around the nursing home feeling more sure of myself than ever before. Despite the terrible circumstances, I felt proud and elated. My mind critiqued this scene: How can I feel happy when my mother is dying a terrible death? Then, in a flash, it hit me: At last, after a lifetime of longing, I have a mother who accepts and embraces me. Everyone can see that I am her daughter.

For ten days I took care of Mother's physical body, watching her medications and making sure the nurses did what was needed to control her pain. Though she couldn't speak, she could understand me, so I stood at her bedside and told the old stories, weaving the web of the generations of our family. I talked about Blanche and Gram, Josephine—Blanche's mother—and my grandfather Blaine. I reminisced with her about our visits in Wapello, the doll clothes that Bernie had made, and the long prayers that Grandpa said over dinner. I showed Mother photographs of my children and told her stories about their lives. I told her about my life, too, stories I'd never shared before—my life as a therapist, my writing, books, and music.

One afternoon, a priest from the parish down the street administered the last rites to Mother, as had been done with Gram, marking a cross on her forehead in oil. During this process, Mother began to choke. Margie and the nurses turned her over, exposing her bare back. I couldn't bear to see my beautiful mother like that, bereft of her dignity, with no control over her body. I left the room and stood in the hall to cry. When the priest was finished with Mother, I told him some of our story. He listened patiently, compassion and concern in his eyes. I knew there was nothing he could do, but it helped me to tell another impartial person our sad generational saga.

Several days later, it was clear that Mother was about to die, though the doctors couldn't predict the course of events or how long it would take. She needed more and more medication to keep her calm. When its effects began to wear off, she cried and wept inconsolably. I tried to prepare myself for what was to come. During the daytime, I was busy with her, but at night I was alone with my thoughts and memories.

One night, I dreamed that Mother was in the next room, crying out for me, dying alone. Convoluted circumstances in the dream kept me from getting to her. I was separated from my mother, powerless to help, while I listened to her terrible death cries.

I woke up from this dream shaking and weeping, wrapped in its horror. I felt again the terror and bone-wrenching mother-loss I'd experienced so often when I was young. Kaleidoscopic images tumbled through my mind, one after the other—Mommy getting off the train in Perry, her soft fingers on my skin soothing the ache I'd been carrying since the last time I saw her. Gram with her cigarette holder, her face showing only a hint of the complex feelings she had for her daughter. Mommy as a little girl, abandoned and lost, aching for her own mother who came to see her so infrequently. Mother had been that girl who felt unwanted, who yearned for love her whole life.

My other mothers appeared—Blanche digging in the garden, eating a strawberry, juice running down her chin. Josephine, that stern-faced pioneer woman, working the land, birthing six children in a farmhouse with only a midwife to attend her. In my mind's eye, I'm at the train station again, where Mommy is leaving me. It's the station in Wichita, that first place of abandonment. The whistle shrieks and I tremble with dread. Mommy is leaving me. My precious Mommy is all I've know for four years, but I can't stop her from tearing us apart. I'm crying, "Don't leave, don't leave. Don't die, Mommy, don't die."

An ancient grief overwhelmed me. I had spent my adult life trying not to love her, trying to reject her before she rejected me, always failing miserably. I had tried to ignore her and I tried to win her, and neither strategy had worked. I understood now in the early hours of the dawn how much a daughter needs her mother, how deep the wounds get buried when she is gone.

Fifty years of suppressed feelings were shaken loose that morning. For a long time, I rocked on the bed, mourning for the losses of the generations, sobbing for my mother. Now that I knew how to love her, I wanted us to start over, to have another chance.

The next morning, Mother's eyes were closed, her breathing labored. As I stroked her face I knew she was gone from me. I thought of all the years we'd shared, and lost, sensing in the depths of my soul that the mother–daughter connection can never really be broken. This primal bond guides and shapes a woman's entire life. When it all goes adrift, when the connection is severed, a lifetime of grief and brokenness must be healed before the next generation can be free.

＊＊＊

As it happens, Mother dies without me at her side. I'm at Aunt Edith's at the time, recovering from the flu. The wind is blowing off the Mississippi, billowing the wet clothes I'm pinning to the clothesline, when the call comes from the nursing home. "Our condolences," says the nurse on the other end of the line. "Your mother has passed."

Aunt Edith, herself weakened from a series of strokes, carries in her arms a basket of fresh-picked tomatoes. The ripe, red tomatoes are voluptuous on the kitchen table where we gather over a cup of coffee and a piece of lemon meringue pie. I sit in her kitchen as I have since I was seven years old, the clocks ticking as they always have, while all around me the ghosts of the past dance through the room. All the mothers, so many memories . . .

＊＊＊

The day Mother is buried is August hot. At the gravesite, I inhale the scents of newly turned earth and freshly mown grass. As I sit under the blue Iowa sky, patches of white clouds scud by, making shadows on a nearby cornfield. A meadowlark sings as the wind whooshes through the cemetery, stirring the leaves of a sycamore tree. Here, Mother's soul flies free, beyond the body she pampered, the body that betrayed her. My mother, Josephine Elizabeth Myers, is finally free of her pain. At last, she can know silence and peace.

In the distance, a train whistle cries its lonely song, calling out across my beloved plains. It is calling out, as it always has, for me and for my mother.

＊＊＊

For a long time after she dies I dream of her. We are riding the train, the wheels click-clacking on the tracks, great ease and peace between us as I rest my head on her shoulder. We are traveling together now, in the same direction. In my dreams we are free, freer in her death than in her life to feel love and compassion for each other. Free at long last to be mother and daughter.

Silent, we watch the tracks coming together at the misty horizon, that place where the past and the future meet.

Epilogue

AFTER MY MOTHER died, I became free of the yearning that had plagued me all my life. No longer did my mother hover in far away Chicago, enticing me with promises that she would never fulfill. I began to feel normal. After all, everyone has a mother who dies someday.

After her death, I became even more determined to get to know her. I became insatiably curious about the lives of all my family members and undertook intensive genealogical research, combing through dusty courthouses in Iowa and scrolling through microfilm in libraries.

Blanche had told me that Gram left my mother when she was a baby, and I'd always believed that, but in the 1920 census I discovered that they were living together in Burlington, Iowa. They were still together when mother was five years old. In shock and disbelief, I put my head down and wept. All my life, I'd believed that Gram had left Mother behind when she was an infant. Perhaps when Blanche said "baby," she just meant "very young child."

Through reading the Wapello Republican, the newspaper owned by my grandfather's family, I tried to find out about my mother's early life. In the old newspapers, the social lives of local people are listed with colorful detail—births, guests, travels, illnesses. I read every weekly newspaper from 1914, when my mother's brother, Harrison, was born and died, through 1921, when the trail grew cold.

For at least three years, Gram and Mother and Blaine were together as a family, living in Wapello, where he worked for the newspaper. At some point, Blaine took a job, perhaps when the marriage began to fail, in Rock Island, Illinois, fifty miles away.

Blaine remarried when Mother was seven, and it is then that she was sent to live with Josephine, her great-grandmother. The discovery that my mother had lived with Gram for seven years gave me insight into her emotional troubles. My mother at age seven was no doubt deeply bonded with Gram. How and why Gram left her when Blaine remarried, no one knows.

❦

Gram's elopement with Blaine in 1911 when she was sixteen had been harshly judged by Blanche and the Iowa relatives, and was still passionately argued about sixty years later. Gram's flight to Chicago, where she took up an entirely new life and identity, did not make her popular among the plain folks who composed her family.

For years, I tried to understand why Gram was such a snob. I had confirmed that she never graduated from high school, but she must have been ashamed of her roots. Our Iowa relatives could sense that—thus the jokes they made at her expense about education and running off to Europe and wearing fancy clothes. Gram's family was working class and owned no land, having only rented the land they'd farmed all those years. They had little money or material possessions. She married into a middle-class professional family—Blaine's father was a newspaper owner, his grandfather an attorney who had served in the Iowa state legislature. They were educated people. She must have felt quite out of place when she lived with them, ignorant of the ways of their refined world.

So Gram reinvented herself as a worldly, sophisticated woman. She was self-educated by virtue of having read hundreds of books, and her travels to Europe helped her develop that English accent and her love of the fine life. Her second husband, a man with money, left her enough at his death so that she did not have to work again; that's when she moved us to Enid to be near Aunt Helen, who had moved there with Uncle Maj after the war.

Gram lived her own fantasy life through me, finding herself in a position to raise me when Mother left, and deciding clearly to take me on full time when I was six, interestingly close to the age that Mother was when Gram left her. I can imagine that she was determined to do it right this time. She wanted me to have the things she'd always yearned for. In her day, a fine, educated lady played the piano, learned foreign languages, and dressed perfectly; she had good manners and knew how to speak to anyone. This was the life Gram had never lived as a child or young woman. Mother didn't go along with Gram's program, except for playing the piano, and even that was against her will. "I always hated the piano," she confessed to me once.

So I became a pawn in the game between my grandmother and the rest of the world. I was the chosen one who was supposed to finally make Gram happy and proud.

<hr/>

The mystery surrounding my father has taken many years to sort out. I'm certain that the root of the conflict between Gram and him was due partly to their perhaps unconscious sexual attraction. She was only twelve years older than he, and still very beautiful. I don't understand why they came to hate each other, but perhaps it had something to do with money. Just before I was sent to Vera's, Gram hired a lawyer to sue my father for child support, which then was paid to Vera.

Relatives of my father told me that he originally thought I might not be his child, probably because he thought my mother was "nutty," as he put it, and loose with her affections. Her flirtatiousness was indeed outrageous enough to arouse his suspicions. Thus, perhaps, his comment on his deathbed: "So, you're a Myers after all."

Daddy's emotional ambivalence about me disappeared when he was dying, but I was not mentioned in his will. I had often wondered if the distance I felt from my parents was just my imagination, but indeed, in their own ways, they both rejected me.

⸻

Mr. Brauninger and Eva were missing from my life for twenty-nine years. During that time, I often dreamed that I was searching for them, as I also searched for Jodie and Keith. Perhaps my rather obsessive searching, before the Internet made locating people much easier, was related to the years I had spent waiting for my parents, yearning to know more about them.

I found Jim and Eva again through Keith's mother, who had their address. One morning in 1991, on my way to Uncle Willard's funeral, I waited for my old mentors in an airport corridor. There they were, as if appearing out of the mists of time: tall, willowy Mr. Brauninger and petite, delicate Eva. We hugged and gazed rapturously at each other. Mr. B.'s red hair was white now, but he exuded love from his blue eyes just as I'd always remembered.

I asked them if they had sensed my grandmother's violent temper and controlling nature. Mr. Brauninger said that he tried to help me just be a little girl and have fun by playing marbles with me. He added, "I used to look into the faces of my students and see the face of God."

For ten years we saw each other about once a year. Once we had a reunion with Keith and his wife. Mr. Brauninger put Bach on his stereo system and closed his eyes. We all sat with him as if in prayer while the music washed over us. Many shared childhood memories were revisited that weekend—all those Saturday mornings at Youth Orchestra, discovering Beethoven and Mozart together. When Keith and I reminisced, we saw and heard the same things—the flow and discovery of amazing music, Mr. Brauninger's bright blue eyes, the open plains, and a time that never will be again.

Mr. Brauninger was eventually diagnosed with stomach cancer. Sensing that he would die soon, I felt a compelling desire to say good-bye and took the train to see him during January, the height of the Iowa winter. For two days after I arrived, he seemed healthy and he and Eva and I had a wonderful visit, but he became ill and had to go back to the hospital. I sat with him there, remembering my hospital vigil for my father. As I was thinking of this, Mr. Brauninger took my hand. Looking into my eyes, he said, "I guess I've been like a father to you, haven't I?"

Tears instantly flooded my eyes. Though he was weak, his grip on my hand was firm. I told him again, as I had many times before, how his love had made my childhood bearable. I kissed him on the forehead, and we sat together, quietly holding hands, until he fell asleep. He died a few months later.

I feel so lucky to have known him. Jim Brauninger touched hundreds of young people in his life, giving them full respect as human beings, imparting his love and musical skill. He was able to read the chapters I wrote about him in this book, so I know he understood the very special place he inhabits in my heart.

❧

Jodie and I have lost and found each other several times over the years. She has been a professional cellist in Italy for thirty years, married a Russian violinist, and has a daughter and grandson. Thanks to the Internet, recently we renewed our special friendship. I am grateful to know her again after our long absences. We often reminisce about our good times together long ago in Enid, which seem to both of us like a dream. We talk about looking in the mirror these days, marveling how the faces of our mothers appear in our own, wondering where the years have gone since we met. When we were nine years old, we were protected and nurtured under Mr. Brauninger's wings, and now our lives reflect his gifts to us.

❧

It took determined research to find out what happened to Aunt Helen. When I last spoke with her in the early 1980s, she hardly remembered me, which broke my heart. After that, all contact faded. I learned a few years ago that she died in 1989 in a nursing home in Tyler, Texas, and is buried in the heart of the Texas plains, which she so loved. There are many nights when I want to talk to her, to find out more from her perspective. I often reread her letters. In one she tells me, "Your mother is nutty and your grandmother depressed, but don't you go living your life that way. You have a lot to offer, so go do it. You have a lot of common sense and you have your father's get up and go." Thank you, Aunt Helen, for saving me many times over with your glop, your belly hugs, and "God love ya, darlin'."

For a long time after my mother died, she hovered as a ghostly figure in my mind and my dreams, just as she had when I was growing up. Any day she might show up at my door wearing a jaunty hat, any day I might get on the train to go see her in Chicago. She had lived for so long in my imagination, far more alive there than in my flesh-and-blood life, that I had a hard time realizing she was truly gone. It was a relief not to have a mother who kept rejecting me. Still, she was my mother, and I grieved for her—for what we never had and never would. I had to learn to quit waiting for her to transform into the mother I kept hoping for.

For seven years I delayed setting her gravestone in the Wapello cemetery. I visited her grave once a few years after she died, ashamed that there was no stone for her. I was uncertain about what to say on the stone, but I began to realize I was delaying this final step as a way to hold on to the ghost she had always been.

For a long time I tried to find the right words to encapsulate a lifetime in a single phrase. When I visited the stone carvers, they asked me what I wanted to say. I thought for a few minutes, and then realized that, finally, I could have the last word:

JOSEPHINE ELIZABETH MYERS,
DAUGHTER OF LULU AND BLAINE,
MOTHER OF LINDA JOY

A fitting end to a story of mothers and grandmothers is to tell about my grandson, Miles. Rachel gave birth to him on February 25, 2003. I was in the room, helping him emerge into the world to the strains of Debussy's "Claire de Lune." Connected to us in the room were all the generations of our foremothers. I could almost see Blanche and Gram and Mother hovering around. It is said that it takes seven generations to heal a family, and Miles represents the seventh generation from the original Josephine who began it all on a patch of land near the Mississippi.

Miles is now nearly two. His eyes light up when he sees me, his face opening into a big smile. Within minutes of my arrival, he picks up one of his books and nestles in my lap. "Read," he commands me.

I love the feeling of his sturdy body nestled next to me, the dark glow of his brown eyes. "Nana, Nana, Nana," he repeats over and over again as he touches my cheek. My daughter says that he asks for me when I'm gone, but for some reason, I keep being surprised that he remembers me at all. My old insecurities have not completely left me. "Of course he remembers you!" Rachel laughs. "You were there when he was born."

I read *Goodnight Moon* to Miles. This wonderful book is a gift from his Uncle Andrew, who recently married a woman who adores him. Andrew waited a long time to get married, waiting to be quite certain in his relationship, determined not to repeat the family pattern of divorce.

As Miles snuggles against me, tears fill my eyes. Rachel gives me that look that says, "Oh, Mom, you're so sentimental."

"It's so beautiful—we're the first generation in one hundred years to have this."

"You'll never get over parts of your past, will you?" she says tenderly, giving me a kiss.

Miles looks up at me, squinching his face like a monkey. I want to laugh and cry from sheer joy. I am the bridge between my painful past and the vibrant present.

"I love you much," Rachel says, beaming at Miles.

"Much," he says back, meaning, "I love you."

I know my children have internalized the shadows of my life. We have all talked about it—too much, according to them. I have taken full responsibility for the mistakes I made, but I can't escape the fact that my sons and daughter were damaged by them. My fifty years of internal stress and struggle about my mother, my father, and Gram—not to mention the emotional and physical violence they inflicted—has marked me indelibly, despite my great strides in healing. My children are marked, in turn, but they are doing well, living their lives, working out the kinds of problems that everyone faces as adults.

I wrote this book to honor the people I have loved, to give them life again, to honor them in memory. I offer it as a legacy and a lesson, and let it go.

Today, I feel free of the past as I cuddle Miles and kiss his soft cheek.

He giggles. "Read more." His small finger points to the page.

"I love you," I say before I begin: "Once upon a time . . ."

But Miles interrupts me. "Much," he says, cuddling closer. "Nana."

Appendix I

Tips for writing a healing memoir
- If you feel that call inside you to tell your story, don't
  let the critic voice within and without stop you.
- Find your voice; don't worry about how it sounds. Just write.
- Write vignettes, small pieces that can
  be quilted together later.
- Know that writing is more about process than product.
- It's okay to be scared; it's part of writing
  true and authentic stories.
- Tell your story; it does not have to be chronological—
  write where the heat is. Write where the fear is.
- Share carefully with supportive people who care; strangers
  may be safer than family, especially during early stages.
- The most important thing is to get a first draft completed.
- Don't tell those who will criticize you and
  your writing what you are doing.
- Create a protected, sacred space around you and write real.
- Accept that shame and fear are part of the process.
- Writing to heal trauma may mean that you
  write the same story repeatedly.
- It may help to heal trauma to write in first person, present
  tense. Write in scenes, using sensual details. Be specific.
- Writing as meditation. Just be with it, then let go.
- Experiment with being a distant narrator
  rather than in the body and of the child.
- Realize that your story may take on a life of its own.
- Keep the faith that writing it is important and healing to you
- Writing for healing is the first step in writing
  a memoir. Publication comes later.

My website is:
www.memoriesandmemoirs.com
Visit me, look at family photos, and learn more about writing
and healing, classes and other writing groups. Let me know about
your story.

Appendix II Resources

General Mental Health Resources
American Psychiatric Association
www.psych.org
1000 Wilson Boulevard, Suite 1825 Arlington, Va. 22209-3901
Phone: 703-907-7300

American Psychological Association
www.apa.org
750 First Street, NE
Washington, DC 20002-4242
Phone: 800-374-2721; 202-336-5500

National Mental Health Association
www.nmha.org
2001 N. Beauregard Street, 12th Floor
Alexandria, VA 22311
Phone: 703-684-7722
Fax: 703-684-5968

The National Alliance for the Mentally Ill
www.nami.org
NAMI
Colonial Place Three
2107 Wilson Blvd., Suite 300
Arlington, VA 22201-3042
Phone: 703-524-7600
1-800-950-NAMI (6264)

Manic-Depressive foundations
Depression and Bipolar Support Alliance
www.dbsalliance.org
730 N. Franklin Street, Suite 501
Chicago, Illinois 60610-7224
800-826-3632
312-642-0049

National Foundation for Depressive Illness, Inc. – NAFDI
www.depression.org
PO Box 2257

New York, NY 10116
Phone: 800-239-1264
Fax: 212-268-4434

Depression Alliance
http://www.depressionalliance.org/
PO Box 1022
London, UK, SE1 7QB
Phone: 0171 721 7672 (answering machine only)
Depression Alliance is the largest charity in Britain that is run by and for sufferers of depression and their caregivers.

The National Alliance for Research on Schizophrenia and Depression
http://www.narsad.org/
60 Cutter Mill Road, Suite 404
Great Neck, New York 11021
Phone: 516-829-0091
Toll-free Infoline: 1-800-829-8289
Fax: 516-487-6930
E-mail: info@narsad.org?subject=TherapistFinder.net%
NARSAD was formed from four major citizens' groups (National Alliance for the Mentally Ill, National Mental Health Association, National Depressive and Manic Depressive Association, and the Schizophrenia Research Foundation) in 1986. NARSAD raises and distributes funds for scientific research.

Depression and Bipolar Support Alliance (DBSA)
www.dbsalliance.org
(Formerly the National Depressive and Manic-Depressive Association)
730 N. Franklin Street, Suite 501
Chicago, Illinois 60610-7224
Phone: 800-826-3632 E-mail: questions@dbsalliance.org

Depression and Related Affective Disorders Association (DRADA)
www.drada.org
2330 West Joppa Rd., Suite 100
Lutherville, MD 21093
Phone: 410-583-2919
DRADA is a community organization serving individuals affected by

a depressive illness, family members, health care professionals, and the general public.

Web Resources
Search for "manic depression" (without the quotation marks) to find many sites about this illness. Here are a few:

www.pendulum.org
www.harbor-of-refuge.org
www.manicdepression.com
www.mcmanweb.com

Therapist Resources
American Association for Marital and Family Therapy
www.aamft.org
112 South Alfred Street
Alexandria, VA 22314-3061
Phone: 703-838-9808

California Association for Marital and Family Therapy
www.camft.org
7901 Raytheon Road
San Diego, CA 92111-1606
Phone: 858-292-2638

American Counseling Association
www.counseling.org
5999 Stevenson Ave.
Alexandria, VA 22304
Phone: 800-347-6647

Bibliography and Suggested Readings

Adams, Kathleen. 1990. *Journal to the Self*. New York: Warner Books.

———. 1998. *The Way of the Journal*. Lutherville, MD: The Sidran Press.

———. 2000. *The Write Way to Wellness*. Lakewood, CO: Center for Journal Therapy.

Albert, Susan Wittig. 1997. *Writing from Life: Telling Your Soul's Story*. New York: Jeremy P. Tarcher/Putnam.

Baldwin, Christina. 1998. *Life's Companion: Journal Writing as a Spiritual Quest*. New York: Bantam Doubleday Dell.

Brande, Dorothea. [1943] 1981. *Becoming a Writer*. Reprint, with a foreword by John Gardner, New York: Jeremy P. Tarcher/Putnam.

Cameron, Julia. 2002. *10th anniversary edition*. The Artist's Way: A Spiritual Path to Higher Creativity. New York: Jeremy P. Tarcher/ Putnam.

Chandler, Marilyn. 1990. *A Healing Art: Regeneration Through Autobiography*. New York: Garland Publishing.

Conroy, Pat. 1986. *The Prince of Tides*. New York: Houghton Mifflin.

DeSalvo, Louise. 2000. *Writing as a Way of Healing: How Telling Our Stories Transforms Our Lives*. Boston: Beacon Press.

Duke, Patty. 1992. *A Brilliant Madness and Call Me Anna*. New York: Bantam Books

Fox, John. 1997. *Poetic Medicine*. New York: Jeremy P. Tarcher/ Putnam.

Herman, Judith. 1992. *Trauma and Recovery*. New York: Basic Books.

Hanh, Thich Nhat. 1997. *Teachings on Love*. Berkeley: Parallax Press.

Hoffman, Bob. 1976. *Getting Divorced from Mom and Dad*. New York: E. P. Dutton.

Jamison, Kay Redfield. 1995. *The Unquiet Mind*. Vintage New York

King, Laurie. 2002. *Gain Without Pain? Expressive Writing and Self-Regulation.* In *The Writing Cure: How Expressive Writing Promotes Health and Emotional Well-Being,* eds., Stephen J. Lepore and Joshua M. Smyth. Washington, D.C.: American Psychological Association.

Ledoux, Denis. 1991. *Turning Memories into Memoirs.* Lisbon Falls, ME: Soleil Press.

Lepore, Stephen J., and Joshua M. Smyth, eds. 2002. *The Writing Cure: How Expressive Writing Promotes Health and Emotional Well-Being.* Washington, D.C.: American Psychological Association.

Metzger, Deena. 1992. *Writing for Your Life.* New York: HarperCollins.

Miller, Alice. 2001. *The Truth Will Set You Free.* New York: Basic Books.

Myers, Linda Joy. 2002. *Becoming Whole: Writing Your Healing Story.* San Diego SilverThreads

Pennebaker, James W. 1990. *Opening Up: The Healing Power of Expressing Emotions.* New York: The Guilford Press.

———. **2004.** *Writing to Heal: A Guided Journal for Recovering from Trauma and Emotional Upheaval.* Oakland, CA: New Harbinger Press.

Rainer, Tristine. 1997. *The New Diary: Your Life as Story.* New York: Jeremy P. Tarcher/Putnam.

———. **1998.** *Your Life as Story: Discovering the "New Autobiography" and Writing Memoir as Literature.* New York: Jeremy P. Tarcher/Putnam.

Rico, Gabriele. 2000. *Writing the Natural Way.* New York. Jeremey P. Tarcher/Putnam

Ueland, Brenda. 1987. *If You Want To Write: A Book about Art, Independence and Spirit.* St. Paul, MN: Graywolf Press.

Wakefield, Dan. 1990. *The Story of Your Life: Writing a Spiritual Autobiography.* Boston: Beacon Press.

Weldon, Michele. 2001. *Writing to Save Your Life: How to Honor Your Story Through Journaling.* Center City, MN: Hazeldon.

Acknowledgments

Many people have encouraged me on my long and winding path to this healing memoir, particularly Ron Kane, who saw me whole, offered compassion, and helped me stay on the healing path. Susan Wittig Albert of Story Circle Network believes in the healing power of memoir writing, and has been supportive of me as a writer and teacher for several years. Denis LeDoux promotes memoir writing through his workshops and classes, and has long been a supporter of this memoir and of me as a teacher and writer. Elizabeth Fischel was a positive mentor for many of the stories in this book, and always believed that the book was important. I wish Josephine Carson were still here to thank. She was my mentor at Mills College who set me on the path of this version of the book. Bless you wherever you are

The Fourth Street Writers, and my close friends Betsy Fasbinder and Amy Peele; the California Writers Club, particularly Barbara Truax and Teresa LeYung Ryan; and the Women's National Book Association have offered the kind of support that an author dreams of. Thanks Christopher Gortner for being a lifeline, helping me get the book completed and published. Thank you Melanie Rigney for urging me to complete the book and get it out in the world. Even the toughest critics were helpful because they forced me to revise my writing and decide to work even harder to finish the book. They shall remain unnamed.

I gratefully thank Doreen Hamilton, Terry Basile, Tad Toomay, Jodie Bevers, Keith Moore, and Eva Brauninger, all of whom helped this memoir come to fruition.

Thank you James Dallesandro, Barbara Gates, Jessica Inclan, Jacqueline Marcell, Beth Proudfoot, Tristine Rainer, Elayne Savage, and Michele Weldon for having faith in me and my work, and contributing to the publication of this book.

So much gratitude goes to my wonderful, patient, and enormously helpful editors: Lisa A. Smith, for helping me learn about editing, finalizing, and publishing a book; and Mindy Toomay, for shaping wayward sentences and sculpting paragraphs so they said what I meant, and the best soup in town.

And to my children, I say thank you for your patience, for understanding and putting up with me through all the highways and byways of our lives, and for the love you have brought into my life. To Miles, I say, "Much."

Author's Page

Linda Joy Myers, Ph.D.

Linda Joy is a therapist in the San Francisco Bay Area, and the author of *Becoming Whole: Writing your Healing Story*. She teaches memoir-as-healing groups and presents workshops throughout the United States. Excerpts from *Don't Call Me Mother* have won several prizes, including first prize in the Jack London Nonfiction Contest and ranked in the top 5% of the annual Writers Digest Writing Contest. She is close to her three grown children, and enjoys reading with her grandson, Miles.

For more information about writing memoirs, writing and healing classes, local and on-line workshops, e-books, and teleseminars, please visit Linda at: www.memoriesandmemoirs.com.